THE ALCHEMY PRESS
BOOK OF THE DEAD 2021

Cover by Chris Achilleos (1947–2021) for the first paperback edition of Fantasy Tales (Autumn 1988) edited by Stephen Jones and David A. Sutton.

THE ALCHEMY PRESS BOOK OF THE DEAD 2021

Compiled by
STEPHEN JONES

The Alchemy Press

Copyright © Stephen Jones 2022

First Edition
10 9 8 7 6 5 4 3 2 1

ISBN: 978-1-911034-14-8

All rights reserved by Stephen Jones. The right of Stephen Jones to be identified as the Author of this Work has been asserted by him in accordance with the Copyright, Designs and Patents Act 1988.

With thanks to Peter Coleborn, Michael Marshall Smith, David Barraclough, Mandy Slater, Andrew I. Porter, Amanda Foubister, Jo Fletcher, Gerry Adair, Jean-Daniel Brèque, Gary Couzens, Séphera Girón, Peter Risby Hansen, Nancy Kilpatrick, David Langford, Terence McVicker, Michael Moorcock, Lisa Morton, Cornelia Queen, Andy Richards, David J. Schow, Cat Sparks and Jonathan Strahan for all their help and support.

Special thanks are also due to *Classic Images*, *Ansible*, *Locus*, and other sources that were used for reference.

Cover design by Smith & Jones

About the Cover

Italian 4-foglio poster by Enzo Nistri for Hammer Films'
Dracula Prince of Darkness (1966), which starred British actress
Barbara Shelley (1932–2021) and Christopher Lee.
All Shelley's screams in the film were overdubbed by co-star
Suzan Farmer, but can still be heard in the German trailer.

The Alchemy Press
Staffordshire, England

Published in England

Visit our website at www.alchemypress.co.uk
Visit the author's website at www.stephenjoneseditor.com

Contents

Introduction	13
Lee Aaker	15
Chris Achilleos	15
Peter Adams	15
Michael G. Adkisson	16
Rick Aiello	16
Paul Alexander	16
Wanda June Alexander	17
Carlo Alighiero	17
Brad Allan	18
Keith Allison	18
Sid Altus	18
Victor Ambrus	19
David Von Ancken	19
C. Dean Andersson	20
Jack Angel	20
Lou Antonelli	21
Michael Apted	21
Richard Arnold	22
Ed Asner	22
Bob Avian	23
Peter Aykroyd	23
Christopher Ayres	24
Dale Baer	24
David Bailie	24
Bob Baker	25
Lisa Banes	25
Douglas Barbour	26
Miquel Barceló	26
Pilar Bardem	26
Graham Garfield Barnard	27
Edward Barnes	27
Olga Barnet	28
David G. Barnett	28
Claudia Barrett	28
Susan Bartholomew	30
Bart the Bear II	30
Anne Beatts	30
Ned Beatty	31
William R. Beck	31
Charles Beeson	32
Jean-Paul Belmondo	32
Catherine Belsey	33
Benício	33
Fran Bennett	33
Walter Bernstein	34
Dennis Berry	34
Kit Berry	34
Val Bisoglio	35
Lionel Blair	35
Rick Boatright	36
Margaret Wander Bonanno	36
Frank Bonner	36
Perry Botkin, Jr.	37
Linda Boyce	37
Blade Braxton	37
Shane Briant	38
Leslie Bricusse	38
Johnny Briggs	40
Harry V. Bring	40
Brick Bronsky	40
Bob Brown	41
Denise Bryer	41
Wiktor Bukato	42
Allan Burns	42
Kathy Burns	42
John Bush	43
David Butler	43
Jeremy G. Byrne	43
JoAnna Cameron	44
Carmine Capobianco	44
René Cardona III	45
Linda Carlson	45
Ralph Carmichael	45
Carol Carr	46
Raffaella Carrà	46
Jean-Claude Carrière	46
Steve Carver	48
Nino Castelnuovo	48
Judi B. Castro	48
Raymond Cavaleri	49
Meloney Crawford Chadwick	49
John Challis	50
Geoffrey Chater	50
Sung-Young Chen	50
Maria Chianetta	51
Sonny Chiba	51
Richard Citron	51

John Clabburn	53	Jerry Douglas	78
Sanford Clark	53	Robert Downey, Sr.	78
Don Collier	54	Olympia Dukakis	79
Mary Collinson	54	David Dukas	79
Gary Compton	54	Alistair Durie	79
Neil Connery	56	Phil Eason	79
Michael Constantine	56	Marilyn Eastman	80
Storm Constantine	58	Mark Eden	80
William G. Contento	58	Avril Elgar	82
Richard Conway	59	Mark Elliott	82
Alex Cord	60	John Erman	82
Joe Cornelius	60	Richard Evans	83
Charlotte Cornwell	60	Trader Faulkner	83
Bob Couttie	62	Gerald Feil	83
Frank Cox	62	Derrick Ferguson	84
J. Randolph Cox	62	Kate Ferguson	84
Robert W. Coye	63	Michael Ferguson	84
Douglas S. Cramer	63	Tony Ferrer	85
Johnny Crawford	64	Harry Fielder	85
Stephen Critchlow	64	Vergena Fields	86
Roger Cudney	64	Gérard Filipelli	86
Ian Curteis	65	Lail Finlay	86
Alan Curtis	65	Colin Fletcher	87
Lou Cutell	66	Robert Fletcher	87
Arlene Dahl	66	Larry Flynt	87
Blackie Dammett	66	James Follett	88
Stuart Damon	68	Bryn Fortey	88
Gene D'Angelo	68	Gérald Forton	89
Henry Darrow	68	David Fox	89
Desmond Davis	69	Myra Francis	90
Peter S. Davis	69	Heath Freeman	90
Anish Deb	70	Mary K. Frey	90
Lois de Banzie	70	Penny Frierson	91
Kellam de Forest	70	Charles W. Fries	91
Martha De Laurentiis	71	Mira Furlan	92
Nathalie Delon	71	Robert Fyfe	92
Jeffrey Dempsey	72	John Gabriel	93
Jo-Carroll Dennison	72	Diana G. Gallagher	93
David H. DePatie	72	Jimmy Garrett	93
Giannetto De Rossi	73	Willie Garson	94
Dustin Diamond	75	Luis Gaspar	94
DMX	75	Anna Gaylor	94
Ron Dominguez	75	Sally Miller Gearhart	95
Mike Don	76	Larry Gelman	95
Tim Donnelly	75	Nicholas Georgiade	96
Richard Donner	77	George Gerdes	96
Carole Nelson Douglas	77	Richard Gilliland	96

Milton Moses Ginsberg	97
Brian Goldner	97
Arlene Golonka	97
Kathleen Ann Goonan	98
Reg Gorman	98
Desiree Gould	98
Saginaw Grant	99
Leon Greene	99
John Gregg	101
Jon Gregory	101
Alberto Grimaldi	101
Charles Grodin	102
Fernand Guiot	102
David Gulpilil	102
Sally Gwylan	103
Bob Haberfield	103
Jean Hale	103
Cleve Hall	104
Robert Hall	104
Richard Halliwell	105
Jesse Hamm	106
Wynn Hammer	106
James Hampton	106
Bridget Hanley	107
Judith Hanna	107
Haya Harareet	107
Tony Harding	108
Don Harley	108
Marie Harmon	108
Al Harrington	109
Cynthia Harris	109
Peter Harris	109
Romaine Hart	110
Alan Hawkshaw	110
Kay Hawtrey	111
Billie Hayes	111
Jeffrey M. Hayes	112
Damaris Hayman	112
Jack Hedley	113
Monte Hellman	113
Gloria Henry	115
Mike Henry	115
Bob Herron	115
Tom Hickey	117
Steve Hickman	117
Chuck Hicks	118
Billy Hinsche	118
Pat Hitchcock	119
John Hitchin	119
Vegar Hoel	119
Basil Hoffman	120
Robert J. Hogan	120
Hal Holbrook	121
Roy Holder	121
Bernard Holley	121
Howard Honig	123
John Hora	123
Patrick Horgan	123
Sally Ann Howes	124
Elizabeth Anne Hull	124
Joye Hummel	124
Mike Humphreys	126
Paul Huntley	126
Halyna Hutchins	127
Ken Hutchison	127
Toshihiro Iijima	127
Alvin Ing	128
Ravil Isyanov	128
Andrei Izmailov	128
Kevin Jackson	129
Frank Jacobs	129
Sondra James	130
Larry D. Johnson	130
Don Jones	130
Langdon Jones	131
Rick Jones	131
Robert C. Jones	132
Fred Jordan	132
Rémy Julienne	132
Nathan Jung	133
Norton Juster	133
Bernie Kahn	134
Irma Kalish	134
Alan R. Kalter	134
Lorina Kamburova	135
Sayaka Kanda	135
Marvin Kaye	135
Ira Keeler	137
Patricia Kennealy	138
Mamat Khalid	138
Shunsuke Kikuchi	139
Larry King	139
Bruce Kirby	139
Tommy Kirk	140

Tawny Kitaen	142		George Mandel	160
Reuben B. Klamer	142		Isidore Mankofsky	160
Vladimir Korenev	142		Lisa Mannetti	161
Erle M. Korshak	143		Biz Markie	161
Yaphet Kotto	143		Alan Marques	162
David Anthony Kraft	144		Simon Marshall-Jones	162
Willy Kurant	144		George Martin	162
Fred Ladd	145		Elizabeth I. McCann	163
Art LaFleur	145		Helen McCrory	163
Jackie Lane	145		John A. McGlashan	164
Timothy Lane	146		Biff McGuire	164
Tommy Lane	146		Joe McKinney	164
Gil Lane-Young	146		Frank McRae	165
Joe Lara	147		Eddie Mekka	165
Milan Lasica	147		Ed Meskys	166
Silvio Laurenzi	147		Art Metrano	166
Cloris Leachman	148		Curt Meyer	167
Libertad Leblanc	148		Diana Millay	167
Denise Lee	149		Frank Mills	167
Peter A. Lees	149		Mike Mitchell	168
Richard Lee-Sung	149		Kentaro Miura	168
John Paul Leon	150		Sharyn Moffett	168
Larry Levine	150		Alec Monteath	170
Reg Lewis	151		Inés Morales	170
David Lightfoot	151		Joey Morgan	170
Steve Lightle	151		Jane Morpeth	171
Gunnel Lindblom	152		Rowena Morrill	171
Steve Lines	152		Christine Morrison	171
Joanne Linville	153		Dean Morrissey	173
Christopher Little	153		Gerardo Moscoso	173
Gary Littlejohn	153		Jill Murphy	173
Douglas Livingstone	154		Alan Robert Murray	174
Norman Lloyd	154		Guillermo Murray	174
John Logan	155		Michael Nader	176
Phil Lonergan	155		Kichiemon Nakamura II	176
William Lucking	156		Peggy Neal	176
Hugh Lund	156		Salman A. Nensi	178
Frank Lupo	156		Michael Nesmith	178
Betty Lynn	157		Leslie Newman	178
Norm MacDonald	157		Ivo Niederle	179
Ray MacDonnell	158		Masanari Nihei	179
Joyce Mackenzie	158		William F. Nolan	179
Doug MacLeod	158		Scott Allen Nollen	180
Gavin MacLeod	158		Denis O'Brien	182
Catherine MacPhail	159		Denis O'Dell	182
Wes Magee	159		Gavan O'Herlihy	183
Ugo Malaguti	160		Walter Olkewicz	183

Colette O'Neil	184	J.W. Rinzler	206
Henry Orenstein	184	Paul Ritter	208
Ota	184	Tanya Roberts	208
Scott Page-Pagter	185	Charles Robinson	209
Nicola Pagett	185	Doug Robinson	209
Peter Palmer	186	Richard Robinson	211
John Paragon	186	Enrique Rocha	211
Darroll Pardoe	187	Robson Rocha	212
Victoria Paris	187	Robert Rodan	212
Eddie Paskey	187	Jean-Claude Romer	212
Gary Paulsen	188	Jeanine Ann Roose	214
Allen Payne	188	Ronald Roose	214
Trevor Peacock	188	Clifford Rose	214
John C. Pelan	189	Giuseppe Rotunno	215
Christopher Pennock	189	Yvonne Rousseau	215
Clare Peploe	190	Richard Rush	215
Morris Perry	190	Will Ryan	217
Pierre Philippe	191	Antonio Sabáto, Sr.	217
Jay Pickett	191	Takao Saitô	217
Ronald Pickup	191	Don Sakers	218
Paolo Pietrangeli	192	Jay Sandrich	218
Marc Pilcher	192	Sompote Sands	218
Jerry Pinkney	192	Camille Saviola	219
Doris Piserchia	193	Roy Scammell	219
Gian Filippo Pizzo	193	Liam Scarlett	220
Edward L. Plumb	194	Renato Scarpa	220
Christopher Plummer	194	Walter Schneiderman	221
Markie Post	196	Enzo Sciotti	221
Anthony Powell	196	Peter Scolari	221
Jane Powell	198	Clive Scott	223
Norman S. Powell	198	Geoffrey Scott	223
Don Poynter	198	George Segal	223
Joe Praml	199	Tony Selby	224
Zdenka Procházková	199	Lee Server	224
Al Pugliese	199	Barbara Shelley	224
Timothy Patrick Quill	200	Antony Sher	226
Rosita Quintana	200	Steve Sherman	226
Kumar Ramsay	200	Ina Shorrock	227
Marion Ramsay	201	Jan Shutan	227
Joel Rapp	201	Gregory Sierra	228
Alex Rebar	201	Felix Silla	228
Juli Reding	202	Cliff Simon	228
John Reilly	202	L. Neil Smith	229
Jonathan Reynolds	202	Wilbur Smith	229
Anne Rice	204	William Smith	230
John Richardson	204	Paul Soles	232
Peter Mark Richman	206	Stephen Sondheim	232

Name	Page
Si Spencer	233
Peggy Spirito	233
Anne Stallybrass	233
Lynn Stalmaster	233
Bill Starr	234
Dorothy Steel	234
Jim Steinman	235
Dr. Aaron Stern	235
Jan Stirling	236
Dean Stockwell	236
Matthew Strachan	238
Julie Strain	238
Una Stubbs	239
Bertrand Tavernier	239
Bill Taylor	240
T. Mark Taylor	240
James R. Terry	240
Andreas Teuber	241
Mikis Theodorakis	241
Frank Thorne	241
Robert Thurston	242
Kartal Tibet	242
Bill Titcombe	242
Stacy Title	244
Greta Tomlinson	244
Ruthie Tompson	245
Lorna Toolis	245
Bill Tortolini	245
Linda S. Touby	246
Michael Tylo	246
Cicely Tyson	246
Andrew Vachss	247
Nikki Van der Zyl	247
"Buddy" Van Horn	248
Melvin Van Peebles	248
Isela Vega	248
Chick Vennera	250
Peter Vere-Jones	250
Henri Vernes	250
Marie Versini	251
Emi Wada	251
Jessica Walter	252
Gloria Warren	252
Norman J. Warren	252
Joan Washington	254
Dilys Watling	254
Peter Watson-Wood	254
Woody Welch	255
Joan Weldon	255
Lina Wertmüller	257
Betty White	257
Jack Whyte	257
Yvonne Wilder	258
Bergen Williams	258
Cara Williams	258
Clarence Williams III	259
Karl Williams	259
Michael K. Williams	260
Betty Willingale	260
Marc Wilmore	260
Mark Wilson	261
S. Clay Wilson	261
Romy Windsor	261
Jane Withers	263
Robin Wood	263
Victor Wood	265
Henry Woolf	265
Samuel E. Wright	265
May Wynn	266
Andy Yanchus	266
Masayoshi Yasugi	267
Viktor Yevgrafov	267
John Sacret Young	267
Jeanne Youngson	267
Index by Date	269
About the Author	277

Commemorating the passing of writers, artists, performers and technicians who, during their lifetimes, made significant contributions to the horror, science fiction and fantasy genres (or left their mark on popular culture in other, often fascinating, ways) . . .

Swedish one-sheet poster by Moje Åslund for the 1934 Paramount movie
Death Takes a Holiday starring Fredric March as "Prince Sirki",
the personification of Death.

Introduction

"What could terror mean to me, who have nothing to fear?"
—Prince Sirki (Fredric March) in *Death Takes a Holiday* (1934)

SOMETIMES IT FEELS like I've been writing obituaries for most of my life.

That's probably because I *have*.

I can still remember how it all began . . . I was visiting my grandmother (a formidable old lady) in West Sussex with the rest of my family, when the BBC evening news announced that Stan Laurel had died at the age of 74.

I was just starting to get interested in going to the movies and reading magazines like Forrest J Ackerman's *Famous Monsters of Filmland* and the more sophisticated *Castle of Frankenstein*.

I obviously knew who Stan Laurel was—the skinny one in the classic comedy duo of Laurel and Hardy. But those were *silent* movies—seen as grainy, flickering images from a time unimaginable decades earlier. (The irony is, of course, that I'm now almost two decades further away from that evening in February 1965 than I was back then from the beginning of Laurel and Hardy's iconic partnership in 1927.) I had presumed that Stan must have been dead for *years* (his last film had been released three years before I was born).

That he had still been living *up to that very day*—that, given the right circumstances, I might have *met* him—fascinated me. The thought captured my imagination, and it never let go again. (Of course, 74 is considered no age at all nowadays.)

Over the next few years I got to know my actors—particularly the character and supporting players whose names often never even appeared in the credits. Thanks to magazines like *Famous Monsters*, *Castle of Frankenstein* and their various imitators, I started putting faces to names; and when it came to my favourite genres of horror, science fiction and fantasy, I soon began to realise that the same familiar faces would turn up time and again, often in productions from different studios.

Famous Monsters would often feature an obituary column that sometimes took its name from Fredric March's vacationing Grim Reaper in the 1934 movie *Death Takes a Holiday*. Forry would note the passing of the great and the good of filmmaking with a mini-bio and photos from his extensive collection. I remember coming across one particularly traumatic example in the November 1967 issue that included tributes to the recently deceased Tom Conway, Basil Rathbone, Charles Beaumont, Nelson Eddy, Mischa Auer, Walt Disney, Barbara Payton and Spencer Tracy!

I was only just starting to learn who some of these people were, and now it seemed like Prince Sirki had taken his scythe to my childhood!

Almost exactly four years to the day after I visited my Gran and heard about Stan Laurel's demise, I was on the 36 bus coming home from school on Monday evening when, just as we rounded London's Marble Arch, I saw that the newspaper placards were announcing FAMOUS FILM STAR DIES. That's how they would do it in those days—purposely not name the actor so that you would have to buy a copy of the newspaper to discover their identity.

I was wondering who it could possibly be, when I happened to glance across at the woman in the seat in front of me who was reading a copy of the evening newspaper. As soon as I saw the photo of Boris Karloff I started crying.

The next day I went out and bought a copy of every national newspaper, cut out all the obituaries for Karloff, and pasted them into my scrapbook.

Beginning in the mid-1970s, I started contributing my own obituaries to such fanzines as *The British Fantasy Society Bulletin*, *Starship Exeter Organisation Newsletter* and *Fantasy Media*, before moving upmarket to *Halls of Horror*, *Science Fiction Chronicle*, *Locus* and a regular column in *Shock Xpress* (tastefully titled 'Dead People').

In 1990, when I launched my "Year's Best" anthology series *Best New Horror* with co-editor Ramsey Campbell, we inaugurated an annual 'Necrology' column to appear in every volume. My old friend and collaborator Kim Newman—Britain's undisputed expert on genre movies and popular media—came on board (along with a number of other correspondents from around the world) to help me out, and over the next thirty-one years we kept track of the passing of as many notable names as we could.

And here I am, still doing it today.

As I explained in the previous volume in this series, *The Alchemy Press Book of the Dead* came about after I moved my obituaries over to Facebook following the outbreak of the COVID-19 pandemic in 2020; and although things have calmed down somewhat since then, Death, alas, continued to take no holiday in 2021...

This time there are more than 500 mini-biographies in this present volume, as we note the passing of James Bond's brother...a pair of actors who appeared in an unsold 1967 TV pilot for *Dick Tracy*...two iconic fantasy artists...a former child actor who starred in two different versions of H.P. Lovecraft's *The Dunwich Horror*...two movie Tarzans and a Jane...the twin sister of a Hammer vampire...the two stars of the Japanese sci-spy movie *Terror Beneath the Sea*...an actor who played both Frankenstein's Monster *and* Count Dracula...the two teenage stars of *Village of the Giants*...and, as always, far too many friends and colleagues.

Once again, Prince Sirki calls...

Stephen Jones
London, England
December 2021

Lee Aaker

American former child actor Lee [William] Aaker, who starred as "Rusty" in the 1954-59 TV series *The Adventures of Rin Tin Tin*, died alone and unclaimed of complications from a stroke on April 1, aged 77. He was listed as an "indigent decedent" upon his death in Arizona. Aaker not only appeared in such classic Westerns as *High Noon*, *Hondo* and *Destry* (he lost out to Brandon De Wilde on *Shane*), but he was also in *The Atomic City* and *Hans Christian Andersen* (1952). After working as an assistant to the producer on the TV show *Route 66*, he retired from the screen in the early 1960s and became a carpenter and taught skiing to underprivileged children and people with disabilities.

Chris Achilleos

Greek Cypriot-born British illustrator, painter and movie conceptual artist Chris Achilleos (Christos Achilléos) died of a stroke on December 8, aged 74. After attending Hornsey College of Art in the 1960s, he began creating covers for hundreds of fantasy books by Robert E. Howard, Edgar Rice Burroughs, John Norman, Michael Moorcock, Anne McCaffrey, Karl Edward Wagner, John Jakes and many other authors. Achilleos also produced covers for the original Target Books *Doctor Who* novelisations, the reissues of James Blish's *Star Trek* volumes, and various "Fighting Fantasy" gamebooks. He worked as a conceptual/costume artist for the 1980 animated movie *Heavy Metal* and created the iconic poster for the film. Other movies he worked on include *Willow* and the historical dramas *King Arthur* (2004) and *The Last Legion*. Achilléos' artwork has been showcased in such volumes as *Beauty and the Beast* (1978), *Sirens* (1986), *Medusa* (1988) and *Amazona* (2004).

Peter Adams

British film executive and scriptwriter Peter Adams died of cancer on June 11, aged 75. His credits include the

low budget horror movies *S.N.U.B!* (2010) and *Aux* (aka *Soldier of War*, 2018), both co-written with his son John (who also directed the latter).

Michael G. Adkisson

American SF publisher, writer and artist Michael G. (George) Adkisson died on February 7, aged 65. From 1986-92 he edited and published the small press magazine *New Pathways into Science Fiction and Fantasy* (later *New Pathways*). Adkisson used some of his own fiction and artwork in the periodical during its early years.

Rick Aiello

American supporting actor Rick Aiello, the son of actor Danny Aiello, died of pancreatic cancer on July 26, aged 63. He appeared in *Silent Madness*, *K-9000* and *Twin Peaks: Fire Walk with Me*, along with episodes of TV's *Tales from the Crypt*, *Strange Luck* and *Early Edition*.

Paul Alexander

American science fiction artist Paul R. Alexander died on June 14, aged 83. Best known for his high-tec hardware and machinery illustrations, one of his earliest published covers was for Edward L. Ferman's *The Best from Fantasy and Science Fiction: A Special 25th Anniversary Anthology* from Ace Books (1977). Alexander also created the cover for the first issue of *Asimov's SF Adventure Magazine* the following year, and he worked for Berkley, Ballantine, Fawcett, Del Rey and many other imprints. Examples

Wanda June Alexander, a former high school English teacher who worked as a freelance editor for Tor Books from 1984-2006, died of complications from Idiopathic Pulmony Fibrosis on February 14, aged 69.

Carlo Alighiero

of Alexander's covers for David Drake's "Hammer's Slammers" series and Keith Laumer's "Bolos" series, done for Baen Books in the 1990s, were chosen for the *Spectrum* art anthologies. In 1983 he also collaborated with Laurie Bridges on three YA horror novels in Bantam Books' "Dark Forces" series: *Magic Show*, *Devil Wind* and *Swamp Witch*. By the late 1990s Alexander had largely retired from the art field.

Wanda June Alexander

Italian supporting actor Carlo Alighiero (Carlo Animali) died on September 11, aged 94. He appeared in Dario Argento's *The Cat o' Nine Tails* and Sergio Martino's *The Strange Vice of Mrs. Wardh* and *Torso*. Alighiero also had a second career as a prolific dubbing actor, and amongst the many titles he worked on (uncredited) are the James Bond film *Diamonds Are Forever*, *Something Creeping in the Dark*, *Web of the Spider*, *What Have You Done to Solange?*, *La casa stregata* and *Fracchia vs. Dracula*.

Brad Allan

Australian stuntman and stunt co-ordinator Brad Allan (Bradley James Allan) died on August 7, aged 48. The first non-Asian member of Jackie Chan's stunt team, he worked with the actor on such movies as *The Tuxedo*, *The Medallion* and *Chinese Zodiac*. Allan's other credits include *Peter Pan* (2003), *The Chronicles of Riddick*, *Eragon*, *Hellboy II: The Golden Army*, *Bedtime Stories*, *A Christmas Carol* (2009), *Avatar*, *Kick-Ass*, *A Nightmare on Elm Street* (2010), *Scott Pilgrim vs. the World*, *I Am Number Four*, *Mars Needs Moms*, *The Adventures of Tintin*, *Pacific Rim*, *The World's End*, *Iceman*, *Kingsman: The Secret Service*, *Insidious: Chapter 3*, *Sinister 2*, *Wonder Woman*, *Kingsman: The Golden Circle*, *Solo: A Star Wars Story*, *Shang-Chi: The Legend of the Ten Rings* and *The King's Man*. He was also a second-unit director on *Scott Pilgrim vs. the World*, *The World's End*, *Wolves*, *Kingsman: The Secret Service*, *Kingsman: The Golden Circle*, *Solo: A Star Wars Story*, *Shang-Chi: The Legend of the Ten Rings* and *The King's Man*.

Keith Allison

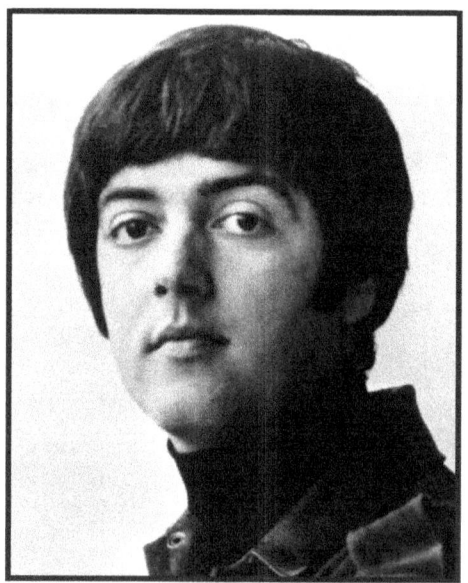

American singer, songwriter and guitarist Keith Allison, a former member of Paul Revere & the Raiders (1968-75), died on November 17, aged 79. He worked on *Head* (1968) with the Monkees, appeared as a country & western singer in *Phantom of the Paradise* (1974) and turned up in the finale of *Sgt. Pepper's Lonely Hearts Club Band* (1978).

Sid Altus

American SF fan and publisher Sid (Sidney) Altus died on July 13, aged 71. In 1978 he and Alex Berman co-founded the Michigan small press

imprint Phantasia Press Inc., which published just over eighty limited edition science fiction and fantasy hardcovers by, amongst others, L. Sprague De Camp, Jack Williamson, Isaac Asimov, Phillip José Farmer, Fredric Brown, Arthur C. Clarke, Harlan Ellison, Stephen King (a boxed edition of *Firestarter*, limited to 725 copies), Robert Silverberg and Roger Zelazny. The final book from Phantasia Press appeared in 1989.

Victor Ambrus

Hungarian-born British illustrator and writer Victor (Győző László) Ambrus, who illustrated the first edition of Michael Morpurgo's *War Horse*, died of complications from Parkinson's disease on February 10, aged 85. Best known for his work on more than 300 children's books, he also created artwork for television programmes (BBC's *Jackanory*, Channel 4's *Time Team*), museum displays, postage stamps and Christmas cards. A winner of the the Kate Greenaway medal twice, amongst the many books he illustrated were *Dracula: Everything You Always Wanted to Know, But Were Too Afraid to Ask* (1980), *Dracula's Bedtime Story Book* (1981) and *What Time is It Dracula?* (1992), along with *Witch Fear*, *A Book of Magicians*, *A Tolkien Bestiary*, *Dead Men of Dunharrow*, *Gulliver's Travels* (1987), *A –Z of Tolkien*, *The Wizard of Oz* (1999) and *A Guide to Tolkien*.

David Von Ancken

American TV producer and director David Von Ancken died of stomach cancer on July 26, aged 56. He co-executive produced the first season of WGN's *Salem* (2014), Syfy's *Ghost Wars* (2017-18), ABC's *The Crossing* (2018), NBC's *The InBetween* (2019) and Netflix's *The Order* (2019-20), also directing episodes of all those shows plus *The Vampire Diaries* and *The Purge*.

C. Dean Andersson

American horror and fantasy author C. (Cloyce) Dean Andersson died after a long illness on July 5, aged 75. He had been suffering from heart disease. As "Asa Drake", in the early 1980s Andersson published the "Bloodsong Saga" (*Warrior Witch of Hel*, *Werebeasts of Hel* and *Death Riders of Hel*), as well as *Crimson Kisses* and *The Lair of Ancient Dreams* (both with his wife Nina Romberg). His other books include the "Dallas Horror Trilogy" (*Torture Tomb*, *Raw Pain Max*, *Fiend*), *Buried Screams*, *I am Dracula* and *I am Frankenstein*. Andersson's short fiction appeared in such anthologies as *Scare Care*, *Dark Seductions*, *Dark Destiny*, *Children of Dracula*, *The Many Faces of Van Helsing*, *Cross Plains Universe: Texans Celebrate Robert E. Howard* and other titles, along with an issue of *Cemetery Dance* magazine.

Jack Angel

American voice actor Jack T. Angel died on October 19, aged 90. His credits include *The Secret of NIMH*, *The Transformers: The Movie*, *Beetlejuice*, *Who Framed Roger Rabbit*, *The Little Mermaid* (1989), *The Rescuers Down Under*, *Beauty and the Beast* (1991), *Aladdin* (1992), *A Troll in Central Park*, *Toy Story*, *The Hunchback*

of Notre Dame (1996), *Quest for Camelot*, *A Bug's Life*, *Tarzan* (1999), *The Iron Giant*, *Alvin and the Chipmunks Meet Frankenstein*, *Toy Story 2*, *Shrek*, *A.I. Artificial Intelligence*, *Spirited Away*, *Monsters Inc.*, *Lilo & Stitch*, *Treasure Planet*, *Looney Tunes: Back in Action*, *Ice Age: The Meltdown*, *Horton Hears a Who!*, *Toy Story 3*, *The Lorax* and *Monsters University*, along with episodes of the animated TV shows *The All-New Super Friends Hour* and *Challenge of the Superfriends* (as "Hawkman"), *Spider-Man* (1981–82), *The Real Ghostbusters*, *The Transformers* (1985–87), *Back to the Future*, *Peter Pan and the Pirates*, *Darkwing Duck*, *Spider-Man: The Animated Series* (as "Nick Fury", 1997), *Avatar: The Last Airbender* and *Transformers Project Nemesis*, amongst many other titles.

Lou Antonelli

American speculative fiction author and journalist Lou Antonelli (Louis Sergio Antonelli) died of pneumonia on October 6, aged 64. His short fiction appeared in *RevolutionSF*, *Asimov's Science Fiction*, *Jim Baen's Universe*, *Nova Science Fiction*, *Zombified: An Anthology of All Things Zombie* and elsewhere, and was collected in *Fantastic Texas*, *Texas & Other Planets*, *The Clock Struck None* and *In the Shadow of the Cross*. Antonelli's writing memoir, *Letters from Gardner: A Writer's Odyssey* (2014), included short fiction and writing advice and was a Hugo Award finalist, while his debut novel, *Another Girl, Another Planet*, appeared in 2017. Dissatisfied with the Science Fiction & Fantasy Writers of America, he founded his own rival organization, the Society for the Advancement of Speculative Storytelling, in 2012. Three years later, as part of the Hugo's "Sad Puppies/Rabid Puppies" controversy, Antonelli wrote a letter to the Spokane Police Department telling them to be on the lookout for someone who may incite violence—the World Science Fiction Convention's Master of Ceremonies, David Gerrold—who he described as "insane and a public danger and needs to be watched when the convention's going on". He later publicly apologized to Gerrold.

Michael Apted

British-born director Michael [David] Apted, whose credits include the 1999 James Bond movie *The World is Not Enough*, died in Los Angeles on January 7, aged 79. He began his career as a TV director in the early

1960s, and his other credits include *Blink*, *The Chronicles of Narnia: The Voyage of the Dawn Treader* and the 1974 hour-long ghost story *Haunted: Poor Girl* for TV. Apted was also an executive producer on Francis Ford Coppola's *Bram Stoker's Dracula* (1992).

Richard Arnold

Canadian Richard Arnold, who worked with Gene Roddenberry for fifteen years and was Paramount's sometimes-controversial *Star Trek* archivist up to the early 1990s, died on January 26, aged 66. He had small cameos in *Star Trek: The Motion Picture* (1979) and *Star Trek* (2009), and contributed to a number of *Star Trek* documentaries, including *Trekkies* and *Trekkies 2*. Arnold was credited as a research consultant on *Star Trek: The Next Generation*.

Ed Asner

American character actor and political activist Ed Asner (Yitzhak Edward Asner) died on August 29, aged 91. He became an unlikely star on TV playing gruff former television station manager turned newspaper editor "Lou Grant" on CBS' *Mary Tyler More Show* (1970–77) and then getting his own spin-off sitcom, *Lou Grant* (1977–82). Asner was also in episodes of *Studio One* ('The Night America Trembled', based on Orson Welles' 1938 *War of the Worlds* broadcast),

Alfred Hitchcock Presents, The Alfred Hitchcock Hour, The Outer Limits, Voyage to the Bottom of the Sea, The Girl from U.N.C.L.E., The Wild Wild West, The Invaders, Here Come the Brides ('The Legend of Big Foot'), Highway to Heaven, The X Files, Touched by an Angel, The Dead Zone and Doom Patrol. His movie credits include The Satan Bug, The Venetian Affair (with Boris Karloff), Daughter of the Mind, The Last Child, Haunts of the Very Rich, Elf, Not Another B Movie and Angels on Tap. In later years, Asner voiced many cartoon series (including Batman: The Animated Series, Captain Planet and the Planteers, Gargoyles, Freakazoid!, Spider-Man: The Animated Series, Superman: The Animated Series and Max Steel) and video games, he was the voice of "Jabba the Hutt" in the Star Wars: Return of the Jedi radio series (1996), and he voiced "Carl Fredricksen" in Disney/Pixar's Oscar-winning Up (2009). In a career that spanned more than six decades, he never stopped working.

Bob Avian

Tony Award-winning American dancer-turned choreographer and producer Bob Avian (Robert Avedisian), best known for his work on Broadway's A Chorus Line (with creative partner Michael Bennett) and Dreamgirls, died of cardiac arrest on January 21, aged 83. In 2000 he choreographed the West End production of The Witches of Eastwick, starring Ian McShane.

Peter Aykroyd

Canadian-born scriptwriter, actor and psychic researcher Peter [Jonathan] Aykroyd, the younger brother of Dan Aykroyd, died on November 20, the day after his 66th birthday. An alumni of the Second City comedy troupe in Toronto, he was a regular writer and performer during the fifth season of NBC-TV's Saturday Night Live (1979–80). Aykroyd also turned up in supporting roles in Coneheads, Nothing But Trouble, Kids of the Round Table and an episode of The New Avengers, and with Christopher Chacon he co-created/executive-produced the 1996–2000 TV series Psi Factor: Chronicles of the Paranormal.

Christopher Ayres

Prolific American *anime* voice actor and ADR director Christopher [Owen] Ayres died of end-stage COPD (chronic obstructive pulmonary disease) on October 18, aged 56. He voiced the English versions of such Japanese series and video games as *Gatchaman* (1973-74), *Super Dimension Fortress Macross* (1983), *Trinity Blood* (2005), *Speed Grapher* (2005), *Innocent Venus* (2006), *Ghost Hunt* (2007), *Moonlight Mile* (2007), *Ghost Hound* (2007-08), *Highschool of the Dead* (2020), *Bodacious Space Pirates* (2012), *Chaika: The Coffin Princess* (2014) and various *Dragon Ball Z* titles, amongst many others.

Dale Baer

American animator Dale [Leonard] Baer died on January 15, aged 70. He worked on *Bedknobs and Broomsticks*, *Journey Back to Oz*, *Pete's Dragon* (1977), *The Lord of the Rings* (1978), *Mickey's Christmas Carol*, *The Black Cauldron*, *The Great Mouse Detective*, *Who Framed Roger Rabbit*, *Beauty and the Beast* (1991), *Species*, *Tarzan* (1999) and *Treasure Planet*, amongst many other titles.

David Bailie

South African-born character actor David Bailie, who played the speechless "Cotton" in the *Pirates of the Caribbean* films *The Curse of the Black Pearl*, *Dead Man's Chest* and *At World's End*, died on March 6, aged 83. His other film credits include *The Creeping Flesh* (with Christopher Lee and Peter Cushing), *Son of Dracula* (1973), *Legend of the Werewolf* (again with Cushing), *The Beyond* (2017), *The House That Jack Built* and *In the Trap*. On TV, Bailie appeared in episodes of *Doctor Who*, *Blakes 7* and *Sinbad* (2012), and he was also in *Doctor Who* radio plays as the mad scientist "Taren Capel" and the "Celestial Toymaker".

Bob Baker

Oscar-winning British scriptwriter Bob Baker (Robert John Baker), who created the robot dog "K9" with writing partner Dave Martin for the BBC's *Doctor Who* in 1977, died on November 3. He was 82. Baker won various awards for co-writing the animated "Wallis & Gromit" short films *The Wrong Trousers* (1993), *A Close Shave* (1995) and *A Matter of Loaf and Death* (2008), along with the feature film *The Curse of the Were-Rabbit* (2005). With Martin (who died in 2007), he also co-created the children's series *Sky* (1975) and *King of the Castle* (1977) for HTV, and the 1987 pilot *Succubus*. Baker's other scriptwriting credits include episodes of TV's *Arthur of the Britons* and *Scorpion Tales*, while additionally coming up with the original idea and scripting fifteen episodes of *Into the Labyrinth* (1981–82). He was also a technical consultant on Disney's 1971 movie *Bedknobs and Broomsticks*. Baker's autobiography, *K9 Stole My Trousers*, was published in 2013.

Lisa Banes

65-year-old American actress Lisa Banes died of traumatic brain injury on June 14, after being struck ten days earlier by an e-scooter that went through a red light in New York City. She starred in the 1992 TV movie *Danger Island* (aka *The Presence*) and also appeared in *Last Exit to Earth*, *Dragonfly* and *A Cure for Wellness*, along with episodes of *Star Trek: Deep Space Nine*, *Once Upon a Time*, *The Orville* and *Them*.

Douglas Barbour

Canadian academic, poet and critic Douglas [Fleming] Barbour died on September 25, aged 81. He wrote the non-fiction study *Worlds Out of Words: The SF Novels of Samuel R. Delany*, co-edited *Tesseracts 2* (1987) with Phyllis Gotlieb, reviewed for various SF magazines and served on the editorial board for *OnSpec Magazine*. The Book Publishers Association of Alberta announced that its Speculative Fiction Book of the Year award has been renamed the Douglas Barbour Award for Speculative Fiction in his memory.

Miquel Barceló

Spanish SF editor, translator and writer Miquel Barceló died of liver disease on November 22, aged 72. A scientist and engineer by profession, in 1986 he founded the Nova science fiction series for publisher Ediciones B, editing the annual *Premio UPC* anthologies. Barceló also wrote the non-fiction studies *Paradojas: Ciencia en la ciencia-ficción*, *Paradojas II: Ciencia en la ciencia ficción* and *Ciencia ficción: Nueva guía de lectura*, and edited the fanzine *Kadama* (1980–84).

Pilar Bardem

Spanish actress Pilar Bardem [Muñoz], the mother of actor Javier Bardem, died of lung disease on July 17, aged 82. She was in *Exorcism's Daughter*, *Blue Eyes of the Broken Doll*, *The Mummy's Revenge* (with Paul Naschy), *Cosa de brujas*, *Hexe Lilli: Der Drache und das magische Buch* and the sequel *Hexe Lilli: Die Reise nach Mandolan*, along with the SF TV series *El inquilino* (2004) and the haunted house series *Hay alguien ahí* (2009-10)

Graham Garfield Barnard

Australian TV producer Graham Garfield Barnard died of cancer on September 16, aged 59. He was one of the co-creators of the weekly *The Schlocky Horror Picture Show* (with Tim Newsom), which showed old horror movies on a number of Australian and New Zealand TV stations from 2007 until Barnard's death. From episode 26 onwards, he also provided the voice of skeleton host "Nigel Honeybone". In 2013, Barnard was awarded the Rondo Hatton Classic Horror Award for International Fan of the Year, and he was inducted into the Official Horror Host Hall of Fame in 2019.

Edward Barnes

Edward Barnes (Herbert Edward Campbell Barnes), who was head of BBC television's children's programmes from 1978-86, died of COVID-19 on September 7, aged 92. A former actor, early in his career at the BBC Barnes worked as a stage manager on the 1953 serial *The Quatermass Experiment*. He went on to produce and direct *Blue Peter* from 1962-68, and he helped to commission such shows as *Rentaghost* (1976-84) and "The Chronicles of Narnia" (*The Lion the Witch and the Wardrobe*, *Prince Caspian and the Voyage of the Dawn Treader* and *The Silver Chair*, 1988-90).

Olga Barnet

Russian stage and screen actress Olga [Borisovna] Barnet, who appeared in *Solaris* (1972) under the name "O. Barnet", died after a long illness on June 25, aged 69.

David G. Barnett

American writer, editor and book cover designer David G. Barnett died in a car crash in February, aged 53. His short fiction appeared in the first three volumes of Cemetery Dance's *Shivers* anthologies and the chapbooks *Spying on Gods* and *The Baby* (with Edward Lee), and was collected in *Dead Souls*. Barnett also wrote the novels *Tales of the Fallen Book 1: Awakenings* and *Tales of the Fallen Book 2: Neon Wings*. He edited five issues of "The Magazine of Extreme Horror" *Into the Darkness* (1994–96), and the anthologies *Damned: An Anthology of the Lost*, *Into the Darkness Vol. 1* (with C. Dennis Moore), *Chopping Block Party* (with Brendan Deneen) and *The Big Book of Blasphemy* (with Regina Garza Mitchell). Barnett founded Necro Publications in 1993, along with the imprints Bedlam Books and Weird West Books, publishing such authors as Edward Lee, Joe R. Lansdale, Charlee Jacob, Gerard Houarner, Mehitobel Wilson, Jeffrey Thomas, Patrick Lestewka and others. As Fat Cat Graphic Design he also created covers for Necro and a number of other small press publishers.

Claudia Barrett

American actress Claudia Barrett (Imagene Williams), who co-starred in the infamous *Robot Monster* (1953), died on April 30, aged 91. 25-year-old producer/director Phil Tucker's post-apocalyptic movie was shot in black and white 3-D over four days in Los Angeles' Bronson Canyon for a reported budget of $16,000. Barrett also appeared on TV in an episode of *Science Fiction Theatre*. She retired from acting in 1964, and in 1981 joined the Academy of Motion

Astor Pictures' Robot Monster (1953) was shot in a cheap 3-D process and marked a rare starring role for American actress Claudia Barrett (1929–2021).

Picture Arts and Sciences (AMPAS) where, for fourteen years, she worked on the annual Oscars for scientific and technical advances.

Susan Bartholomew

Self-published British author and poet Susan Bartholomew died after a long illness on September 26. She was the author of the medieval fantasy trilogy "Swords of Elyx" trilogy (*The Lake of Destiny*, *The World Below* and *Taliesin's Heir*). Bartholomew also published the online novels *Codename Chameleon*, *Meat Machines*, *Vine Manor* and *The Emerald Cross*, along with a number of short stories. Another novel, *Witch Gate*, apparently remains unpublished. She also wrote interactive fiction and text games under the name "Endelyon".

Bart the Bear II

Alaskan brown bear Bart the Bear II (aka "Little Bart") died on November 14, aged 21. Trained by Doug and Lynne Seus of Wasatch Rocky Mountain Wildlife, Inc., who also raised the first "Bart the Bear", he appeared in *Dr. Dolittle 2*, *Into the Grizzly Maze*, *Pete's Dragon* (2016) and an episode of HBO's *Game of Thrones*.

Anne Beatts

Saturday Night Live actress and writer Anne [Patricia] Beatts died on April 7, aged 74. She co-scripted the American

version of the French/Belgium animated film *Tarzoon: Shame of the Jungle* (1975), and her other scriptwriting credits include *Nightlife* (1989) and episodes of TV's *Faerie Tale Theatre*, *Happily Ever After: Fairy Tales for Every Child* and the 1993 pilot *The Elvira Show*.

Ned Beatty

American character actor Ned (Thomas) Beatty died on June 13, aged 83. He made a memorable screen debut in 1972 in *Deliverance* ("Squeal like a pig"), and went on to appear in the Richard Matheson-scripted *Dying Room Only*, *Exorcist II: The Heretic*, *Superman* and *Superman II* (as Lex Luthor's bumbling sidekick "Otis"), *The Incredible Shrinking Woman*, *The Haunting of Barney Palmer*, *The Unholy* (1988), *Purple People Eater*, *Time Trackers*, *Repossessed*, *Captain America* (1990), *Prelude to a Kiss*, *Ed and His Dead Mother*, *Replikator* and *Thunderpants*. On TV, Beatty turned up in episodes of *Tales of the Unexpected*, *Lucan*, *Faerie Tale Theatre*, *Alfred Hitchcock Presents* (1985), *Highway to Heaven* and the 1999 mini-series *Gulliver's Travels*.

William R. Beck

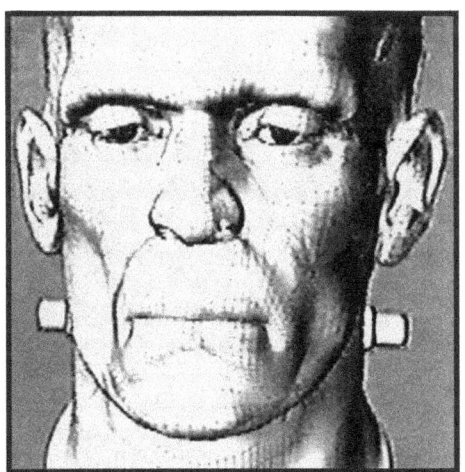

American special effects model maker William R. Beck (aka "Bill Beck") died on September 19, aged 84.

While at ILM he worked on *Star Wars: The Empire Strikes Back, Raiders of the Lost Ark, Dragonslayer, Star Wars: Return of the Jedi, Star Trek III: The Search for Spock, Cocoon, Explorers, The Golden Child, Back to the Future Part II* and *Star Wars Episode I–The Phantom Menace*. In 1987, Beck became a set director, and he contributed to *Leonard Part 6, Jack* (1996) and *Sphere*, and he was an electrician on *James and the Giant Peach* (1996). Beck also worked as a set designer on an all-digital 1998 film at ILM called *CGI Frankenstein* (aka *Frankenstein vs. The Wolfman*), but the project was soon abandoned and only a short animation test exists.

Charles Beeson

British-born television director and producer Charles Beeson died of a heart attack on April 26, aged around 64. After working as a first assistant director on the BBC series *The Invisible Man* (1984), he directed five episodes *Afterlife* (2005–06, created by Stephen Volk) and such US shows *Smallville, Terminator: The Sarah Connor Chronicles, The Vampire Diaries, The Secret Circle, Fringe, The Whispers, Containment, Timeless, Supernatural* and *Around the World in 80 Days* (2021).

Jean-Paul Belmondo

Suave French leading man Jean-Paul Belmondo died on September 6, aged 88. Jean-Luc Godard's "New Wave" classic *Breathless* (1960) made the former boxer an international star, and he was best known for his comedy and crime films, including the James Bond spoof *Casino Royale* (1967), the serial-killer thriller *The Night Caller* (1975) and the SF comedy *Peut-être* (1999). Belmondo was made a Commander of France's Légion d'Honneur in 2007.

Catherine Belsey

British literary scholar and lecturer Catherine Belsey died of a stroke on February 14, aged 80. Her books include the transformative *Critical Practice* (1980), *Shakespeare?* (2007) and *Tales of the Troubled Dead: Ghost Stories in Cultral History* (2019), which looked at how ghost stories "unsettle conventional ways of understanding the world" by allowing us to "think beyond the limited categories orthodoxy takes for granted".

Benício

Brazilian artist Benício (José Luiz Benício da Fonseca) died on December 7, aged 84. He created thousands of paperback covers (notably for the "Brigitte" spy series), more than 300 national cinema posters, and hundreds of record covers. Benício started painting movie posters in the late 1960s, and

amongst the many titles he worked on are *Aladim e a Lâmpada Maravilhosa*, *O Signo de Escorpião*, *Elke Maravilha Contra o Homem Atômico* and *O Profeta da Fome*, *The Strange Hostel of Naked Pleasures* and *Infernal Carnal* (the last three starring José Mojica Marins), along with such entries in the popular 1980s comedy series as *Os Trapalhões na Guerra dos Planetas*, *O Incrível Monstro Trapalhão*, *Os Trapalhões e o Mágico de Oróz* and *Os Trapalhões na Terra dos Monstros*. His work has been collected in the books as *Sex & Crime: The Book Cover Art of Benício* and *E Benício criou a mulher* (aka *Benicio: Um perfil do mestre das pin-ups e dos cartazes de cinema*), while *Benício, O Mestre das Pin-ups* is a 2010 documentary about the artist and his work.

Fran Bennett

American character actress Fran Bennett died on September 12, aged 84. Often cast as judges, she appeared

in *Wes Craven's New Nightmare*, *8MM*, *Crazy as Hell* and *The Manor*, along with episodes of TV's *Shadow Chasers*, *The Twilight Zone* (1986), *Highway to Heaven*, *ALF*, *Star Trek: The Next Generation*, *Quantum Leap*, *Team Knight Rider* and *Early Edition*. From 1996-2003, Bennett was head of acting and director of performance at the California Institute of the Arts School of Theater.

Walter Bernstein

Blacklisted American writer Walter [Saul] Bernstein, who scripted the 1964 movie *Fail Safe* and the 2000 TV remake, died on January 22, aged 101.

Dennis Berry

American-born TV producer, writer and director Dennis (Charles) Berry died in Paris, France, on June 12, aged 76. His credits include the TV movie remakes of *Angel on My Shoulder* (1980) and *Midnight Lace* (1981), along with episodes of *Stargate SG-1*, *Highlander* and *Highlander: The Raven*. Berry also turned up in a small role in Roger Vadim's 'Metzengerstein' episode of *Spirits of the Dead* (1969). He was married to actress Jean Seberg from 1972-79 and Anna Karina from 1982-2019, both of whom predeceased him.

Kit Berry

British author Kit Berry (Kirtsen Espensen) died on October 29. A former school teacher, the popularity of her self-published young fantasy

novels *Magus of Stonewylde* (2005), *Moondance of Stonewylde* (2006) and *Solstice at Stonewylde* (2007) led to a six-figure publishing deal with Gollancz/Orion that included the original trilogy, plus the sequels *Shadows at Stonewylde* (2011) and *Shaman of Stonewylde* (2012). Berry also created merchandise, festivals and online forums based around the "Stonewylde" series.

Val Bisoglio

American character actor Val Bisoglio (Italo Valentino Bisoglio) died on October 18, aged 95. He studied acting under drama coach Jeff Corey and appeared in the 1966 Broadway production of *Wait Until Dark* (opposite Lee Remick and Robert Duvall). On TV, Bisoglio was in episodes of *The Sixth Sense*, *Kolchak: The Night Stalker* ('The Zombie') and *Galactica 1980*.

Lionel Blair

Canadian-born British actor, dancer and choreographer [Henry] Lionel Blair [Ogus] died on November 4, aged 92. He created the musical numbers for Hammer's Jekyll & Hyde comedy *The Ugly Duckling* (1959) and was choreographer for *The Magic Christian* and an episode of TV's *Space: 1999*. In 2004, Blair took over the role of the "Child Catcher" in the London stage production of *Chitty Chitty Bang Bang*. Along with actor-singer Leon Greene (who died in June), he is credited as helping to introduce pantomime to Canada.

Rick Boatright

American author Rick Boatright (James Richard Boatright, Jr.) died of pancreatic cancer on July 22, aged 66. He contributed a number of short stories to to Eric Flint's multi-author, alternate-history "Assiti Shards (1632) Universe" from Baen Books, along with the 2016 novel *1636: The Chronicles of Dr. Gribbleflotz* (with Kerryn Offord).

Margaret Wander Bonanno

American writer Margaret Wander Bonanno died on April 8, aged 71. She wrote a number of *Star Trek* tie-ins (*Dwellers in the Crucible*, *Strangers from the Sky*, *Probe*, *Catalyst of Sorrows*, *Burning Dreams* and *Unspoken Truth*) along with *The Others*, *OtherWhere*,

OtherWise, *Saturn's Child* (with Nichelle Nichols), *Preternatural*, *Preternatural Too: Gyre*, *Preternatural 3*, *Ailuranth* and the "Young Astronauts" YA novels *Destination Mars* and *Citizens of Mars* (as by "Rick North"). Bonanno also wrote *Angela Lansbury: A Biography*.

Frank Bonner

American supporting actor and TV director Frank Bonner (Frank Woodrow Boers, Jr.), who played

"Herb Tarlek" on the CBS-TV sitcom *WKRP in Cincinnati* (1978-82), died of complications from Lewy body dementia on June 17, aged 79. He also appeared in *Equinox* (1967/70, with Fritz Leiber, Jr.), along with episodes of *Man from Atlantis*, *Fantasy Island* and *Harry and the Hendersons*. Bonner directed eleven episodes of the latter show.

Perry Botkin, Jr.

American music producer and composer Perry Botkin, Jr., who arranged Glen Campbell's 'Wichita Lineman', died on January 18, aged 87. He composed the music for TV's *Quark* (1977-78) and *Mork & Mindy* (1978-82), and his others credits include *Tarzan the Ape Man* (1981), *Dance of the Dwarfs* and *Silent Night Deadly Night*, along with an episode of *My Brother the Angel*.

Linda Boyce

It was reported in early December that 1960s "sexploitation" actress Linda Boyce had died. Her credits include *Electronic Lover*, *The Curse of Her Flesh*, *To Hex with Sex*, *Bacchanale* and *The Amazing Transplant*. Boyce appeared in a number of "roughie" movies and used a variety of names, including "Lena Brice", "Claudia Cheer", "Linda Mactavish", "Linda Burns", "Liz Cole", "Linda Wilson", "Lydia Bove", "Lyse Boule", "Helga Ripp", "Mary Poey", "Lois Boyd" and "Linda Boyers". She retired from acting in 1970, after six years in the adult film business, but returned briefly in the 1970s as a sound recordist under the "Helga Ripp" pseudonym.

Blade Braxton

American professional wrestler Blade Braxton (Troy Ferguson, aka "The Midnight Rose") died on March 28, aged 46. As an actor, he appeared in

such low budget indie movies as *Mediatrix*, *I.D.S. Rising* (as "Satan"), *House of Forbidden Secrets*, *The Girl Who Played with the Dead* (as "Satan" again), *Hole in the Wall*, *Aztec Revenge*, *Sleepless Nights* ('It Hits the Fan' segment), *Grindsploitation* ('Durville Sweet & The Lost Temple of Ass Pirates' segment), *Dreaming Purple Neon*, *Return to Return to Nuke 'em High aka Vol. 2*, *Drive-In Movie Maniacs: Super Boo Sunday*, *Kabukiman's Cocktail Corner: Loaded in Las Vegas* and *Shakespeare's Sh*tstorm*.

Shane Briant

British-born leading man and novelist Shane Briant died after a long illness on May 27, aged 74. In the early 1970s Hammer Films put him under contract and tried to turn him into a star with such films as *Straight on Till Morning*, *Demons of the Mind*, *Captain Kronos: Vampire Hunter* and *Frankenstein and the Monster from Hell*. Briant also portrayed "Dorian Gray" in the 1973 Dan Curtis production of *The Picture of Dorian Gray*, and his other credits include *Hawk the Slayer*, *Out of Body*, *Chameleon II: Death Match*, *Chameleon 3: Dark Angel* and *Subterano*, along with the TV mini-series *Maria Marten or Murder in the Red Barn* (1980) and episodes of *Time Trax*, *Twisted*, *The Lost World* (2001) and *Farscape*. He immigrated to Australia in 1983.

Leslie Bricusse

British-born music composer, lyricist and scriptwriter Leslie [Charles] Bricusse OBE died in France on

Frankenstein and the Monster from Hell (1974) *was the last in Hammer's long-running series and co-starred Shane Briant (1946–2021) as an asylum inmate helping Peter Cushing's Baron Frankenstein with his experiments.*

October 19, aged 90. The double Academy Award-winner's credits include the theme songs for the James Bond films *Goldfinger* and *You Only Live Twice*, and the love theme from *Superman* (1978). He also worked on *Doctor Dolittle* (1967), *Scrooge* (1970), *Willy Wonka & the Chocolate Factory*, *Peter Pan* (1976), *Babes in Toyland* (1986), *Hook*, *Harry Potter and the Philosopher's Stone* and *Jekyll & Hyde: The Musical*. Brucusse's songs have been recorded by Sammy Davis Jr., Petula Clark, Nina Simone, Frank Sinatra, Nancy Sinatra, Shirley Bassey, The Turtles and many others. His first wife was Hammer Films actress Yvonne Romain.

Johnny Briggs

Former British child actor Johnny Briggs (John Ernest Briggs) MBE, who appeared with Christopher Lee in Hammer's *The Devil-Ship Pirates* (1964), died after a long illness on February 28, aged 85. His other film appearances include uncredited roles in the crazy fantasy *Helter Skelter* (1949), the "Bulldog" Drummond sci-spy *Some Girls Do* and *Quest for Love* (based on a short story by John Wyndham). On TV, Briggs enjoyed long-running co-starring roles in such dramas and soap operas as *No Hiding Place* (1962–66), *Crossroads* (1972–74) and, notably, 2,349 episodes of the soap opera *Coronation Street* (1974–2006).

Harry V. Bring

American TV producer Harry V. Bring died of cancer on February 16, aged 78. After working as an assistant director and unit production manager on earlier seasons, he moved up to a producer on *The X Files* (2000–02). Bring's other credits as a second unit or assistant director include *Strange Brew*, *Little Monsters* and TV's *Max Headroom* (1987–88).

Brick Bronsky

57-year-old American character actor and professional wrestler Brick Bronsky (Jeffrey M. Beltzner) died of

American book dealer Bob Brown (Robert Lee Brown) died of esophageal cancer in early June, aged 78. Although he worked in advertising, he started selling used books in the 1970s and co-founded the Seattle Book Center in the early 1980s. He became a full-time bookseller a decade later, opening his own store specialising in used and rare science fiction, fantasy, horror and mystery books, pulp magazines and original art.

complications from COVID-19 on August 23, after going into a coma the previous day. He co-starred in Troma Studio's *Sgt. Kabukiman N.Y.P.D.*, *Class of Nuke 'Em High Part II: Subhumanoid Meltdown*, *Class of Nuke 'Em High Part 3: The Good, the Bad and the Subhumanoid* and *Return to Nuke 'Em High Volume 1*, along with the 2019 "slasher" *Masked Mutilator* (which he also co-produced and directed under his real name).

Bob Brown

Denise Bryer

British voice actress Denise [Pauline Rosalie] Bryer died on October 16, aged 93. She voiced the title character in Gerry Anderson's now mostly lost puppet series *The Adventures of Twizzle* (1957–58) and went on to work with Anderson again on *Four Feather Falls* (1960), *Terrahawks* (1983–86) and *G-Force Intergalactic* (1993). Bryer's other voice credits include *Gulliver's Travels* (1977), *Hercules* (1983), Disney's *Return to Oz*, *Labyrinth* and the *anime*

TV series X Bomber. She was married to Nicholas Parsons from 1954-89.

Wiktor Bukato

Polish SF fan, translator and publisher Wiktor [Cezary] Bukato died on July 26, aged 72. A former English teacher, he worked as an editor at the publishing houses Wydawnictwo Iskray and Wydawnictwie Alfa, creating the "Zeszytową Iskier" and "Biblioteki Fantastyki" series respectively, before becoming the head of the Warsaw branch of Phantom Press (1991-92) and then editor-in-chief at Alkazar (1992-95). Bukato translated books by Poul Anderson, Arthur C. Clarke, Harlan Ellison, James E. Gunn, Theodore Sturgeon, Stanley G. Weinbaum, James White, Donald A. Wollheim and many other authors. His own books include Sztuka Science Fiction Art and the anthology Rakietowe dzieci. In 1987, Bukato was presented with the Karel Award for best translator by World SF.

Allan Burns

American scriptwriter and producer Allan Burns, who is credited with coming up with the original format for TV's The Munsters (1964-66) with Chris Hayward, and who created My Mother the Car (1965-66), died on January 30, aged 85. Burns was also a story consultant on Get Smart and created the breakfast cereal character "Cap'n Crunch".

Kathy Burns

Kathy Burns, the wife of legendary gorilla-suit actor and movie memorabilia collector Bob Burns since 1956, died on May 12 - her husband's 86th birthday. During the 1950s she helped pioneering special make-up effects creator Paul Blaisdell on such movies as Not of This Earth and Invasion of the Saucermen, and with her husband hosted Shock Theater in the late 1950s on a local Texas TV channel. When William Castle came to town to promote The Tingler (1959), Bob turned his wife

into "Miss Shock" and they greeted the producer/director at the airport and presented him with the "Skeleton Key" to the city. Castle reportedly loved it! Kathy Burns also co-scripted the 2009 video documentary *Bob Burn's Hollywood Halloween* and made small cameo appearances in Peter Jackson's *King Kong* (2005) and *The Lovely Bones, Fire City: End of Days* and the mini-series *Monstrkyd Manor*.

John Bush

John Bush, who took over as Chairman and Joint Managing Director (with Livia Gollancz) of Victor Gollancz Ltd. in 1963, died in Canada on April 29, aged 105. For many years he ran the Gollancz SF list, until his retirement in 1982, when he handed it over to Malcolm Edwards. "JB", as he was known, was Guest of Honour at the 1977 Eastercon.

David Butler

South African actor David Butler died of cancer on May 27, aged 61. He appeared in *The Canterville Ghost* (1983), *Project Shadowchaser II, Friend Request, Maze Runner: The Death Cure, Dust* and the 2005 mini-series *The Triangle*. On TV, Butler co-starred in the series *Room 9* (2012–13) and *Dead Places* (2021), and he also turned up in two episodes of *The Prisoner* (2009).

Jeremy G. Byrne

Australian editor and publisher Jeremy G. (George) Byrne died after a

70-year-old American actress JoAnna [Kara] Cameron, best remembered for starring as "Andrea Thomas"/"Isis" in the Saturday morning superhero TV series *The Secrets of Isis* (1975–76), died in Hawaii of complications from a stroke on October 22. She recreated her role as the goddess in three episodes of *Shazam!*, and her other credits include episodes of *Search* and *The Amazing Spider-Man*. Cameron retired from acting in 1980, and in later years worked in hotel marketing.

long illness on November 25, aged 57. With Richard Scriven, Jonathan Strahan and others, he co-founded the small press Eidolon Publications and co-edited *Eidolon: The Journal of Australian Science Fiction and Fantasy* (1990–2000). Eidolon published books by Terry Dowling and Robin Pen. With Strahan, Byrne also edited the anthologies *The Year's Best Australian Science Fiction and Fantasy Volume 1* and *Volume 2*, and *Eidolon 1*.

JoAnna Cameron

Carmine Capobianco

American actor and video-store owner Carmine Capobianco died of cancer on January 9, aged 62. He appeared in such low-budget movies as *Disconnected*, *Psychos in Love*, *Galactic Gigolo*, *Cemetery High*, *Thrill Kill Jack in Hale Manor*, *The Land of College Prophets*, *Bikini Bloodbath Shakespeare*, *Bikini Bloodbath*, *Bikini Bloodbath Car Wash*, *I Spill Your Guts*, *Cool As Hell*, *The Sins of Dracula*, *Seven Dorms of Death*, *Bite School*, *Model Hunger*, *Killer Waves*, *Mind Melters*, *Cool As Hell 2*, *Sexy Time* and *Brotherhood Bloodlines: A*

Hunters' Crossing Story. Copabianco also co-scripted *Psychos in Love*, *Galactic Gigolo* and *Cemetery High*, which were released by various Charles Band distribution companies in the 1980s.

René Cardona III

Mexican actor, screenwriter and director René Cardona III, the son of director René Cardona Jr. and the grandson of director René Cardona, died of a heart attack on May 16, aged 59. As an actor, he had supporting roles (sometimes billed as "Al Coster") in *Santo vs. Capulina*, *The Bermuda Triangle* (1978), *Terror en los barrios*, *Cemetery of Terror*, *Beaks: The Movie* and *Vacaciones de terror* (aka *Horror Holiday*). Cardona also directed *Vacaciones de terror* along with *El beso de la muerte: historias espeluznantes*, *Alarido del terror*, *Colmillos el hombre lobo*, *El asesino del teatro* and many other direct-to-video movies.

Linda Carlson

American character actress Linda Carlson died of ALS on October 26, aged 76. She was in *Honey I Blew Up the Kid* and episodes of TV's *Space: Above and Beyond* and *The Pretender*.

Ralph Carmichael

American composer, conductor and arranger Ralph Carmichael died on October 18, aged 94. His credits include the scores for the cult 1950s SF movies *The Blob* and *4D Man*, along with the theme music for the

1965-66 TV series *My Mother the Car*. Carmichael was later regarded as one of the pioneers of contemporary Christian music.

Carol Carr

American author Carol Carr (Carol Stuart), the widow of author and editor Terry Carr, died of lung cancer on September 1, aged 82. She became involved in SF fandom in the early 1960s and sold her first story to Damon Knight's anthology *Orbit 5* in 1969. Her other stories (two in collaboration with her husband or Karen Harber) appeared in *Orbit 8*, *Science Fiction Tales*, *Magicats!*, *The Ultimate Alien*, *The Magazine of Fantasy & Science Fiction* and *Omni*, and were included in the 2014 volume *Carol Carr: The Collected Writings*. She was married to Terry Carr from 1961 until his death in 1987, and she married SF fan Robert Lichtman in 2000.

Raffaella Carrà

Italian actress, singer and entertainer Raffaella Carrà (Raffaella Roberta Pelloni) died on July 5, aged 78. She appeared in the 1960s *peplums Atlas Against the Cyclops*, *Mole Men Against the Son of Hercules* and *Ulysses Against Hercules*.

Jean-Claude Carrière

Honorary Oscar-winning French screenwriter and novelist Jean-Claude [François] Carrière died on February 8, aged 89. The prolific Carrière worked

La Nuit de Frankenstein (1957) was the third of six sequels written by French novelist Jean-Claude Carrière (1931–2021) under the house name "Benoît Becker".

on Jess Franco's *The Diabolical Dr. Z* and *Jack the Ripper*, *The Monk* (1972) and Luis Buñuel's *The Phantom of Liberty*. Under the shared pseudonym "Benoît Becker" he also wrote six "Frankenstein" novels for Fleuve Noir from 1957–59: *La tour de Frankenstein*, *Le pas de Frankenstein*, *La nuit de Frankenstein*, *Le sceau de Frankenstein*, *Frankenstein rôde* and *La cave de Frankenstein*.

Steve Carver

American photographer and exploitation movie director Steve Carver died of a heart attack on January 8, aged 75. His movies include the 1971 short *The Tell-Tale Heart* (based on the story by Edgar Allan Poe) and several films for Roger Corman (*Big Bad Mama*, *Capone*, etc.). Carver supplied the photos for C. Courtney Joyner's 2019 volume, *Western Portraits: The Unsung Heroes and Villains of the Silver Screen*.

Nino Castelnuovo

Italian leading man Nino Castelnuovo (Francesco Castelnuovo) died after a long illness on September 6, aged 84. Best known for co-starring opposite Catherine Deneuve in *The Umbrellas of Cherbourg* (although his performance was completely re-dubbed by another actor), his other credits include *The Creatures* (1966), *Psychout for Murder*, *The Bloodstained Lawn*, *Strip Nude for Your Killer*, *Star Odyssey* and *With the Killer's Eyes*. Castelnuovo also appeared as "William Wilson" in two episodes of the 1979 TV mini-series *I racconti fantastici di Edgar Allan Poe*.

Judi B. Castro

Judi B. Castro (Judi Beth Goodman), who co-wrote a story in John Joseph Adams' 2017 anthology *Cosmic Powers* with her husband, writer Adam-Troy Castro, died after a brief illness on July 15, aged 58. The couple were also part of a group of writers who collaborated on a deliberately bad novel, *Atlanta Nights* (2005), designed

to embarrass publishers who cared little about the prose they printed, with proceeds going to the SFWA Emergency Medical Fund. She was active in Florida fandom and chaired Tropicon XVI in 1997. Following his wife's death, Adam-Troy Castro set up a GoFundMe page.

Raymond Cavaleri

1960s American child actor Raymond Cavaleri died on July 19, aged 74. He played "Billy" alongside John Carradine and Bruce Dern in the 1961 *Thriller* episode 'The Remarkable Mrs. Hawk' (based on a *Weird Tales* story by Margaret St. Clair). Cavaleri also appeared in an episode of *Alfred Hitchcock Presents* and several other TV shows and movies before retiring from the screen in the mid-1970s to become a talent agent.

Meloney Crawford Chadwick

American comics editor and publisher Meloney Crawford Chadwick died of COVID-19 in February, aged 66. She worked for such companies as Harris Publications and Dark Horse Comics on such titles as *Vampirella Classic*, *Chains of Chaos*, *The Vengeance of Vampirella* and *The Heretic*.

John Challis

British character actor John Challis, best remembered as second-hand car dealer "Boycie" in the BBC sitcom *Only Fools and Horses* (1981-2003), died on September 19, aged 79. He made his screen debut in the low budget horror movie *Where Has Poor Mickey Gone?* (1964), and his other film credits include the 1974 version of *Dracula* (with Jack Palance as the Count). On TV, Challis also appeared in episodes of *Doctor Who* ('The Seeds of Doom'), *Thriller* (1976) and *The New Avengers*. The actor was made an honorary citizen of Serbia, where *Only Fools and Horses* remains hugely popular.

Geoffrey Chater

British character actor Geoffrey Chater (Geoffrey Michael Chater Robinson) died on October 16, aged 100. Often cast as Establishment figures such as ministers, vicars, lawyers, bankers and doctors, his many credits include *The Strange World of Planet X* (aka *Cosmic Monsters*), *The Day the Earth Caught Fire*, *If . . .*, *Endless Night*, *Dr. Jekyll and Mr. Hyde* (1973), *O Lucky Man!* and *The Aerodrome*, along with episodes of TV's *Sherlock Holmes* (1951), *Adam Adamant Lives!*, *The Avengers*, *The Champions*, *Big Brother* (1970), *Doomwatch*, *The Wide World of Mystery*, *Orson Welles Great Mysteries*, *Father Brown* ('The Curse of the Golden Cross', 1974), *Haunted: The Ferryman*, *Thriller* (1974-75) and *Tales of the Unexpected*.

Sung-Young Chen

Taiwanese actor Sung-Young Chen (Chen Sung-young) died after a long illness on December 17, aged 80. A former child actor, his credits include *Burning of the Red Lotus Monastery*, *The 3-D Army* and the 1985 "hopping vampire" comedy *Hello Dracula*.

Maria Chianetta

Italian actress and scriptwriter Maria Chianetta (Chianetta Mara) died on September 17, aged 82. From 1957-84 she appeared in a number of movies (including the early *giallo*, *Libido*), under various names ("Mara Ombra"/"Chianetta"/"Mara Marilli"/"Mara Maryl") and, in collaboration with her husband, writer and director Ernesto Gastaldi, she contributed to the scripts for Sergio Martino's *The Great Alligator* (1979) and *The Scorpion with Two Tails* (1982).

Sonny Chiba

Japanese movie star and martial arts expert Sonny Chiba (Sadaho Maeda, aka "Shin'ichi Chiba") died of complications from COVID-19 on August 19, aged 82. He starred in *Invasion of the Neptune Men*, *Terror Beneath the Sea*, *The Golden Bat*, *Wolf Guy*, *Message from Space*, *Virus* (1980), *Samurai Reincarnation*, *Ninja Wars*, *Legend of the Eight Samurai* (1983) and *The Storm Riders*. Chiba also co-starred as "Space Sheriff Voicer" in the 1982-83 TV series *Space Sheriff Gavan* and various spin-off series and films, and he also turned up in an episode of *Robot Detective*.

Richard Citron

American movie and TV marketing executive Richard "Rusty" Citron died of Lewy body dementia on December 16, aged 68. As a marketing executive, he led the team that revitalized the Marvel Comics

Invasion of the Neptune Men (1961) was an early credit for Japanese action star Sonny Chiba (1939–2021).

film franchise, and Citron also worked at 20th Century Fox, LucasFilm, Walt Disney, MGM, Sony Pictures and Universal Studios. His career encompassed everything from designing national mall promotions for George Lucas' *Return of the Jedi* (1983) to personal representation for Mel Brooks, Anne Bancroft, Dom DeLuise, Larry Gelbart and others. A memoir about Citron's time in showbusiness was entitled *The Elephant Won't Do Cable!: My Life in Hollywood from Zsa Zsa to Alice Cooper*. He donated his brain for research to the Brain Donor Project, in hopes of a cure and more support to treat Lewy body dementia.

John Clabburn

52-year-old Australian second unit and first assistant director John Clabburn died after a freak accident while trimming his garden hedges on April 6. He fell ten feet from a tree at home in Sydney and cut his hand on a power saw, but subsequently died in hospital from cardiac arrest as a result of blood loss. Clabburn's credits include the 2005 horror film *Feed* and episodes of TV's *Return to Jupiter* and *Ash vs Evil Dead*.

Sanford Clark

85-year-old American country-rockabilly singer and guitarist turned bit-actor Sanford Clark, who made his screen debut playing one of the eponymous "Cannibalistic Humanoid

Underground Dwellers" in the 1984 cult horror movie *C.H.U.D.*, died of complications from COVID-19 on July 4, while undergoing treatment for cancer. He also turned up in Playboy's direct-to-video *Inside Out IV* (the 'My Cyberian Rhapsody' segment) and episodes of TV's *Murder She Wrote* ('Night of the Headless Horseman'), *Beauty and the Beast* (1987) and *Freddy's Nightmares*. During the 1950s Clark had a few minor hits with 'The Fool' (later covered by Elvis Presley), 'The Cheat' and 'Son of a Gun'. In later years he worked in construction business while continuing to record songs.

Don Collier

American supporting actor Don Collier, who played ranch foreman "Sam Butler" in NBC's *The High Chaparral* (1967–71), died of lung cancer on September 13, aged 92. Although mostly known for his work in Westerns on both the big and small screens, he also appeared in the 1988 horror movie *The Cellar* and episodes of TV's *Death Valley Days* ('The Man Who Wouldn't Die'), *Land of the Giants* and *Highway to Heaven*.

Mary Collinson

Maltese-born British actress Mary Collinson died on November 23, aged 69. With her indentical twin Madeleine (who died in 2014), she co-starred with Peter Cushing as the innocent "Maria Gellhorn" in Hammer's *Twins of Evil* (1972). Arriving in Britain in April 1969, the sisters appeared in a handful of softcore sex movies in the late 1960s and early '70s, and became the first pair of identical twins to pose as "Playmates of the Month" in *Playboy* (October, 1970). Mary Collinson later moved to Milan, Italy, to run a model agency.

Gary Compton

British small press publisher, editor and author Gary [Stephen] Compton

German poster art by Klaus Dill for Hammer's Twins of Evil (1971), in which Mary Collinson (1952–2021) portrayed the demure twin opposite her sister Madeleine's seductive vampire.

died in hospital after a short illness on May 25, aged 62. Through his Tickety Boo Press imprint (2014–18) he published novels by Jo Zebedee, P.J. Strebor, Ralph Kern, Dave De Burgh, Ian Sales and many other authors. Compton also stepped in to help Simon Marshall-Jones (who died in November) after the latter's Spectral Press imprint ran into financial problems in 2016.

Neil Connery

Neil Connery, the look- and sound-alike younger brother of Sean, died after a long illness on May 10, aged 83. He was paid $5,000 to star in the 1967 Italian James Bond spoof, *Operation Kid Brother* (aka *OK Connery*) alongside such Bond alumni as Daniela Bianchi, Adolfo Celi, Bernard Lee, Anthony Dawson and Lois Maxwell. Connery also held his own against George Sanders, Maurice Evans and Patrick Allen in Tigon's *The Body Stealers* (1969), and he turned up as "Mr. Bond" in the 1984 comedy *Mad Mission 3: Our Man from Bond Street*. For many years he ran a plastering business in Glasgow, Scotland.

Michael Constantine

Greek-American character actor Michael Constantine (Constantine Joanides) died on August 31, aged 94. He appeared in *Death Cruise* (1974), *The Night That Panicked America*,

Neil Connery (1938–2021) traded on his older brother Sean's fame in the Italian-made sci-spy film Operation Kid Brother (aka OK Connery, 1967).

Conspiracy of Terror and *Thinner* (based on the novel by Stephen King). On TV, Constantine was in episodes of *The Twilight Zone*, *The Outer Limits*, *Voyage to the Bottom of the Sea*, *My Favorite Martian*, *The Invaders*, *The Flying Nun*, *Rod Serling's Night Gallery*, *Electra Woman and Dyna Girl* (as "The Sorcerer"), *Fantasy Island*, *Darkroom*, *The Powers of Matthew Star*, *Highway to Heaven*, *Probe* ('Plan 10 from Outer Space'), *Friday the 13th: The Series*, *Free Spirit* and the 1967 pilot *Ghostbreakers*.

Storm Constantine

British fantasy and horror author and publisher Storm Constantine died after a long illness on January 14, aged 64. She began writing stories as a child, and in 1987 created the "Wraeththu Chronicles" with a trilogy of novels that encompassed *The Enchantments of Flesh and Spirit*, *The Bewitchments of Love and Hate* and *The Fulfilments of Fate and Desire*. She continued the series in further novels, short stories and anthologies (co-edited with Wendy Darling), and Constantine's other novels include *Hermetch*, *Burying the Shadow*, *Sign for the Sacred*, *Calenture*, *Thin Air*, *The Thorn Boy*, *Beast and Sekhmet: Eyes of Ra* (with Eloise Coquio) and *Silverheart* (with Michael Moorcock). Her short fiction is collected in *Colurastes*, *Three Heralds of the Storm*, *The Oracle Lips*, *The Thorn Boy and Other Dreams of Dark Desires*, *Mythanima*, *Mythophidia*, *Mythangelus*, *Mytholumina*, *Mythanimus*, *Splinters of Truth* and *Mythumbra*, and she edited the anthologies *Night's Nieces*, *Dark in the Day* (with Paul Houghton) and *The Darkest Midnight in December: Ghost Stories for the Winter Season*. Many of her books were published by her own Immanion Press, which she created in 2003 after finding that UK publishers were losing interest in her work, and she republished some of Tanith Lee's books under the same imprint. In the 1990s, Constantine also founded and edited the magazine *Visionary Tongue*.

William G. Contento

American bibliographer William G. (Guy) Contento died of prostate cancer on December 13, aged 74. A computer hardware technical support engineer, he published such reference books as *Index to Science Fiction*

Anthologies and Collections, Index to Science Fiction Anthologies and Collections: 1977–1983, Index to Crime and Mystery Anthologies (with Martin H. Greenberg), the HWA Bram Stoker Award-winning *The Supernatural Index: A Listing of Fantasy, Supernatural, Occult, Weird, and Horror Anthologies* (with Mike Ashley), *Science Fiction, Fantasy, & Weird Fiction Magazine Index 1890–1998* and *Science Fiction, Fantasy, & Weird Fiction Magazine Index* series (1998–2008, with Stephen T. Miller), plus various volumes with Charles N. Brown, including *Science Fiction in Print: 1985*, the *Science Fiction, Fantasy, & Horror* series (1987–92), and *The Locus Index to Science Fiction* series (1998–2008). From 2000 onwards, Contento worked with Phil Stephenson-Payne on the FictionMags Index project.

Richard Conway

British-born visual effects supervisor Richard [Stanley Palmer] Conway died in America on December 22,

aged 79. His many credits include *Thunderbirds Are GO*, *Captain Nemo and the Underwater City*, *Arabian Adventure*, *Flash Gordon* (1980), *Conan the Barbarian*, *Britannia Hospital*, *The Meaning of Life*, *Indiana Jones and the Temple of Doom*, *Brazil*, *Little Shop of Horrors* (1986), *Superman IV: The Quest for Peace*, the Oscar-nominated *The Adventures of Baron Munchausen*, *Mary Shelley's Frankenstein*, *Loch Ness*, *Mary Reilly*, *Alice in Wonderland* (1999), *A Christmas Carol* (1999), *28 Days Later . . .*, *The Gathering*, *Agent Cody Banks 2: Destination London*, *Five Children and It*, *Sunshine*, *28 Weeks Later*, *Attack the Block*, *Dredd*, *Ex Machina*, *The Lovers* and *Containment*. On TV, Conway worked on such shows as *Stingray*, *Thunderbirds*, *Doctor Who*, and the mini-series *The Odyssey*, *Merlin* (1998), and *Jason and the Argonauts* (2000).

Alex Cord

American leading man Alex Cord (Alexander Viespi, Jr.), best known for co-starring as "Michael Coldsmith Briggs III" aka "Archangel" in the 1984–86 CBS-TV series *Airwolf*, died on August 9, aged 88. He appeared in *The Dead Are Alive!*, Gene Roddenberry's *Genesis II*, *Chosen Survivors*, *Inn of the Damned*, *Uninvited* (1987), *Hologram Man* and a 1971 short film of Edgar Allan Poe's *The Tell-Tale Heart*. On TV, Cord was in episodes of *Rod Serling's Night Gallery*, *The Six Million Dollar Man*, *Fantasy Island*, *War of the Worlds* (1988), *Monsters* (as a fine "John Thunstone" in Manly Wade Wellman's 'Rouse Him Not'), *Freddy's Nightmares* and the mini-series *Goliath Awaits* (with Christopher Lee and John Carradine). His second wife (1968–75) was actress Joanna Pettet.

Joe Cornelius

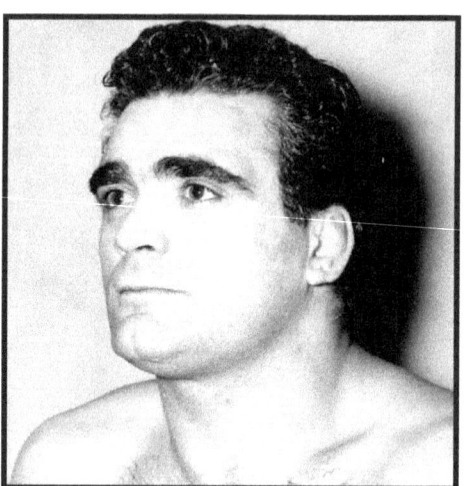

British professional wrestler turned actor Joe Cornelius ("Dazzler Joe"), who played the titular apeman in Joan Crawford's last movie, *Trog* (1970, also featuring Michael Gough), died on October 30, aged 93. He also appeared in *Casino Royale* (1967) and on TV in episodes of *Adam Adamant Lives!* and *The Avengers*. Cornelius retired from the ring as undefeated Southern England Heavyweight Champion in 1967 and went into pub management.

Charlotte Cornwell

British actress Charlotte [Elizabeth] Cornwell, the half-sister of author John le Carré (David Cornwall), died

As the eponymous troglodyte, Joe Cornelius (1928–2021) got a bigger share of the poster for Trog *(1970) than imported Hollywood star Joan Crawford.*

of cancer on January 16, aged 71. Best known for co-starring in the cult 1976 TV series *Rock Follies* and its sequel, she supplied voice work to John Carpenter's *Ghosts of Mars*, *Dante's Inferno: An Animated Epic* and *Dead Space: Aftermath*.

Bob Couttie

British novelist, scriptwriter and bit-actor Bob Couttie (Robert Couttie) died in the Philippines following a short illness on September 21, aged 71. He co-wrote the 1992 film *Future War* (which he also produced and appeared in) and *Doomsdayer* (2000). Couttie is also credited as art director on the 2016 Cambodian horror movie *The Forest Whispers*.

Frank Cox

British TV director and producer Frank Cox, whose credits include

episodes of *Doctor Who* and *Doomwatch*, died on April 29, aged 80.

J. Randolph Cox

American pulp historian, editor, publisher and author J. Randolph Cox died on September 14, aged 85. A long-time reference and government documents librarian and professor emeritus at St. Olaf College in Northfield, Minnesota, he was the editor and publisher of *The Dime Novel Round-Up* for more than twenty years. Cox was also the author of such non-fiction guides as *Man of Magic and Mystery: A Guide to the Work of*

Walter B. Gibson (the creator of "The Shadow"), *The Dime Novel Companion: A Source Book* and *Flashgun Casey, Crime Photographer: From the Pulps to Radio and Beyond* (with David S. Siegel, about the character originally created for *Black Mask* by George Harmon Coxe). He also edited *Masters of Mystery and Detective Fiction: An Annotated Bibliography* and *Dashing Diamond Dick and Other Classic Dime Novels*, and contributed fiction to *The Further Misadventures of Ellery Queen*. In 2014, Cox was presented with the Munsey Award at PulpFest. He donated his collection of comic books and newspaper strips, fanzines, pulps and other materials to the University of Minnesota Libraries, and his collection of Walter Gibson books and *Shadow* pulps and comics to Gibson's *alma mater*, Colgate University.

Robert W. Coye

Robert "Bob" W. Coye, the son of famed *Weird Tales* and Arkham House illustrator Lee Brown Coye (1907-81), died on June 3, aged 89. A retired computer-drafting instructor, he not only managed the estate but also read his father's stories for Cadabra Records' limited edition vinyl recordings *Where is Abby? & Other Tales* (2015), *Scrying Stones & Dolmen* (2018) and *Orange Hair* (2020). In 2005, Robert Coye curated an exhibition of his father's work in New Woodstock, New York.

Douglas S. Cramer

Veteran American producer Douglas S. Cramer (Douglas Schoolfield Cramer, Jr.) who, with Aaron Spelling, co-executive produced such successful TV series as *The Love Boat* (1977-87), *Hotel* (1983-88) and *Dynasty* (1981-89), died of heart and kidney failure on June 7, aged 90. As an executive, he was also responsible for such successful series as *Star Trek* (1968-69), *The Immortal* (1969-71) and *Wonder Woman* (1976-79).

Cramer's other credits include such TV movies *Dr. Crook's Garden*, *Escape*, *Terror in the Sky*, the ridiculously entertaining *The Cat Creature* and *The Dead Don't Die* (both scripted by Robert Bloch), *Search for the Gods*, *Snowbeast*, *Cruise Into Terror*, *The Power Within*, *Massarati and the Brain* (featuring Christopher Lee), *Don't Go to Sleep* (1982) and *Dark Mansions*. At one time his $100 million modern-art collection was considered amongst the largest in the world.

Johnny Crawford

American actor and singer Johnny Crawford (John Ernest Crawford), who as a child actor co-starred in the Western TV series *The Rifleman* (1958–63), died on April 29, aged 75. He had been suffering from Alzheimer's disease and dementia. Crawford was also in *The Space Children*, Bert I. Gordon's *Village of the Giants*, *The Thirteenth Floor* (1999) and an episode of *Mister Ed*.

Stephen Critchlow

British actor Stephen Critchlow died on September 19, aged 54. He co-starred as "William Cave" in the 2001 TV mini-series *The Infinite Worlds of H.G. Wells*, and his other credits include episodes of *Red Dwarf* and *Journey to the Centre of the Earth* (2017, as "Professor Otto Lidenbrock"). Critchlow also recorded a number of *Doctor Who* and *Torchwood* audio dramas with Big Finish, and he contributed voice work to numerous video games.

Roger Cudney

American character actor Roger Cudney, who was often cast as doctors and ambassadors, died of a heart attack in Mexico City on July 6, aged 85. He appeared in Juan López Moctezuma's *Mary Mary Bloody Mary* (with John Carradine), *The Bees* (again with Carradine), *Amityville II: The Possession*, *Remo Williams: The Adventure Begins*, *Ghost Fever*, *Deathstalker and the Warriors from Hell*,

Controversial British scriptwriter and director Ian [Bayley] Curteis, who directed most of the troubled 1966 SF movie *The Projected Man*, died on November 24, aged 86. He also directed an episode of TV's *Out of the Unknown* and scripted an episode of *Doomwatch*. Curteis' second wife was novelist Joanna Trollope.

Alan Curtis

British character actor Alan Curtis died on February 18, aged 90. He appeared in the Euro sci-spy thriller *Ypotron–Final Countdown*, *Aladdin and His Wonderful Lamp* (1966), *Die Screaming Marianne*, *Four Dimensions of Greta*, *The Flesh and Blood Show*, *Tiffany Jones* and *Professor Popper's Problem*. On TV, Curtis was in episodes of *Doctor Who*, *The Corridor People* and *Six Dates with Barker* ('1899: The Phantom Raspberry Blower of Old London Town'). Between 1967–95 he also served as an announcer for the MCC at Lord's Cricket Ground.

Barbarian Queen II: The Empress Strikes Back, *Total Recall* (1990), *Los demonios del desierto*, *Muerte infernal*, *Immortal Combat*, *The Arrival*, *Baño de sangre*, *Los pajarracos*, *Species: The Awakening*, *The Wailer 2*, *Soul Walker* and *The Containment*. In later years he turned up in numerous Mexican *telenovelas*.

Ian Curteis

Lou Cutell

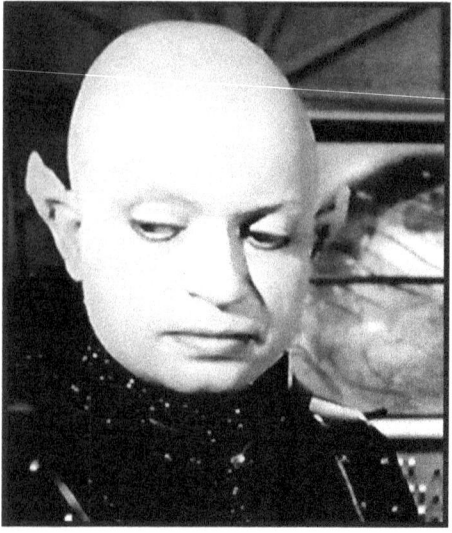

American character actor Lou Cutell died on November 21, aged 91. Probably best known for his portrayal of the alien "Dr. Nadir" in his movie debut, *Frankenstein Meets the Spacemonster* (1965), he also appeared in *Rhinoceros* (1974), *Young Frankenstein*, *Peewee's Big Adventure*, *Maxie*, *Frankenstein General Hospital*, *My Mom's a Werewolf* and *Honey I Shrunk the Kids*. On TV, Cutell was in episodes of *The Wild Wild West*, *Tales from the Darkside*, *Starman*, *Eerie Indiana*, *Lois & Clark: The New Adventures of Superman* and *Weird Science*.

Arlene Dahl

American leading lady Arlene [Carol] Dahl, the mother of actor Lorenzo Lamas, died on November 29, aged 96. The former fashion model made her movie debut in 1947 and she co-starred with James Mason and Pat Boone in the 1959 version of *Journey to the Center of the Earth*. Dahl's other credits include the 1971 TV movie *The Deadly Dream* and an episode of *Fantasy Island*. In the 1950s she became a beauty columnist and writer, later establishing Arlene Dahl Enterprises, which marketed lingerie and cosmetics. The first two of Dahl's six husbands were actors Lex Barker (1951-52) and Fernando Lamas (1954-60).

Blackie Dammett

French grande affiche by Boris Grinsson for
Journey to the Centre of the Earth (1959), *which co-starred
Arlene Dahl (1925–2021) as the obligatory female lead.*

American supporting actor Blackie Dammett (John Michael Kiedis), the father of Anthony Kiedis from the Red Hot Chili Peppers, died on May 12, aged 81. He was in *Midnight Lace* (1981), Jim Wynorski's *The Lost Empire*, *The American Scream* and *A Night at the Magic Castle*. On TV, Dammett turned up in episodes of *Alfred Hitchcock Presents* (1986) and *ALF*.

Stuart Damon

American leading man Stuart Damon (Stuart Michael Zonis), who co-starred as the super-powered "Craig Stirling" in ITV's *The Champions* (1968–69), died of renal failure on June 29, aged 84. His other credits include the TV movies *Cinderella* (1965) and *Fantasies*, along with episodes of *UFO*, *Thriller* (1975), *Space: 1999*, *The New Avengers* and *Fantasy Island*. He later became a popular soap opera actor in such long-running shows as *Port Charles*, *Days of Our Lives*, *As the World Turns* and *General Hospital* (as "Dr. Alan Quartermaine").

Gene D'Angelo

American comics colourist and inker Gene D'Angelo (Eugene D'Angelo) died in early November, aged 97. He started working at King Features Syndicate, adding shading on the black-and-white daily strips. D'Angelo went on to colour numerous strips for King Features, including 'The Phantom', 'Flash Gordon', 'Mandrake the Magician' and 'Brick Bradford'. In 1977, after twenty-three years working for King Features, he moved to DC Comics, where his credits include *Action Comics*, *Justice League of America*, *Superman*, *World's Finest Comics* and many other titles. He was said to be editor Julius Schwartz's favourite colourist.

Henry Darrow

American supporting actor Henry Darrow (Enrique Tomás Delgado), who co-starred in such TV series as *The High Chaparral* (1967–71) and *Harry O* (1974–75), died on March 14, aged 87. He appeared in the vampire-Western *Curse of the Undead*, *The Invisible Man* (1975), *Halloween with the New Addams Family*, *Beyond*

the Universe and *The Hitcher*. Darrow was the first Latino actor to portray "Zorro" on TV (over three different shows!), and he also turned up in episodes of *The Outer Limits*, *Voyage to the Bottom of the Sea*, *The Wild Wild West*, *Rod Serling's Night Gallery* (as "Dr. Juan Munos" in H.P. Lovecraft's 'Cool Air'), *Kung Fu* ('The Brujo'), *The Six Million Dollar Man*, *Gemini Man*, *Wonder Woman*, *The Bionic Woman*, *The Incredible Hulk*, *Knight Rider*, *Star Trek: The Next Generation*, *Time Trax*, *Star Trek: Voyager*, *Babylon 5*, *Nightman* and *Beyond Belief: Fact or Fiction*.

Desmond Davis

British film director Desmond [Stanley Tracey] Davis died on July 3, aged 95. He began his career in the mid-1940s as a clapper-loader on such films as the ghost comedy *Don't Take It to Heart!*, working up to focus-puller and camera operator on *Colonel March Investigates* (starring Boris Karloff), *The Trollenberg Terror* (aka *The Crawling Eye*), *Behemoth the Sea Monster* (aka *The Giant Behemoth*) and Hammer's *Taste of Fear* (aka *Scream of Fear*, starring Christopher Lee). Davies went on to direct the 1981 version of *Clash of the Titans* (featuring stop-motion effects by Ray Harryhausen) and *The Sign of Four* (1983, with Ian Richardson as "Sherlock Holmes"), along with episodes of such TV series as *Wessex Tales* (Thomas Hardy's 'The Withered Arm') and *The New Avengers* ('The Eagle's Nest' with Peter Cushing). He retired in 1994.

Peter S. Davis

Peter S. Davis, who was the CEO and President of Davis-Panzer Productions, died in his sleep on February 21, aged 79. A co-producer of the original *Highlander* (1986), he was also credited on the sequels

Highlander II: The Quickening, Highlander IV: Endgame, Highlander: The Source, the animated *Highlander: The Adventure Begins* and *Highlander: The Search for Vengeance,* along with the TV series *Highlander* (1992–98), *Highlander: The Raven* (1998) and *Highlander: The Animated Series* (1994–96). Davis also executive produced the 1989 horror movie *Cutting Class.*

Anish Deb

Indian Bengali writer, editor and physicist Anish Deb died of complications from COVID19 on April 28, aged 69. He produced more than fifty books since 1968, including the short story collection *Kishore Kalpabigyan Samagra* (2005). Deb also edited numerous anthologies of crime, ghost and horror fiction.

Lois de Banzie

Scottish-born character actress Lois de Banzie died in California on April 3, aged 90. She appeared in *The Return of the Man from U.N.C.L.E.: The Fifteen Years Later Affair, Arachnophobia* and *Addams Family Values,* along with episodes of TV's *The Six Million Dollar Man, Fantasy Island* and *Amazing Stories.*

Kellam de Forest

American movie and TV researcher Kellam de Forest, who worked on *The Legend of Lizzie Borden* and *The*

Stepfather (1987), died of complications from COVID-19 on January 19, aged 94. Along with his small team, he was also an uncredited continuity adviser on the original *Star Trek* TV series and is credited with creating the show's "stardates" concept (based on the Julian calendar). In 1998, de Forest was interviewed in the documentary *Inside Star Trek—The Real Story*.

Martha De Laurentiis

American film producer Martha De Laurentiis (Martha Schumacher), who co-founded the Dino De Laurentiis Company (DDLC) in 1980 with her then-partner and later, husband, Dino De Laurentiis, died of cancer on December 4, aged 67. A former production accountant of such movies as *Wolfen*, *Amityville II: The Possession* and *Amityville 3-D*, her producing credits include the Stephen King titles *Firestarter* (1984 and 2022), *Cat's Eye*, *Silver Bullet* and *Maximum Overdrive*, along with *King Kong Lives*, *Date with an Angel*, *Hannibal*, *Red Dragon*, *Hannibal Rising* and the *Hannibal* TV series (2013–15).

Nathalie Delon

French leading lady Nathalie Delon (Francine Canovas) died of cancer on January 20, aged 79. Her credits include *The Hand* (1969), *Bluebeard*

(1972), *The Monk* (1972) and *A Whisper in the Dark*. She was married to actor Alain Delon from 1964-69.

Jeffrey Dempsey

British editor and publisher Jeffrey Dempsey died in January from encephalitis complicated by COVID-19. With David Cowperthwaite he was co-editor of the fanzine of macabre fiction and poetry *Dark Dreams*, which ran for nine issues from 1984-92. Dempsey also founded the Liverpool small press Crimson Altar Press, which between 1982-91 published chapbooks by John Gale, John [Nic] Howard, Mary Ann Allen, Mark Valentine and David G. Rowlands, along with his own anthologies *Darkness Comes* and *When Shadows Creep*. He was also a co-founder of The Ghost Story Society.

Jo-Carroll Dennison

American actress and former Miss America 1942, Jo-Carroll Dennison, died on October 18, aged 97. She was in *Prehistoric Women* (1950) and appeared as "Breathless Mahoney" in two episodes of the 1950 TV series *Dick Tracy*, before retiring from the screen in the early 1950s. The oldest surviving Miss America, Dennison was one of the first winners to object to wearing a swimsuit during her reign. She was married (1945-50) to comedian Phil Silvers. Ray Bradbury used to give her guidance on which books to read, while "Flash Gordon" creator Alex Raymond drew her portrait at the 1942 Miss America pageant.

David H. DePatie

Oscar-winning American animation producer David H. (Hudson) DePatie who, with Friz Freleng, co-created the iconic cartoon character "Pink Panther", died on September 23, aged 91. Originally part of the credits for Blake Edwards' 1963 heist comedy of

went on to produce or co-produce such 1960s cartoon shorts for the studio as *The Abominable Snow Rabbit*, *The Pied Piper of Guadalupe*, *Martian Through Georgia*, *I Was a Teenage Thumb*, *Transylvania 6-5000*, *Dr. Devil and Mr. Hare* and *A-Haunting We Will Go* (1966).

Giannetto De Rossi

the same name, the Pink Panther went on to appear in a number of short films and TV series. DePatie-Freleng Enterprises also created the animated opening credits for *I Dream of Jeannie* and such cartoon series as *Super President* (1967), *Inspector Clouseau* (including 'Transylvania Mania' and 'Cherche le phantom'), *The Ant and the Aardvark*, *Roland and Rattfink*, *Doctor Dolittle* (1970), *Return to the Planet of the Apes* (1975), *The Fantastic Four* (1978), *Spider-Woman* (1979-80), *Spider-Man* (1981-82), *G.I. Joe: A Real American Hero* (1983), *Spider-Man and His Amazing Friends* (1981-83), *The Incredible Hulk* (1982-83), and several "Dr. Seuss" shorts (including *Halloween is Grinch Night*). The company is also credited with developing the lightsabre effect for the first *Star Wars* movie, before DePatie-Freleng was sold to Marvel Comics in 1981. DePatie started his career as a sound and film editor at Warner Bros., where he worked on several movies, including *Them!* (1954), and

Italian special effects and make-up designer, scriptwriter and director Giannetto De Rossi died on April 11, aged 78. He worked on *Doctor Faustus* (1967), *When Women Had Tails* and the sequel *When Men Carried Clubs and Women Played Ding-Dong*, Jorge Grau's *The Living Dead at Manchester Morgue* (aka *Let Sleeping Corpses Lie*), *The Humanoid*, Lucio Fulci's *Zombie*, *The Beyond* and *The House by the Cemetery*, Antonio Margheriti's *Cannibals in the Streets*, *Piranha II: The Spawning*, *Atlantis Interceptors*, *Conan the Destroyer*, *Dune* (1984), *King Kong*

Original Spanish poster for Jorge Grau's
The Living Dead at Manchester Morgue *(1974),
which featured zombie make-ups by Giannetto De Rossi (1941–2021).*

Lives, *Killer Crocodile*, *Dr. M*, *DragonHeart*, *Kull the Conqueror* and *Curse of the Ring* (aka *Sword of Xanten*). De Rossi also directed *Cy Warrior*, and wrote and directed *Killer Crocodile 2* and *Tummy*.

Dustin Diamond

American character actor Dustin [Neil] Diamond, best known for playing the annoying "Samuel 'Screech' Powers" in the teen sitcom *Saved by the Bell* (1989–92) and various spin-offs, died of lung cancer on February 1, aged 44. A former child actor, he appeared in *Big Top Pee-wee*, *Purple People Eater*, *Attack of the Killer B-Movies*, *Little Creeps*, *Hamlet A.D.D.*, *Scavenger Killers*, *College Fright Night*, *Bleeding Hearts* and *Joker's Wild* (aka *Joker's Poltergeist*), along with episodes of TV's *The Munsters Today* and *Your Pretty Face is Going to Hell*.

DMX

New York rapper DMX (Earl Simmons) died on April 9, aged 50. He had been hospitalised after suffering a heart attack seven days earlier. As an actor, he appeared in a number of movies and TV shows, including *Lockjaw: Rise of the Kulev Serpent*, *The Bleeding* and *Chronicles of a Serial Killer*. He reportedly fathered fifteen children, and in 2015 was sentenced to six months in prison for failing to pay child support. He also served a year-long sentence for tax evasion in 2018.

Ron Dominguez

"Disney Legend" Ron Dominguez died on January 1, aged 85. Known as "Mr. Disneyland", he grew up on the Anaheim property that would become Disneyland, and his family home was moved to the park to serve as the first administration offices. He became a ticket-taker for the initial

theme park. In 1957, Dominguez became the assistant supervisor of Frontierland, moving up to the manager of Tomorrowland in 1962. He became the manager of the westside of Disneyland and, in 1974, was named vice president of Disneyland and chairman of the park operating committee. In 1990, Dominguez became Executive Vice President Walt Disney Attractions, West Coast, and he retired from The Walt Disney Company in 1994 after thirty-nine years.

Mike Don

Scottish-born bookseller Mike Don died around the end of June, aged 77. A former underground magazine editor and publisher, in 1974 he joined a collective to take over the management of Manchester's radical Grass Roots bookshop. In 1982 he left to start the science fiction mail-

order (later online) secondhand book business, Dreamberry Wine, which lasted until late 2020.

Tim Donnelly

American supporting actor Tim Donnelly (Timothy David Donnelly), who played "Fireman Chet Kelly on NBC's *Emergency!* (1972–78) died on September 19, aged 77. He appeared in *The Toolbox Murders* (1978), *The Clonus Horror* and three episodes of

TV's *Project U.F.O.* Donnelly retired from acting in the early 1980s.

Richard Donner

He was the man who made us believe that a man could fly! American director and producer Richard "Dick" Donner (Richard D. Schwartzberg), who directed *Superman* (1978) and most of the original version of *Superman II* (1980) before he was replaced by Richard Lester, died on July 5, aged 91. He began his career in series television in the 1960s, working on such shows as *The Twilight Zone* (Richard Matheson's 'Nightmare at 20,000 Feet', etc.), *The Man from U.N.C.L.E.*, *Get Smart*, *It's About Time*, *The Wild Wild West* ('The Night of the Returning Dead', etc.) and, later, *The Sixth Sense*, *Circle of Fear* (Matheson and Jimmy Sangster's 'The Concrete Captain') and *Tales from the Crypt*. Donner's breakout movie was *The Omen* (1976), and after the *Superman II* debacle, he went on to produce and direct *Ladyhawke*, *The Goonies*, *Scrooged*, *Two-Fisted Tales* ('Showdown' segment) and *Timeline* (based on the novel by Michael Crichton). He also produced or executive produced, sometimes in collaboration with his wife, Lauren Shuler Donner, *The Final Conflict*, *The Lost Boys*, *Tales from the Crypt: Demon Knight*, *The Omen* (1995), *W.E.I.R.D. World*, *Bordello of Blood*, *X-Men*, *Matthew Blackheart: Monster Smasher*, *Ritual*, *X-Men Origins: Wolverine* and the TV series *Tales from the Cryptkeeper*, *Tales from the Crypt*, *Secrets of the Cryptkeeper's Haunted House* and *Perversions of Science*. In tribute, Steven Spielberg called him "The greatest Goonie of all".

Carole Nelson Douglas

Best-selling American author Carole Nelson Douglas died in October, aged 76. She wrote the "Sword & Circlet" fantasy series, beginning with the *Six of Swords* (1982) and continuing with *Exiles of the Rynth*, *Keepers of Edanvant*, *Heir of Rengarth* and *Seven of Swords*, and the "Delilah Street, Paranormal Investigator" series (*Dancing with Werewolves*, *Brimstone Kiss*, *Vampire Sunrise*, *Silver Zombie* and *Virtual Virgin*). Douglas is probably best known for her mystery series of "Irene Adler" Sherlockian novels and the "Midnight Louie" series about "the twenty-pound black tomcat with the wit of Damon Runyon". Her other books include the novels *Probe*, *Counterprobe*, *Cup of Clay* and *Seed Upon the Wind*, the collection *Once Upon a Midnight Noir*, and the anthology *Midnight Louie's Pet Detectives*.

Jerry Douglas

American soap opera actor Jerry Douglas (Gerald Rubenstein) died after a long illness on November 9, aged 88. Best known for playing "John Abbott" on *The Young and the Restless* (1981-2016), his other credits include *Black Zoo* (with Michael Gough), *The Stranger* (1973), *The Dead Don't Die* (1975, scripted by Robert Bloch), *Looker* and *Silent But Deadly*, along with episodes of TV's *The Outer Limits* (1963), *Land of the Giants*, *The Bionic Woman*, *The Secrets of Isis*, *Lucan*, *The Incredible Hulk* and *The Greatest American Hero*. Douglas' first wife (1962-73) was actress Arlene Martel.

Robert Downey, Sr.

American actor, writer and director Robert Downey, Sr. (Robert John Elias, Jr.), the father of actor Robert Downey, Jr., died of Parkinson's disease on July 7, aged 85. He directed three episodes of the 1980s revival of TV's *The Twilight Zone* and appeared in another episode.

Olympia Dukakis

Oscar-winning American character actress Olympia Dukakis died on May 1, aged 81. She appeared uncredited in *Lilith* (1964) and Brian De Palma's *Sisters* (aka *Blood Sisters*), along with *The Librarian: Quest for the Spear*, *The Librarian: Return to King Solomon's Mines*, *The Last Keepers* and an episode of TV's *Touched by an Angel*.

David Dukas

South African supporting actor David Dukas died of heart failure on July 20, aged 51. He appeared in *Cold Harvest*, *Merlin: The Return*, *Slash*, *Berserker*, *Blood of Beasts*, *District 9* and *Bloodshot*, along with episodes of TV's *Legend of the Hidden City* and *Doctor Who* (2018).

Alistair Durie

British book collector and historian Alistair Durie died of cancer on August 5, aged 76. In 1979 he published *Weird Tales*, an oversized collection of covers of "The Unique Magazine". Durie had a huge collection of fanzines and magazines, many acquired from the sale of Sam Moskowitz's estate, including the only complete set of *Hutchinson's Adventure Story Magazine* known to exist.

Phil Eason

British film and TV puppeteer Phil Eason (Philip Eason) died on April 5, aged 60. He worked on *Labyrinth*, *Little Shop of Horrors* (1986), *The Neverending Story III*, *Lost in Space*

(1998), *Star Wars Episode 1–The Phantom Menace*, *The Hitchhiker's Guide to the Galaxy*, *Somnus* and episodes of TV's *Wizadora*, *Yonderland* and *The Dark Crystal: Age of Resistance*.

Marilyn Eastman

American actress Marilyn Eastman (Marilyn Marie Johnson), who co-starred as "Helen Cooper" in George A. Romero's iconic zombie movie *Night of the Living Dead* (1968), died on August 22, aged 87. Eastman was one of the ten members of the Image Ten production company that was formed to make the movie, and she also worked on the make-up and in other uncredited capacities during filming. She also later turned up in John A. Russo's 1996 horror movie *Santa Claws*.

Mark Eden

British leading man Mark Eden (Douglas John Malin) died on January 1, aged 92. He had been suffering from Alzheimer's disease. Eden co-starred with Boris Karloff, Christopher Lee, Barbara Steele and Michael Gough in *Curse of the Crimson Altar* (aka *The Crimson Cult*, 1968), loosely based on H.P. Lovecraft's 'The Dreams in the Witch-House'. He made his TV debut in *Quatermass and the Pit* (1958), and he went on to appear in episodes of *One Step Beyond*, *Dimensions of Fear*, *Doctor Who* (as "Marco Polo"), *Out of the Unknown*, *The Prisoner*, *The Rivals of Sherlock Holmes*, the 1973 mini-series *Jack the*

Mark Eden (1928–2021) co-starred with horror legends Boris Karloff, Christopher Lee, Barbara Steele and Michael Gough in Curse of the Crimson Altar (1968).

Ripper and Mark Gattiss' *Doctor Who* tribute, *An Adventure in Space and Time* (2013). Eden's first wife (1953–59) was Joan Long, who subsequently married actor John Le Mesurier. She died on July 9, aged 90.

Avril Elgar

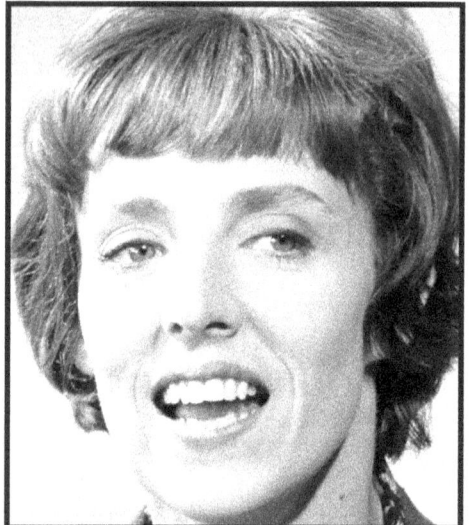

British character actress Avril Elgar (Avril Williams) died on September 17, aged 89. Although best known for her stage work, her film and TV credits include Jonathan Miller's *Alice in Wonderland* (1966), *The Medusa Touch* and two episodes of *Tales of the Unexpected*. She retired from acting in 2011. Elgar was married to actor James Maxwell from 1952 until his death in 1995.

Mark Elliott

81-year-old Mark Elliott (John Harrison Frick, Jr.), the iconic voice of Disney movie trailers and TV promos

from the late 1970s to the early 2000s, died on April 6, after suffering two heart attacks. He had also been battling lung cancer. Elliott, who was a former disc jockey, also did the voice-over for the original American radio spots for George Lucas' *Star Wars* (1977).

John Erman

Emmy Award-winning American TV producer and director John Erman (aka "Bill Sampson") died after a short illness on June 25, aged 85. A former actor (*The Cosmic Man*, 1957), he directed episodes of *The Outer Limits* (he was also a production associate on the show), *My Favorite Martian*, *Star Trek* ('The Empath'), *The Flying Nun*, *The Ghost & Mrs. Muir*, *The Girl with Something Extra* and *Good Heavens*.

Richard Evans

American character actor, director and author Richard "Dick" Evans (Richard Rodell Evans) died of cancer on October 2, aged 86. A familiar face on TV during the 1960s and '70s, he appeared in episodes of *Alfred Hitchcock Presents*, *Star Trek* and *The New People*, along with the 1965 movie *The Return of Mr. Moto*.

Trader Faulkner

Australian-born character actor [Ronald] Trader Faulkner, a close friend of such stars as Laurence Olivier, Peter Finch (whose biography he wrote), Vivien Leigh and Noël

Coward, died in London, England, on April 14, aged 93. He appeared in *Macbeth* (1960) and episodes of TV's *Colonel March of Scotland Yard* (with Boris Karloff), *The Avengers* and *The Return of Sherlock Holmes*.

Gerald Feil

87-year-old American cinematographer Gerald Feil died in Canada after a short illness on February 9. His credits include Peter Brook's *Lord of the Flies*

(1963, which he also associate produced and edited), *He Knows You're Alone* (1980), *Friday the 13th: Part III* and *Silent Madness*. In the 1980s, Feil also helped refine and design camera systems, lighting and framing techniques used in the production of such 3-D films as *Friday the 13th: Part III* and *Jaws 3-D*.

Derrick Ferguson

American "New Pulp" author Derrick Ferguson, who belatedly novelised the obscure 1997 regional Bigfoot movie *Search for the Beast* almost twenty years after it was made, died on April 4, aged 62. He also published a number of novels, collections and short stories in the small press.

Kate Ferguson

Australian actress and musician Kate Ferguson died of cancer on July 2, aged 66. She co-starred in Norman J. Warren's 1979 softcore SF comedy *Outer Touch* (aka *Spaced Out*). Ferguson retired from the screen in the late 1980s to teach music, become a voice coach and mentor young talent. [Thanks to Gary Couzens.]

Michael Ferguson

British TV producer and director Michael Ferguson died on October 4, aged 84. He originally started as an assistant floor manager on the BBC's *Doctor Who* in 1963 ("playing" the first Dalek ever seen on screen) before directing more than twenty episodes of the show between 1966-71, including 'The Seeds of Death' and 'The Claws of Axos' serials. Ferguson also directed four episodes of *Out of the Unknown* (1969-71), copies of which no longer exist. He turned up as a party guest in the 2013 TV movie *An Adventure in Space and Time*, which looked at the early years of *Doctor Who*.

Tony Ferrer

Filipino actor Tony Ferrer (Antonio D. Laxa), who starred as James Bond-inspired secret agent "Tony Fallon"/"Agent X-44" in a long-running series of movies during the 1960s and '70s, died of a heart ailment on January 23, aged 86. He is probably best remembered for co-starring as "Inspector Ramos" in *The Vengeance of Fu Manchu* (with Christopher Lee, 1967).

Harry Fielder

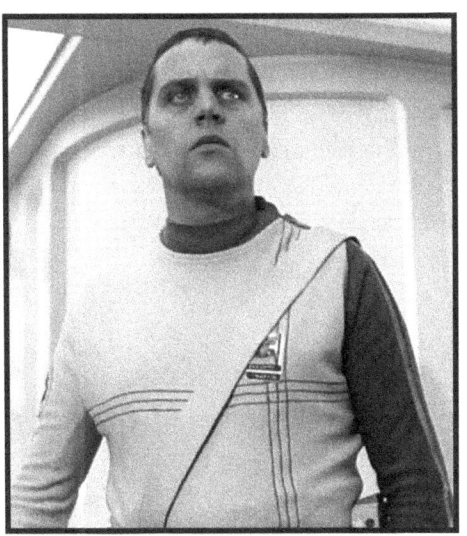

Prolific British bit-actor Harry Fielder died on February 6, aged 80. He appeared in (usually uncredited) small parts or extra roles in such films as Hammer's *Quatermass and the Pit*, *The Vengeance of She*, *Frankenstein Must Be Destroyed*, *Twins of Evil*, *Blood from the Mummy's Tomb* and *Dr Jekyll & Sister Hyde*, along with *Billion Dollar Brain*, *2001: A Space Odyssey*, *Chitty Chitty Bang Bang*, *Cry of the Banshee*, *Trog*, *The Blood on Satan's Claw*, *The Devils*, Alfred Hitchcock's *Frenzy*, *The Pied Piper*, *The Mutations* (aka *The Freakmaker*), *Lisztomania*, *Trial by Combat* (aka *A Dirty Knight's Work*), *The Seven-Per-Cent Solution*, *Star Wars*, *The Spy Who Loved Me*, *Superman* (1978), *The Elephant Man*, *Superman II*, *Raiders of the Lost Ark*, *An American Werewolf in London*, *The Hunchback of Notre Dame* (1982), *The Bride*, *The Doctor and the Devils*, *Highlander*, Clive Barker's *Nightbreed*, *Loch Ness*, *Mary Reilly*, *101 Dalmations* (1996) and

Fairytale: A True Story. On TV Fielder turned up in episodes of *The Avengers*, *The Champions*, *Moonbase 3*, *The Phoenix and the Carpet*, *Survivors*, *1990*, *Space: 1999*, *Blakes 7*, *Doctor Who* and *The Tripods*, and he was also actor Mike Pratt's stunt double on *Randall and Hopkirk (Deceased)* (aka *My Partner the Ghost*, 1969–70).

Vergena Fields

31-year-old American indie actress and professional wrestling ring announcer Vergena Fields died, along with her mother, in a car accident in Kentucky on September 28. The Jeep she was driving crashed into the back-end of a 18-wheeler commercial vehicle. Fields appeared in a number of low budget regional movies, including *Hicky: The Hillbilly Vampire*, *House of Whores 2: The Second Cumming*, *Deadly Numbers*, *The Rave* and the zombie comedy *AOTMZ*, along with several horror shorts.

Gérard Filipelli

Gérard Filipelli (Gérard-Pierre-Alexandre Filipelli), a member of the French comedy singing group "Les Charlots" ("The Crazy Boys"), died of cancer on March 30, aged 78. They appeared in a number of films from the late 1960s to the early 1990s, including *Les Charlots contre Dracula* (1980).

Lail Finlay

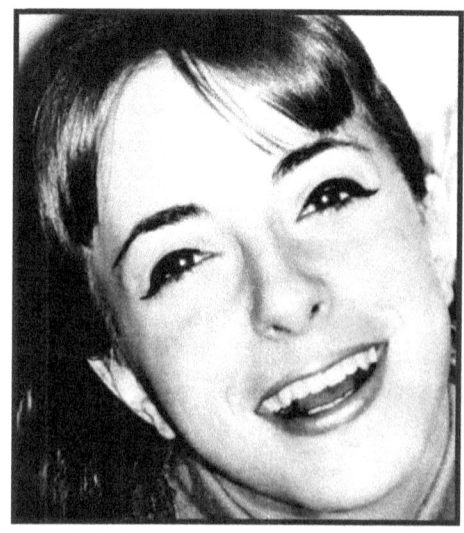

Lail Montgomery Finlay Hernandez, the daughter of pulp artist Virgil Finlay, died on January 13, aged 71. In recent years she had been battling metastatic cancer. She contributed remembrances to *Virgil Finlay Remembered: The Seventh Book of Virgil Finlay* (1981) and *Virgil Finlay's Women of Ages* (1982) and was closely involved with the publication of *The Collectors' Book of Virgil Finlay* (2019). After her house burned down in November 2019 (killing her musician husband), a GoFundMe page was created to help her and her daughter save what they could of her father's art and papers.

Colin Fletcher

British journalist, photographer and *bon vivant* Colin [Adrian] Fletcher died on August 7, aged 84. In 1988 he was the pre-production photographer on the sequel *Hellbound: Hellraiser II*.

Robert Fletcher

American stage and screen costume designer Robert "Bob" Fletcher (Robert Fletcher Wyckoff), the son of Hollywood actor Leon Ames, died on April 5, aged 98. He worked on *Star Trek: The Motion Picture*, *Star Trek II: The Wrath of Khan*, *Star Trek III: The Search for Spock*, *Star Trek: The Voyage Home*, *Caveman*, *The Last Starfighter*, *Fright Night* (1985) and the TV show *The Powers of Matthew Star*.

Larry Flynt

Controversial American publisher Larry Flynt (Larry Claxton Flynt, Jr.) died of heart failure on February 10, aged 78. An outspoken champion of First Amendment rights, he built an adult entertainment empire based around his magazine *Hustler*. In 1996, Flynt created *Rage* magazine, which often published horror and speculative fiction. It only ran for eighteen issues. In 1978 Flynt was paralysed from the waist down and confined to a wheelchair due to

injuries sustained in an assassination attempt. His life was depicted in the 1996 movie *The People vs. Larry Flynt*, which starred Woody Harrelson as Flynt.

James Follett

British science fiction and techno-thriller author James Follett died on January 10, aged 81. Inspired by the works of Eric Frank Russell, his novels include *Ice* (aka *Second Atlantis*), *Earthsearch* and *Earthsearch II: Deathship* (both novelisations of his own radio serials), *Dominator*, *Torus*, *Trojan*, *Savant*, *Mindwarp*, *Sabre*, *Temple of the Winds*, *Wicca*, *The Silent Vulcan* and the e-book *Hellborn*. Follett also scripted two episodes of BBC-TV's *Blakes 7* ('Dawn of the Gods' and 'Stardrive').

Bryn Fortey

Welsh author and poet Bryn Fortey died of kidney failure and sepsis on July 21, aged 83. He started publishing in the late 1960s, and he had stories in such anthologies as *New Writings in Horror and the Supernatural* and *New Writings in Horror and the Supernatural Volume 2* both edited by David A. Sutton; *Frighteners 2* and *The 12th* and *15th Fontana Books of Great Horror Stories* edited by Mary Danby, and *New Writings in SF #28* edited by Kenneth Bulmer. Fortey's son Jim was stabbed to death in 2007 by a friend suffering from paranoid schizophrenia and his wife Maddalena died four years later. Although he had a few stories published in the 1990s with the Welsh Speculative Writers Foundation, he didn't really return to the genre until 2014, when The Alchemy Press published a collection of new and reprint stories and poems entitled *Merry-Go-Round and Other Words*. Further stories appeared in small press magazines and anthologies, and The Alchemy Press issued a second collection, *Compromising the Truth*, in 2018.

Gérald Forton

French-Belgian comics artist Gérald Forton died in America on December 18, aged 90. With scriptwriter Jean-Michel Charlier he created the jungle adventurer 'Kim Devil' (1953–56) and the space exploits of 'Alain Cardan' (1957–59) with Yvan Delporte for the long-running Belgium magazine *Spirou*. Forton moved to the US in 1980, where he worked for DC Comics, Eclipse Comics and First Comics, before becoming a storyboard artist in the animation industry. His many credits as a character designer and storyboard artist include *Pinocchio and the Emperor of the Night*, *He-Man and She-Ra: The Secret of the Sword*, and such cartoon TV series as *He-Man and the Masters of the Universe* (he also drew the short-lived newspaper strip), *She-Ra: Princess of Power*, *Ghostbusters*, *BraveStarr*, *The Pirates of Dark Water*, *Swamp Thing* (1991), *The Real Ghostbusters*, *James Bond Jr.*, *Captain Planet and the Planeteers*, *The Legend of Prince Valiant*, *Skeleton Warriors*, *Teenage Mutant Ninja Turtles*, *Street Fighter: The Animated Series*, *Extreme Ghostbusters*, *Men in Black: The Series* and *RoboCop: Alpha Commando*.

David Fox

Canadian supporting actor David Fox died of cancer on November 13, aged 80. His credits include *My Pet Monster*, *Witchcraft* (1988), *Jungle Boy* (1998), *Rats* (2000), *2001: A Space Travesty*, *Prince Charming*, *Population 436*, *Jack Brooks: Monster Slayer*, *Dream House*, *Mama* and *Pacific Rim*. Fox appeared on TV in episodes of *Alfred Hitchcock Presents* (1988), *Counterstrike* ('Cyborg'), *Beyond Reality*, *Poltergeist: The Legacy*, *PSI Factor: Chronicles of the Paranormal* and *Orphan Black*.

Myra Francis

British TV actress Myra Francis, who was featured in the first female gay kiss to ever air on British television (with Alison Steadman, in 1974), died of cancer on March 30, aged 78. She also appeared in episodes of *Survivors* (1975) and *Doctor Who* ('The Creature from the Pit'). Francis was married to actor Peter Egan from 1976 until her death.

Heath Freeman

American supporting actor Heath Freeman, who portrayed serial killer "Howard Epps" over two series of *Bones* (2005–07), died on November 14, aged 41. He appeared in *All American Christmas Carol*, *Dark Was the Night*, *The Wicked Within* and *The Seventh Day*. On TV, Freemnan also appeared in an episode of *Tru Calling* and voiced "Agent Joe" in the 2011 digital animated series *Torchwood: Web of Lies*.

Mary K. Frey

American fantasy writer Mary K. Frey (Mary Osmanski) died on August 18. She contributed to Marion Zimmer Bradley's anthologies *Sword and Sorceress VII* and *IX*, *Domains of Darkover* and *Leroni of Darkover* during

the early 1990s, and had a story published in *Marion Zimmer Bradley's Fantasy* magazine.

Penny Frierson

American fan Penny Frierson (Penelope Miller Frierson), who published the influential 1972 study of H.P. Lovecraft, *HPL*, with her husband Meade Frierson, died on April 3, aged 79. She was also a founder member of the Birmingham (Alabama) SF Club, and chaired DeepSouthCon 15 (1977) and co-chaired the 1986 World Science Fiction Convention ("ConFederation") in Atlanta.

Charles W. Fries

American movie producer Charles W. (William) Fries died on April 21, aged 92. His many credits include *The People, She Waits, Tales from the Crypt* (1972), *Sandcastles, The Norliss Tapes, The Vailt of Horror* (1973), *Scream of the Wolf* (based on the story by David F. Case), *Chosen Survivors, The Strange and Deadly Occurence, Where Have All the People Gone, The Spell* (1977), *Halloween with the New Addams Family, Night Cries, The Initation of Sarah* (1978 and 2006), *Are You in the House Alone?, Spider-Man Strikes Back, Spider-Man: The Dragon's Challenge, The Two Worlds of Jennie Logan, Cat People* (1982), *Starcrossed, Terror at London Bridge* (aka *Bridge Across Time*), *Timestalkers, Flowers in the Attic* (1987 and 2014), *Phantom of the Mall: Eric's Revenge, Deathstone, Peacemaker, K-9000, Steel and Lace, Screamers* (based on a story by Philip K. Dick) and *Screamers: The Hunting*, *Deadly Web*, *Petals in the Wind*, *If There Be Thorns* and *Seeds of Yesterday*. Fries also executive-produced the TV series *The Amazing Spider-Man* (1977–79) and the 1980 min-series of Ray Bradbury's *The Martian Chronicles*. His memoir, *Chuck Fries: Godfather of the Television Movie, A History of Television*, was published in 2013.

Mira Furlan

Yugoslavian-born actress Mira Furlan, best known for her role as "Ambassador Delenn" in TV's *Babylon 5* (1993–98) and spin-off movies, died in Los Angeles of complications from West Nile virus on January 20, aged 65. She began her screen career in 1976 and immigrated to America in 1991 with her husband, actor Goran Gajic. She also played "Danielle Rousseau" on *Lost* (2004–10) and appeared in episodes of *Sheena*, *Night Stalker* (2006) and *Space Command*.

Robert Fyfe

Scottish character actor Robert [Douglas] Fyfe, best remembered for playing henpecked husband "Howard Sibshaw" in the long-running BBC sitcom *Last of the Summer Wine* (1985–2010), died of kidney disease on September 15, aged 90. He also appeared in *Xtro*, *Around the World in 80 Days* (2004), John Landis' *Burke and Hare*, *Cloud Atlas* and *Pride and Prejudice and Zombies*, along with episodes of TV's *Survivors* (1975), *The Return of Sherlock Holmes* and *Misfits*. In 1975, Fyfe played the horse dealer in the Royal Shakespeare Company's stage production of *Doctor Faustus* in Stratford-upon-Avon and on tour.

John Gabriel

American supporting John Gabriel (Jack Monkarsh) died on June 13, aged 90. Originally cast as the "Professor" in the unaired pilot of *Gilligan's Island* (1964), he also appeared in in episodes of such TV series as *The New Adventures of Charlie Chan*, *The Girl from U.N.C.L.E.*, *The Flying Nun*, *The Girl with Something Extra* and *The Six Million Dollar Man*, along with the TV movies *Fantasies* and *The Incredible Hulk Returns*.

Diana G. Gallagher

American TV tie-in author and filk-singer Diana G. Gallagher died of of chronic obstructive pulmonary disease (COPD) on December 2, aged 75. She wrote many novels in the *Buffy the Vampire Slayer*, *Angel*, *Charmed*, *Sabrina the Teenage Witch*, *Are You Afraid of the Dark?*, *Star Trek* and *The Secret World of Alex Mack* series. Gallagher also published the SF novel *The Alien Dark*, and her short fiction appeared in

anthologies edited by Forrest J Ackerman, Nancy Holder and others. The third of her four husbands was author William F. Wu and, as Diana G. Wu, she won the Hugo Award for Best Fan Artist in 1989.

Jimmy Garrett

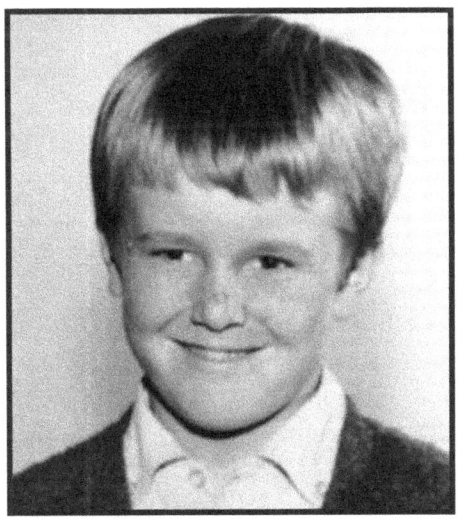

American former child actor Jimmy Garrett (James Coleman Garrett), best known for playing Lucy

Carmichael's son "Jerry Carmichel" in the third and fourth seasons of *The Lucy Show* (1962-65), died on September 17, aged 66. He was also in episodes of *The Twilight Zone* (uncredited) and *Mister Ed*, and the 1966 movie *Munster, Go Home!* (again, uncredited). Garrett switched careers and became a talent agent and then a production accountant, and he worked in the latter capacity on *X2: X-Men United* and various TV series.

Willie Garson

American character actor Willie Garson (William Garson Paszamant), best known for his recurring role as talent agent "Stanford Blatch" on the HBO sitcom *Sex and the City* (1998-2004) and spin-offs, died of cancer on September 21, aged 57. He was also in Adam Simon's *Brain Dead*, *Reposessed*, *Groundhog Day*, *Mars Attacks!*, *Being John Malkovich*, *Fortress 2: Re-Entry*, *What Planet Are You From?*, *Freaky Friday* (2003), *Just Like Heaven* and *Magic Camp*. On TV, Garson was also in episodes of TV's *Twin Peaks* (1991), *Quantum Leap*, *Touched by an Angel*, *VR.5*, *Buffy the Vampire Slayer*, *Star Trek: Voyager*, *Early Edition*, *The X Files*, *Level 9*, *Special Unit 2*, *Taken*, *Stargate SG-1*, *Wizards of Waverly Place*, *Pushing Daises*, *Medium*, *Salvation* and *Supergirl*.

Luis Gaspar

Spanish character actor Luis Gaspar [Osorio] (aka "Luis Caster") died on September 21. Best known for his roles in European Westerns, he also turned up in small parts in *The Werewolf versus the Vampire Woman*, *Dr. Jekyll vs. the Werewolf* and *The Mummy's Revenge* (all starring Paul Naschy).

Anna Gaylor

Veteran French character actress Anna Gaylor (Anna Senioutovitch) died on September 21, aged 89. She was featured in *Shock Treatment* (1973), *The Dogs*, *Frankenstein 90*, *Les visiteurs* and position after being hired by San Francisco State University. Gearhart's SF books include the "Earthkeep" novels, *The Kanshou* and *The Magister*, and the influential short-story collection *The Wanderground: Stories of the Hill Women*. She also co-wrote *A Feminist Tarot* with Susan Rennie.

Larry Gelman

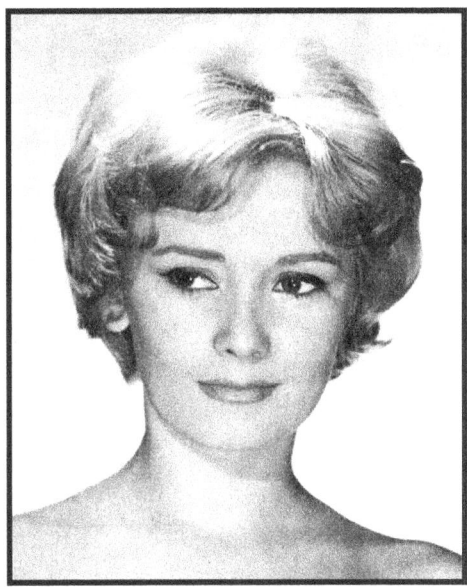

an episode of the TV series *Joséphine, ange gardien*. Gaylor was married to writer and director Alain Jessua.

Sally Miller Gearhart

American feminist author and political gay rights activist Sally Miller Gearhart died on July 14, aged 90. In 1973, she became the first out lesbian to obtain a tenure-track faculty

90-year-old American comedy actor Larry (Sheldon) Gelman died of complications from a fall on June 7. He appeared in William Castle's *The Busy Body*, Disney's *Now You See Him Now You Don't* and *The Strongest Man in the World*, *Alice in Wonderland: An X-Rated Musical Fantasy*, *Chatterbox!*, *Almost Heaven*, *Topper* (1979), *Wholly Moses!* and *Dreamscape*, along with episodes of TV's *I Dream of Jeannie* (as "Sigmund Freud"), *Batman* (1968), *Get Smart*, *The Flying Nun*, *The Love*

Boat ('Ship of Ghouls' with Vincent Price), *Mork & Mindy*, *ABC Weekend Specials* ('Henry Hamilton Graduate Ghost'), *Amazing Stories*, *Tales from the Darkside*, *Weird Science*, *Touched by an Angel* and *Beyond Belief: Fact or Fiction*.

Nicholas Georgiade

Greek-American actor Nicholas Georgiade, who co-starred as "Agent Enrico Rossi" in ABC-TV's *The Untouchables* (1959–63), died on December 19, aged 88. He also turned up in the TV movie *Poor Devil* (with Christopher Lee) and episodes of *Batman* (1967) and *Get Smart*.

George Gerdes

American character actor George Gerdes died of a brain aneurysm on January 1, aged 72. He was a familiar face in such movies as *Single White Female*, *Attack of the 50 Ft. Woman* (1993), *Bats* and *The Passing*, and on

TV in episodes of *The X Files*, *Nowhere Man*, *Threshold*, *Lost*, *True Blood* and *Dexter*.

Richard Gilliland

American supporting actor Richard [Morris] Gilliland died following a brief illness on March 18, aged 71. He appeared in *Bug*, *The White Buffalo*,

Star Kid, *Vampire Clan* and *Case 347*. On TV, Gilliland's credits include episodes of *Fantasy Island*, *Touched by an Angel*, *Dark Skies*, *Early Edition*, *Joan of Arcadia*, *Dexter* and *Torchwood*.

Milton Moses Ginsberg

American filmmaker Milton Moses Ginsberg, who wrote, edited and directed the 1973 satirical movie *The Werewolf of Washington*, died of cancer on May 23, aged 85.

Brian Goldner

Brian [David] Goldner, the chairman and CEO of the toy-and-game company Hasbro, Inc. since 2008, died of prostate cancer on October 12, aged 58. As the architect of the company's strategic "Brand Blueprint", he led the expansion of Hasbro properties into a global entertainment industry. These

included the hugely successful "Transformers", "G.I. Joe", "Battleship" and "Power Rangers" film, TV and gaming franchises, along with such movies as *Ouija* and *Ouija: Origin of Evil*.

Arlene Golonka

American actress Arlene Golonka died on May 31, aged 85. She was in William Castle's *The Busy Body*,

Airport '77 (with Christopher Lee), *Dr. Alien* and *Skeletons*, along with episodes of TV's *The Flying Nun*, *Get Smart*, *The Girl with Something Extra* and *Fantasy Island*.

Kathleen Ann Goonan

American SF author Kathleen Ann Goonan died on January 28, aged 68. She had been recovering from a bone marrow transplant. Her novels include *Queen of Jazz City*, *The Bones of Time*, *Mississippi Blues*, *Crescent City Rhapsody*, *Light Music*, *In War Times* (winner of the John W. Campbell Award for Best Science Fiction Novel) and *The Shared Dream*. Some of her short fiction was collected in *Angels and You Dogs* from PS Publishing.

Damned, *The Comet Kids* and an episode of TV's *Legacy of the Silver Shadow*.

Desiree Gould

Reg Gorman

Australian character actor Reg Gorman died of cancer on August 5, aged 84. He appeared in *Inn of the*

American actress Desiree [Joan] Gould died on May 24, aged 76. After appearing as the eccentric "Aunt

Martha" in the 1983 slasher *Sleepaway Camp* (and in flasbacks in *Sleepaway Camp IV: The Survivor*), she became a real estate agent, returning to acting more than twenty years later in *Under Surveillance* (aka *Dark Chamber*), *Tales of Poe* ('The Tell-Tale Heart' segment) and the short film *Caesar and Otto Meet Dracula's Lawyer*.

Saginaw Grant

Native American character actor [Morgan] Saginaw Grant, the Hereditary Chief and member of the Sac and Fox, Iowa and Otoe-Missouria Nations, died on July 28, aged 85. He appeared in *Purgatory* (1999), *Legend of the Phantom Rider*, *Skinwalkers*, *DreamKeeper*, *The Fallen Ones*, *It Waits*, *Beyond the Quest*, *Slipstream* (2007), *Maneater* (2009), *The Lone Ranger* (2013), *Wind Walkers*, *Crosser* and *Valley of the Gods*, along with episodes of TV's *The Young Indiana Jones Chronicles*, *Miracles* and *American Horror Story*.

Leon Greene

British opera singer and actor Leon Greene (Lenard George Green) died of cancer on June 19, aged 89. Best remembered as "Rex Van Ryn", the loyal assistant to Christopher Lee's aristocratic "Duc de Richleau" in Hammer Film's *The Devil Rides Out* (1968), Greene's bass baritone voice was overdubbed by Patrick Allen, reportedly because the studio was concerned that he sounded too similar to Lee. The 6ft 4in tall Greene also appeared in Hammer's *A Challenge for Robin Hood* (as "Little John"), *The Seven-Per-Cent Solution*, *The Thief of Baghdad* (1978), *Flash Gordon* (1980, in which his voice was dubbed by David de Keyser) and a few *Carry On* films, along with episodes of TV's *The Avengers*, *T. Bag and the Revenge of the T. Set* and Dennis Potter's *Cold Lazarus*. In 1985, he took the title role in Stephen Sondheim's musical

Leon Greene (1931–2021) was dubbed by Patrick Allen in
Hammer Films' The Devil Rides Out (1968),
which starred Christopher Lee.

Sweeney Todd at the Half Moon Theatre in London. Greene spent most of the 1990s in pantomime and, along with Lionel Blair, helped introduce the genre to Canada.

John Gregg

Australian actor John Gregg died on May 29, aged 82. During the 1970s and early '80s he appeared on British TV in episodes of *Doomwatch*, *Dead of Night*, *Doctor Who*, *Leap in the Dark* and *The Hitchhiker's Guide to the Galaxy*. Later credits include episode of *Roar*, *Mirror Mirror*, *Farscape*, *Spirited* and the 1997 TV movie *The Ripper* (as "Dr. William Gull").

Jon Gregory

British film editor Jon Gregory died after a short illness on September 9, aged 77. Born in pre-partition India

(now Pakistan), his credits include *Loch Ness* (1996) and *The Road* (2009).

Alberto Grimaldi

Italian lawyer-turned-film producer Alberto Grimaldi died on January 23, aged 95. He was a producer (uncredited) on *Spirits of the Dead* (Federico Fellini's "Toby Dammit" episode) and *Burnt Offerings*.

Charles Grodin

Likeable American leading man Charles Grodin (Charles Grodinsky) died of cancer on May 18, aged 86. He began his screen career playing an uncredited drummer boy in Walt Disney's *20,000 Leagues Under the Sea* (1954) before going on to appear in *Rosemary's Baby* (1968), *King Kong* (1976), *Heaven Can Wait* (1978), *The Incredible Shrinking Woman*, *The Great Muppet Caper*, *So I Married an Axe Murderer* and *Heart and Souls*. On TV, Grodin was in an episode of *Captain Nice*. He also authored a number of showbusiness autobiographies.

Fernand Guiot

Busy Belgium-born French character actor Fernand Guiot died in Paris on June 26, aged 88. His many credits include *Nemo* (1970) and *The Murders in the Rue Morgue* (1986), an episode of TV's *Histoires extraordinaires* ('The Fall of the House of Usher', 1981), and the 1980 mini-series *Fantômas*.

David Gulpilil

Indigenous Australian actor and dancer David Gulpilil (David Gulpilil Ridjimiraril Dalaithngu) died of lung cancer on November 29, aged 68. Having made his memorable film debut at the age of 16 in Nicolas Roeg's *Walkabout* (1971), he went on to appear in *The Last Wave*, *Dark Age*, *Until the End of the World*, *Cargo*, and episodes of TV's *BeastMaster* and *The Leftovers*.

Sally Gwylan

American SF author Sally Gwylan was hit by a car and killed on October 8. Her short fiction appeared in *Infinite Matrix*, *Asimov's Science Fiction*, *Strange Horizons* and *Clarkesworld*, while her novel *A Wind Out of Canaan* was appeared in 2012. Gwylan also worked as a copy editor for Jane Lindskold, Carrie Vaughn and other writers.

Bob Haberfield

Australian-born commercial artist Bob Haberfield died in Wales during the summer. He was in his early 80s. From 1968 until 1984, Haberfield's distinctively psychedelic covers

appeared on many UK Mayflower, Granada, Panther and W.H. Allen books, especially those by Michael Moorcock (*Stormbringer*, *The Mad God's Amulet*, *The Eternal Champion*, *The Singing Citadel*, *Behold the Man*, *The Final Programme*, *The Knight of Swords*, *The Queen of Swords*, *The Sword of the Dawn*, *The King of Swords*, *The Jewel in the Skull* and many others). His other covers include *Carnacki the Ghost-Finder*, *Dagon and Other Macabre Tales*, *The Lurker at the Threshold*, *Strange Ecstasies* and *The Mind Parasites* (all 1973), *Tales of Science and Sorcery* (1976), *Victorian Nightmares* and *Cold Fear* (both 1977), *The Man-Wolf and Other Horrors* (1978) and *Tales from a Gas-Lit Graveyard* (1979).

Jean Hale

1960s American leading lady [Carol] Jean Hale, who portrayed "Polly", the hatcheck-girl accomplice of David Wayne's "Mad Hatter" on TV's *Batman* (1967), died on August 3, aged 82. She also co-starred in *Violent*

Midnight (aka Psychomania) and the sci-spy In Like Flint, and appeared in episodes of My Favorite Martian, The Alfred Hitchcock Hour, The Wild Wild West, My Brother the Angel and Tarzan (1967). Hale's career stalled in the early 1970s after she rejected the studios' "sexy" image for her. She was married to actor Dabney Coleman from 1961-84.

Cleve Hall

Low-budget American special effects technician, make-up artist and actor Cleve Hall, who starred in his own short-lived Syfy reality series *Monster Man* (2011), died of congestive heart failure on May 31, aged 61. He worked in various capacities on *Nightmare* (1981), *Metalstorm: The Destruction of Jared-Syn*, *The Adventures of Buckeroo Banzai Across the 8th Dimension*, *The Dungeonmaster*, *Ghoulies*, *Zone Troopers*, *Re-Animator*, *Troll*, *Eliminators*, *Terrorvision*, *Evil Spawn*, *Twisted Nightmare*, *Terror Night*, *Roller Blade Warriors: Taken by Force*, *Alienator*, *Demon Wind*, *The Halfway House*, *My Demon Within*, *Bloodstruck*, *2-Headed Shark Attack*, *Big Ass Spider*, *Camp Dread*, *Betrothed*, *Book of Fire*, *Variant*, *Dances with Werewolves* and *Waking Nightmare*. Cleve also turned up in supporting roles or bit-parts in *The Dungeonmaster* (as "Jack the Ripper"), *Pee-wee's Big Adventure*, *Warlords*, *Return of the Living Dead: Necropolis*, *Dead Things*, *Diary of Death*, *The Summer of Massacre* and *The Black Dahlia Haunting*. A GoFundMe was launched by his daughter to cover burial costs.

Robert Hall

American special effects make-up artist and director Robert [Green] Hall died on May 24, aged 47. He worked on the effects of such movies

and *Malibu Horror Story*, along with episodes of TV's *Click*, *The X Files*, *The Phantom Eye*, *Black Scorpion*, *Miracles*, *Buffy the Vampire Slayer*, *Firefly*, *Angel*, *Frankenstein* (2004), *Terminator: The Sarah Connor Chronicles*, *Grimm* and *Teen Wolf*. Hall also wrote and directed *Laid to Rest*, *Chromeskull:Laid to Rest 2* and *Fear Clinic* (based on his FearNet show of the same name), and directed episodes of the *Teen Wolf* TV series.

Richard Halliwell

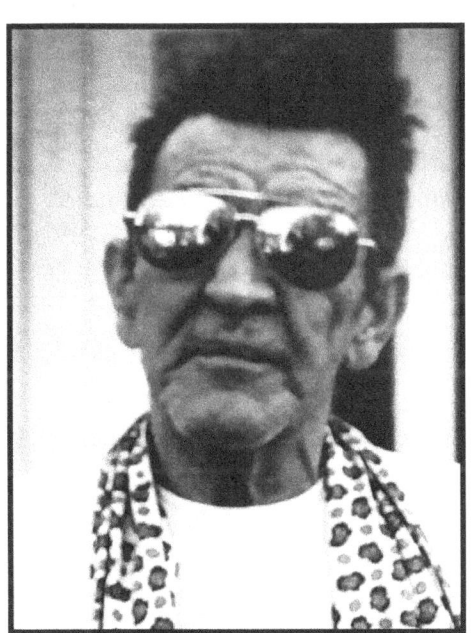

Body Snatchers (1993), *Night of the Scarecrow*, *Caged Heat 3000*, *Jumanji* (1995), *The Island of Dr. Moreau* (1996), *The Relic*, *Starquest II*, *Black Scorpion II: Aftershock*, *Wishmaster*, *Alien Avengers II*, *Storm Trooper*, *Club Vampire*, *Warlock III: The End of Innocence*, *From Dusk Till Dawn 3: The Hangman's Daughter*, *The Bogus Witch Project*, *The Doorway*, *Ghosts of Mars*, *Crocodile 2: Death Swamp*, *Unspeakable*, *Santa Jr.*, *Monster Makers*, *Dead Birds*, *Frankenfish*, *Point Pleasant*, *All Souls Day: Dia de los Muertos*, *House of the Dead 2*, *Wristcutters: A Love Story*, *Voodoo Moon*, *Room 6*, *Last Rites*, *The Darkroom* (2006), *Vacancy*, *Killer Pad*, *Prom Night* (2008), *The Burrowers*, *Quarantine*, *Red Sands*, *The Crazies* (2010), *Devil*, *Paranormal Activity 2*, *Quarantine 2: Terminal*, *Paranormal Activity 3*, *Locke & Key*, *John Dies at the End*, *The Vampire Spider*, *Creep Van*, *No One Lives*, *The Collection*, *Paranormal Activity 4*, *sxtape*, *Wer*, *Area 51*, *Bedeviled*, *Halloween* (2018), *Mary*

British wargame designer Richard Halliwell died on May 3, aged 62. While working at Games Workshop in the early 1980s he wrote the original rulebook for what would become *Warhammer*. Halliwell also created a number of *Judge Dredd* spin-off games for GW, and developed *Dark Future* with Marc Gascoigne.

Jesse Hamm

American comic book writer and artist Jesse [Alan] Hamm died of a blood clot in his lungs on May 12, aged 45. A member of the Portland-based comics collective "Helioscope", he worked for DC and Marvel, as well as various alternative/independent imprints.

Wynn Hammer

American photographer Wynn Hammer died of congestive heart failure on May 2, aged 97. He shot stills on such movies as *Wicked Wicked*, *The Boy Who Cried Werewolf*, *Burnt Offerings*, *Carrie* (1976), *Audrey Rose*, *The Pack*, *Invasion of the Body Snatchers* (1978), Disney's *The Black Hole*, *Blood Beach*, *Oh God! Book II*, *The Ghosts of Buxley Hall*, *Hysterical*, *The Last Starfighter*, *Cloak & Dagger*, *Warning Sign* and *Maxie*.

James Hampton

Likeable supporting actor and TV director James [Wade] Hampton, who portrayed understanding father "Harold Howard" in *Teen Wolf* (1985) and the 1986-87 *Teen Wolf* TV series, died of complications from Parkinson's disease on April 7, aged 84. He was also in Disney's *The Cat from Outer Space* and *Condorman*, *The*

China Syndrome, *Hangar 18*, *The Time Crystal* and *Teen Wolf Too*. On TV, Hampton co-starred as "Trooper Hannibal Dobbs" in the sitcom *F Troop* (1965–67), and he appeared in the mini-series *World War III* and episodes of *The Greatest American Hero*, *Otherworld* and *Superboy*.

Bridget Hanley

American TV actress Bridget [Ann Elizabeth] Hanley died of Alzheimer's disease on December 15, aged 80. She appeared in *Bell, Book and Candle* (1976) and episodes of *Bewitched*, *I Dream of Jeannie*, *The Flying Nun*, *Circle of Fear* and the 1968 pilot *Mad Mad Scientist*. She was married to director/producer E.W. Swackhamer from 1969 until his death in 1994.

Judith Hanna

Australian-born science fiction fan and social and environmental activist Judith Hanna died of liver cancer in London on September 6, aged 67.

During the 1980s she contributed articles and reviews to a number of publications, including *Ansible*, *Vector*, *Matrix* and *Paperback Inferno* (edited by her husband, Joseph Nicholas). Hanna also wrote a guest editorial for *Interzone* #15 (Spring, 1986).

Haya Harareet

Palestinian-born actress Haya Harareet (Haya Neuberg), who starred as "Queen Antinea" in Edgar G. Ulmer's troubled *Journey Beneath the Desert* (the fourth film version of Pierre Benoit's fantasy *L'Atlantide*, 1961), died in England on February 3, aged 89. The exotic-looking actress also co-starred as "Esther" in *Ben-Hur* (1959) before she retired from the screen in 1964. Harareet was married to director Jack Clayton from 1984 until his death in 1995, and is co-credited as a scriptwriter on his offbeat 1967 movie *Our Mother's House*.

Tony Harding

British character actor Tony Harding (Anthony Armatrading), the younger brother of musician Joan Armatrading, died of cancer on May 10, aged 60. He is the voice of "Xalex" in the video games *Star Wars: The Old Republic*, *Star Wars: The Old Republic–Rise of the Hutt Cartel*, *Star Wars: The Old Republic–Shadow of Revan* and *Star Wars: The Old Republic–Knights of the Fallen Empire* (2011–15).

Don Harley

Bruce Cornwell, Eric Eden *and* Don Harley *discuss the first episode of* Dan Dare - Mission of the Earthmen *(Eagle 1960)*

British comics artist Don Harley (Donald Eric Harley) died in January 27, aged 93. Between 1951–59, he was part of Frank Hampson's studio, working on the weekly 'Dan Dare' strip in *Eagle*. Harley's other credits include 'Thunderbirds' in *Countdown*, 'The Investigator' in *TV Century 21*, 'Mark of the Mysterons' in *Solo*, 'Mysterons' in *TV Tornado* and strips in various annuals, include *Blakes 7* in 1979.

Marie Harmon

Republic Pictures contract player Marie Harmon, who had uncredited

bit-parts in "The Shadow" movie *Behind the Mask* (1946) plus *Secret Beyond the Door . . .* (1947), died on January 25, aged 97. She gave up her acting career in the 1950s to launch a dress business. One of Harmon's twin daughters, Cherie Currie, was former lead vocalist of The Runaways.

Al Harrington

85-year-old Western Samoa-born American character actor Al Harrington died in Hawaii on September 21, aged 85. Best known for co-starring as "Ben" in the original TV series of *Hawaii Five-O* (1969–75) and "Mamo Kahike" in the remake (2011–18), he was also in *Escape from Atlantis*, *DreamKeeper* and *The Fall of Night*.

Cynthia Harris

American stage and screen actress Cynthia Harris, who co-starred in such TV series as *Edward & Mrs. Simpson* (1978) and *Mad About You* (1993–2019), died October 3, aged 87. She also appeared in *Doctor Franken*, *Tempest* and *Mannequin: On the Move*, along with episodes of *The Powers of Matthew Star* and *Now and Again*.

Peter Harris

British TV director Peter Harris died on February 23, aged 88. He directed the first seventy-three episodes of *The

Muppet Show (1976–81), along with various specials and spin-off TV movies.

Romaine Hart

British film exhibitor and distributor Romaine Hart OBE died of a heart attack on December 28, aged 88. In 1970, she transformed a rundown 1950s cinema in Islington, north London, into the first-run arthouse The Screen on the Green, described by Quentin Tarantino as "the coolest cinema in London". She went on to open more independent cinemas, and Hart eventually set up her own eclectic distribution company, Mainline Pictures, releasing titles by such maverick directors as David Lynch (*Eraserhead*), Alejandro Jodorowsky (*Santa Sangre*) and Paul Verhoeven (*The 4th Man*).

Alan Hawkshaw

Ubiquitous British TV and film composer/arranger [William] Alan Hawkshaw, who contributed electronic music to *The Monster Club* (1981, based on the stories of R. Chetwynd-Hayes), died of pneumonia on October 16, aged 84. He created the theme music for *Channel 4 News*, *Grange Hill* and *Countdown*, and scored the paranormal documentary series *Arthur C. Clarke's Mysterious World*, *World of Strange Powers* and *Mysterious Universe*. Hawkshaw also composed a companion CD for Shane D. O'Brien's 1997 book *The Venus Legacy: When the Moon Turns to Blood*. In the 1960s he was a member of the rock 'n' roll group Emile Ford & The Checkmates, before joining The Shadows the following decade. Hawkshaw was also Olivia Newton-John's musical director and arranger/pianist, and worked with Cliff Richard, Dusty Springfield, Barbra Streisand, David Bowie, Tom Jones and many other artistes.

Kay Hawtrey

Canadian character actress Kay Hawtrey (Katharine Mary Craven Hawtrey) died on June 11, aged 94. She began her acting career in the mid-1950s, and her credits include *The Intruder*, David Cronenberg's *Videodrome*, *Love at Stake*, *Haunted by Her Past* (aka *Secret Passions*), *Urban Legend*, *American Psycho II: All American Girl* and *The Scream Team*. On TV, Hawtrey appeared in episodes of *The Starlost*, *The New Avengers*, *Faerie Tale Theatre*, *Goosebumps*, *The New Ghostwriter Mysteries* and *The Zack Files*.

Billie Hayes

American character actress Billie Hayes (Billie Armstrong Brosch), best known for playing "Witchipoo" in the Sid and Marty Krofft TV series *H.R. Pufnstuf* (1969–70) and spin-off movie *Pufnstuff* (1970), died on April 29, aged 96. She was "Weenie the Genie" in the Krofft's *Lidsville* (1971–72), and her other credits include episodes of *Bewitched* (as another witch), *Tabitha* and *Murder She Wrote* ('The Murder of Sherlock Holmes'). Hayes also voiced numerous TV cartoon shows, and she was the voice of "Orgoch" in Disney's *The Black Cauldron*.

Jeffrey M. Hayes

American producer Jeffrey M. Hayes, a former executive VP at Paramount Pictures Network Television before forming his own production company Coote/Hayes Productions in 2000, died on March 9, aged 68. He created the 1993-94 series *Time Trax*, and his other credits include the short-lived series *E.A.R.T.H. Force*, *Beastmaster* (1999-02), *Salem's Lot* (2004), *Hercules* (2005), *Nightmares & Dreamscapes: From the Stories of Stephen King* (2006) and *Blood Drive* (2017), along with the TV movies *Cruise Into Terror*, *Snowbeast*, *Nightmare on the 13th Floor*, the two-part *20,000 Leagues Under the Sea* (1997, with Michael Caine as "Captain Nemo"), *The Fury Within*, *The Lost World* (1999) and subsequent TV series, *Max Knight: Ultra Spy*, *Virtual Nightmare*, *On the Beach* (2000), *Dr. Jekyll and Mr. Hyde* (2000, with Adam Baldwin in the title roles), *Code Red*, *Curse of the Talisman*, *The Lost World: Underground*, Mick Garris' *Lost in Oz*, *Evil Never Dies*, *Family Curse*, *Tyrannosaurus Axteca*, *Heatstroke*, *Chasing the Devil* and *The Happytime Murders*.

Damaris Hayman

Veteran British character actress Damaris Hayman, probably best remembered for playing "Miss Hawthorne" in the 1971 *Doctor Who* serial 'The Dæmons', died on June 3, aged 91. In a career stretching back to the early 1950s, she often portrayed eccentric or upper-class characters in such movies as *Mad About Men*, *Bunny Lake is Missing*, *The Pink Panther Strikes Again*, *Full Circle* (aka *The Haunting of Julia*, based on the novel by Peter Straub) and the short *The Man and the Snake* (based on a story by Ambrose Bierce), along with episodes of TV's

Pardon My Genie and *The Witches' Brew*. Hayman recreated her role as Olive Hawthorne in the 2017 *Doctor Who* fan video *White Witch of Devil's End*.

Jack Hedley

Dependable British leading man Jack Hedley (Jack Snowdon Hawkins), who co-starred with Lon Chaney, Jr. in Don Sharp's *Witchcraft* (1964), died of a heart attack on December 11, aged 92. He also appeared in *The Scarlet Blade*, *The Secret of Blood Island* and *The Anniversary* for Hammer Films, along with the James Bond film *For Your Eyes Only* and Lucio Fulci's *The New York Ripper*. On TV, Hedley was in episodes of *Journey to the Unknown*, *UFO*, *The Frighteners* and *Space Precinct*. The actor retired from the screen in 2000.

Monte Hellman

American movie director Monte Hellman (Monte Jay Himmelbaum), whose pair of existential Westerns *The Shooting* and *Ride in the Whirlwind* (both 1966) are classics of the genre, died on April 20, aged 91. During the late 1950s and '60s he worked with producer Roger Corman on such movies as *Beast from Haunted Cave* and *The Terror* (along with half-a-dozen others, 1963), while his later credits include *Silent Night, Deadly Night 3: Better Watch Out!* and *Trapped Ashes* ('Stanley's Girlfriend' segment). Working uncredited, Hellman also shot the title sequence for Corman's *Creature from the Haunted Sea*, was an editor on The Monkees' *Head*, *The Awakening* (1980) and *Grey Knight* (aka *Ghost Brigade*), and a second-unit director on *RoboCop* (1987). He was also an executive producer on Quentin Tarantino's debut, *Reservoir Dogs*.

Jack Hedley (1929–2021) co-starred with Lon Chaney, Jr. in the British-made supernatural thriller Witchcraft (1964).

Gloria Henry

American actress Gloria [Eileen] Henry, best known as wholesome mom "Alice Mitchell" in the TV sitcom *Dennis the Menace* (1959–63), died on April 3, aged 98. During the 1940s and '50s she appeared in a number of "B" Westerns and crime movies and was in *Doin' Time on Planet Earth* (1988).

Mike Henry

1960s movie "Tarzan" Mike Henry (Michael Dennis Henry) died on January 8 of complications from traumatic encephalopathy and Parkinson's disease brought on by head injuries sustained while playing professional football in the NFL and at the University of Southern California. He was 84. Henry portrayed the Lord of the Jungle in *Tarzan and the Valley of Gold*, *Tarzan and the Great River* and *Tarzan and the Jungle Boy*. He went on to appear in a number of other movies, including *Soylent Green*, along with episodes of TV's *The Six Million Dollar Man* and *Fantasy Island*. He retired from acting in the late 1980s as a result of the Parkinson's disease.

Bob Herron

Veteran American stuntman-actor Bob Herron (Robert D. Herron) ironically died of complications from a fall on October 10, aged 97. As a (often uncredited) bit-player, he portrayed a Martian in *Invaders from Mars* (1953), a Mole Person in *The Mole People* (1956) and a Slime Person in *The Slime People* (1963). Herron also appeared in *The Seventh Sign* and *Grave Secrets* (1989), and on TV he was in episodes of *It's About Time*, *The Wild Wild West*, *Star Trek* and *The Six Million Dollar Man*. He was a prolific stunt

Former NFL player Mike Henry (1936–2021) donned the loincloth for the first of three movies in Tarzan in the Valley of Gold *(1967).*

performer, working on *The Ten Commandments* (1956), *The Monolith Monsters*, *The Absent Minded Professor*, *The Silencers*, *In Like Flint*, *Diamonds Are Forever*, *The Groundstar Conspiracy*, *Soylent Green*, *Death Race 2000* (1975), *Doc Savage: The Man of Bronze*, *Obsession*, *Herbie Goes to Monte Carlo*, *Logan's Run*, *The Black Hole*, *The Nude Bomb*, *The Sword and the Sorcerer*, *Poltergeist*, *Cujo*, *Frankenweenie* (1984), *The Goonies*, *Explorers*, *Pee-Wee's Big Adventure*, *Weird Science*, *Poltergeist II: The Other Side*, *Howard the Duck*, *The Kindred*, *Prince of Darkness*, *Pet Sematary* (1989), *Dick Tracy* (1990), *Child's Play 3*, *Batman Returns*, *Batman Forever* and *Small Soldiers*, along with episodes of *I Dream of Jeannie*, *The Man from U.N.C.L.E.*, *Voyage to the Bottom of the Sea*, *The Green Hornet*, *The Girl from U.N.C.L.E.*, *Batman*, *The Invaders*, *Get Smart*, *Wonder Woman*, *Knight Rider*, *Highway to Heaven*, *Amazing Stories*, *Tales from the Crypt*, *They Came from Outer Space*, *Nowhere Man*, *Buffy the Vampire Slayer* and *The X Files*.

Tom Hickey

Irish character actor Tom Hickey died of Parkinson's disease on May 1, aged 77. He appeared in *Gothic*, *High Spirits* and *Possession* (2002).

Steve Hickman

American science fiction and fantasy artist Steve Hickman (Stephen Forrest Hickman) died of prostate cancer on July 16, aged 72. In 1974, Neal Adams introduced Hickman to the art editor at Ace Books, who bought publication rights to several paintings in the artist's portfolio. His first cover actually appeared on the May 1976 issue of *Fantastic*, and he went on to work on numerous books and magazines, including Robert E. Howard's *Cthulhu: The Mythos and Kindred Horrors* (1987), Manly Wade Wellman's *John the Balladeer* (1988), the Winter 2002-03 issue of *Weird Tales* and the Spring 2005 edition of *H.P. Lovecraft's Magazine of Horror*.

Some of Hickman's art is collected in *The Fantasy Art of Stephen Hickman* (1989) and *The Art of Stephen Hickman: Empyrean* (2015), and in 1988 he published his only novel, *The Lemurian Stone*, as by "Stephen F. Hickman". In 1994, Hickman won a Hugo Award for the Space Fantasy Commemorative Booklet of five stamps, the first official recognition of the SF genre by the United States Postal Service. Two years later he created a Cthulhu statuette, inspired by an earlier cover illustration, which was produced and distributed by Bowen Designs.

Chuck Hicks

Veteran Hollywood stuntman-actor Chuck Hicks died on May 4, aged 93. A former boxer (as "Chuck Daley"), he worked (often uncredited) on *Siren of Bagdad*, *Creature with the Atom Brain*, *Zombies of Mora Tau*, *Shock Corridor*, *Our Man Flint*, *The Silencers*, *Murderers' Row*, *In Like Flint*, *Escape* (1971), *The Hound of the Baskervilles* (1972), *Beyond Evil*, *The Sword and the Sorcerer*, *Star Trek II: The Wrath of Khan*, *Star Trek III: The Search for Spock*, *The Beastmaster*, *D.A.R.Y.L.*, *Programmed to Kill*, *Vampire Knights*, *Dick Tracy* (1990), *Bride of Re-Animator*, *Route 666*, *The Ring* (2002), *Snoop Dogg's Hood of Horror*, *Flight of the Living Dead*, *Legion* and many other titles. On TV, Hicks was a semi-regular on the first season of *The Untouchables* (1959), and he also turned up, usually playing henchmen or bodyguards, in episodes of *The Twilight Zone*, *The Green Hornet*, *The Time Tunnel*, *The Man from U.N.C.L.E.*, *Batman* (1966-68), *Search*, *The Six Million Dollar Man*, *Wonder Woman*, *The Powers of Matthew Star*, *Voyagers!*, *Wizards and Warriors*, *Fantasy Island*, *Manimal*, *Star Trek: The Next Generation* and *The Flash* (1990). He retired in 2010.

Billy Hinsche

Filipino-born American singer and musician Billy Hinsche (William Ernest Hinsche), who was a member of the late 1960s singing trio Dino Desi & Billy with celebrity offspring Dean Paul Martin and Desi Arnaz, Jr., died of lung cancer on November 20, aged 70. Dino Desi & Billy turned up in the sci-spy comedy *Murderers' Row* (1966), and Hinsche, who was also a touring musician with The Beach Boys, composed the theme music for the 1983-84 TV series *Automan*. His mother, Celia Hinsche, died on the same day.

Pat Hitchcock

American actress Pat Hitchcock (Patricia Alma Hitchcock), the only daughter of director Alfred Hitchcock and his wife Alma Reville, died on August 9, aged 93. Amongst other small acting roles, she appeared in her father's *Psycho* (1960) and ten episodes of TV's *Alfred Hitchcock Presents*.

John Hitchin

John Hitchin, who worked for just over three decades at Penguin Books as a marketing and publicity manager, died on August 8, aged 88. He joined the company in 1959 and is credited with a number of innovations, including the first paperback gift set, the first display "dump bin", and persuading Sainsbury's supermarket chain to start selling books. From 1974-76 Hitchin was vice-president of Penguin Books USA, and he opened the first Penguin Bookshop in Covent Garden in 1980. He was president of the Booksellers Association from 1992-94 and the European Booksellers Federation from 1993-99.

Vegar Hoel

Norwegian character actor [Geir] Vegar Hoel died after a long illness on November 8, aged 47. He appeared in *Hansel & Gretel: Witch Hunters*, *Dead Snow*, *Dead Snow 2* (which he also co-scripted) and *What Happened to Monday*. Hoel also played

"Baron Magnus of Dracas" on the vampire TV series *Heirs of the Night* (2019-20).

Basil Hoffman

Busy American character actor Basil Hoffman died on September 17, aged 83. He appeared in *Close Encounters of a Third Kind* and *Love at First Bite* (both uncredited), *All of Me*, *Outlaws*, *The Milagro Beanfield War*, *Communion* (1989, based on the novel by Whitley Strieber), *Switch*, *The Double 0 Kid*, *The Elvira Show*, *The Box* (based on Richard Matheson's story 'Button, Button') and *One Wish*, along with episodes of TV's *Good Heavens*, *Alfred Hitchcock Presents* (1985), *The Twilight Zone* (another adaptation of Matheson's 'Button, Button'), *Beauty and the Beast* (1987), *Eerie Indiana*, *Kindred: The Embraced* and *Beyond Belief: Fact or Fiction*. Hoffman was also a successful acting teacher and coach.

Robert J. Hogan

Busy American supporting actor Robert J. [Joseph] Hogan died complications from pneumonia on May 27, aged 87. He was in *Westworld* (1973) and *Species II*. On TV, Hogan appeared in episodes of *The Twilight Zone*, *Batman* (1966), *I Dream of Jeannie*, *Land of the Giants*, *Rod Serling's Night Gallery*, *Tales of the Unexpected*, *The Six Million Dollar Man*, *Turnabout*, *Mork & Mindy*, *The Incredible Hulk* (1980), *Tucker's Witch*, *Automan*,

Knight Rider and *Now and Again*. The main character in CBS' World War II sitcom *Hogan's Heroes* (1965-71) was named after him by his friend, co-creator Bernard Fein.

Hal Holbrook

American actor Hal Holbrook (Harold Rowe Holbrook, Jr.), best known for his performances as Mark Twain and Abraham Lincoln on stage and screen, died on January 23, aged 95. He made his screen debut in the mid-1950s, and his credits include *Wild in the Streets*, *Rituals*, *Capricorn One*, *The Legend of the Golden Gun*, John Carpenter's *The Fog* (1980), George A. Romero's *Creepshow*, and *The Unholy*. On TV, Holbrook appeared in a 2000 episode of *The Outer Limits*.

Roy Holder

British supporting actor Roy [Trevor] Holder, who portrayed sidekick "Chas Diamond" in the second series of the children's TV show *Ace of Wands*

(1972), died of cancer on November 9, aged 75. A former child actor, he appeared in *Psychomania* (aka *The Death Wheelers*), Amicus' *The Land That Time Forgot* (1974), *Trial by Combat* (aka *A Dirty Knight's Work*), *Out of the Darkness* and *Tooth*. On TV, Holder was also in episodes of TV's *Gaslight Theatre* ('Sweeney Todd or, the Demon Barber of Fleet Street'), *Doctor Who*, *The Invisible Man* (1984), *Star Cops*, *The Case-Book of Sherlock Holmes* and *Bugs*.

Bernard Holley

Roy Holder (1946–2021) played a member of a violent motorbike gang resurrected from the dead in Psychomania (1973), which was George Sanders' last film.

British TV actor Bernard Holley died after a long illness on November 22, aged 81. He appeared in episodes of *Out of the Unknown*, *Doctor Who* (as the eponymous alien villain in 'The Claws of Axos'), *Thriller* (1974), *The Phoenix and the Carpet* (1977) and Season 2 of the BBC serial *The Tripods* (1985). Holley also co-starred in the BBC Radio 4 serial *Bram Stoker's Dracula*, and he featured on a couple of *Doctor Who* audio dramas from Big Finish.

Howard Honig

American character actor Howard Honig died on November 29, aged 90. He was in *Curse of the Black Widow*, *Avenging Angel* and *Reel Horror*. On TV, Honig turned up in episodes of *Dark Shadows* (1968), *The Incredible Hulk* and *Supertrain*.

John Hora

American cinematographer John [Charles] Hora died of heart failure on February 9, aged 80. With director

Joe Dante he collaborated on *The Howling*, *Twilight Zone: The Movie*, *Gremlins*, *Explorers*, *The 'Burbs* (additional photography), *Gremlins 2: The New Batch*, *Matinee* and an episode of TV's *Eerie, Indiana*. Hora also worked on *Honey I Blew Up the Kid* and *UHF*, and he turned up in cameo roles in *Innerspace*, *Honey I Blew Up the Kid* and *Burying the Ex*.

Patrick Horgan

British-born actor Patrick Horgan died on October 6, aged 92. He appeared in Hammer's *The Evil of Frankenstein* (uncredited), *The Curse of the Jade*

Scorpion and episodes of TV's *The Girl from U.N.C.L.E.*, *Cimarron Strip* (Harlan Ellison's Jack the Ripper story, 'Knife in the Darkness'), *Star Trek*, *The Wild Wild West* and *Bewitched*. Horgan also narrated Woody Allen's 1983 time-travel fantasy, *Zelig*.

Sally Ann Howes

British-born stage and screen actress and singer Sally Ann Howes, best remembered for playing "Truly Scrumptious" in the 1968 musical movie *Chitty Chitty Bang Bang*, died in Florida on December 19, aged 91. A former child actress, her other film credits include *The Halfway House*, *Dead of Night*, *The Hound of the Baskervilles* (1972) and *Death Ship*. Howes was nominated for a Tony Award for her performance in a 1962 revival of *Brigadoon* at the New York City Opera, and she recreated her role in a 1966 made-for-TV movie.

Elizabeth Anne Hull

84-year-old American writer and academic Dr. Elizabeth Anne Hull, who was married to SF author Frederik Pohl from 1984 until his death in 2013, died on August 2 of complications from a fall a few months earlier. As part of the SF Research Association, she was the newsletter editor from 1981–84 and president from 1989–90, winning the SFRA Clareson Award in 1998. She published stories in *Isaac Asimov's Science Fiction Magazine* and *Aboriginal SF*, and also co-edited the 1986 anthology *Tales from the Planet Earth* with Pohl and *Gateways*, a 2010 volume inspired by her husband's work.

Joye Hummel

Joye Hummel [Murchison Kelly], who was the first woman outside the polygamous partnership enjoyed by creator "Charles Moulton" (William

Australian poster for the classic Ealing Studio's portmanteau picture Dead of Night (1945), which featured a teenage Sally Ann Howes (1930–2021).

Moulton Marston) to produce stories for *Wonder Woman*, died on April 5, one day after her 97th birthday. It was finally revealed in 2014 that, between 1944-47, the typist was responsible for ghostwriting more than seventy issues of the DC comic book for Moulton, earning $50 per strip.

Mike Humphreys

British TV cameraman and operator Mike Humphreys died on September 16. He filmed episodes of *The Guardians*, *The Frighteners*, *ITV Sunday Night Theatre* ('A.D.A.M.'), *Whoops Apocalypse* and *Metal Mickey*.

Paul Huntley

British-born Broadway and movie wig-maker and key hair stylist Paul Huntley, who created the high-piled wigs for singer Dusty Springfield, died in London after a short illness on July 5, aged 88. He worked on such films as *Sheena* (1984), *The Exorcist III*, *The Addams Family* (1991), Disney's *101 Dalmatians* (1996, Glenn Close's wigs as "Cruella DeVil"), *The Cell* and *Jekyll & Hyde: The Musical*. Huntley also created the wigs for Angela Lansbury's "Mrs. Lovett" in the original Broadway production of *Sweeney Todd* in 1979 and styled every feline in the original Broadway production of *Cats* in 1982. In 2003, he received a special Tony Award for his decades of stage work.

Halyna Hutchins

42-year-old Ukraine-born cinematographer Halyna Hutchins was accidentally shot to death by actor and producer Alec Baldwin while filming a Western on location in New Mexico on October 21. The prop gun used by Baldwin reportedly contained a live round. Director Joel Souza was also hit and injured by the bullet, and was treated at a local hospital before being released. Hutchins' credits include *Snowbound*, *Darlin'* (based on characters created by Jack Ketchum and Lucky McKee), *Archenemy* and *The Mad Hatter*. She was named one of *American Cinematographer*'s Rising Stars of 2019.

Ken Hutchison

Scottish-born actor Ken Hutchison (Aitken Hutchison), who starred as "Heathcliff" in the BBC's 1978 serialisation of *Wuthering Heights*, died in London on August 9, aged 72. His

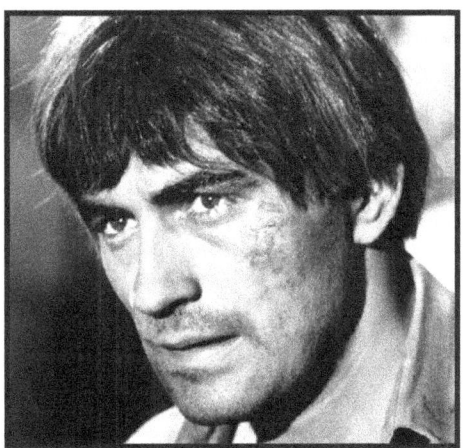

other credits include *Deadly Strangers*, *Ladyhawke* and episode of TV's *The Guardians*, *Arthur of the Britons* (as "Gawain") and *Space: 1999*. He retired from the screen at the end of the 1990s.

Toshihiro Iijima

Veteran Japanese "Ultraman" writer, producer and director Toshihiro Iijima (aka "Kitao Senzoku"/ "Toshihiro Jijima") died of aspiration pneumonia on October 17, aged 89. His credits include such TV series as

Ultra Q (1965–67), *Ultraman* (1965–67), *Ultraseven* (1967–68), *Ultraman Max* (2005–06) and *Operation: Mystery!* (1968–71), along with the movies *Daigoro vs. Goliath* and *Ultraman Cosmos: The First Contact*.

Alvin Ing

Hawaiian-born, Asian-American Broadway singer and character actor Alvin Y.F. Ing died of cardiac arrest on August 1, aged 89. He had been battling pneumonia and breakthrough COVID-19 complications. Ing's screen credits include *The Final Countdown* and episodes of TV's *Fantasy Island*, *Highway to Heaven*, *Strange Luck* and *Agents of S.H.I.E.L.D.*

Ravil Isyanov

Russian-born American character actor Ravil [Akhmedullovitch] Isyanov died of cancer at his home in Los Angeles on September 29, aged 59. He moved to the UK in 1990 and

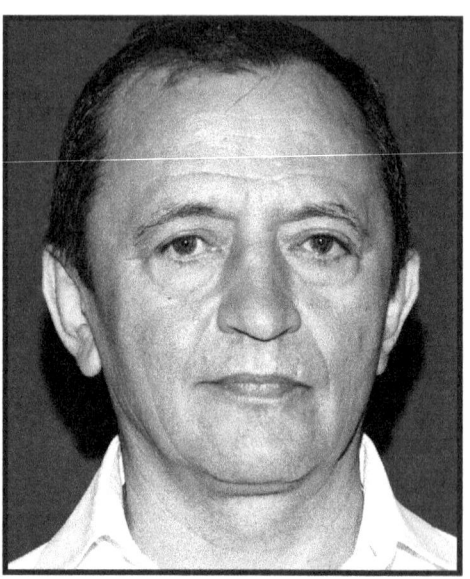

the US eight years later, appearing in the James Bond film *GoldenEye*, *The Omega Code*, *Octopus*, *Arachnid* and *Transformers: Dark of the Moon*. On TV, Isyanov was in episodes of *The Young Indiana Jones Chronicles*, *Seven Days*, *Buffy the Vampire Slayer*, *Fringe*, *Touch*, *Marvel's Agents of S.H.I.E.L.D.* and *The Last Ship* (as "Admiral Konstantin Nikolajewitsch Ruskov", 2014–18).

Andrei Izmailov

Russian author Andrei Izmailov [Narimanovich] died on December 3, aged 68. Best known as an author of contemporary thrillers, in 1979 he took part in the Leningrad seminar of SF writers under the direction of Boris Strugatsky. Izmailov wrote the SF novel *Pokrovitel* and several X Files novelisations.

Kevin Jackson

British writer, broadcaster and filmmaker Kevin Jackson died on May 10, aged 66. He collaborated with cartoonist Hunt Emerson on a series of comic strips about the history of Western occultism for *Fortean Times*, and Jackson's own books include *Bite: A Vampire Handbook* and *Nosferatu (1922): eine Symphonie des Grauens* for the BFI Film Classics series. He also made a number of short films, including *Bite: Diary of a Vampire Housewife*, *Bite: Pavane for a Vampire Queen* and *Dracbeth*.

Frank Jacobs

MAD magazine writer Frank Jacobs (Franklin Jacobs) died on April 5, aged 91. He worked for E.C.'s irreverent humour title from 1957–2014. Amongst nearly 600 pieces for the magazine, Jacobs once critiqued the policies of President Ronald Reagan in a line-by-line satire of Edgar Allan Poe's 'The Raven', while a special pull-out section of song parodies he and Larry Siegel wrote for MAD in 1961 led to an ultimately unsuccessful copyright-infringement lawsuit from Irving Berlin and a group of song publishers.

Sondra James

American character actress and ADR voice casting and looping co-ordinator Sondra James died of lung cancer on September 12, aged 82. She was in *Spider-Man: Homecoming*, *Joker* and an episode of TV's *What We Do in the Shadows*. James also contributed additional voices to numerous movies.

Larry D. Johnson

Larry D. (Don) Johnson, who played "Langston" in the cult Blaxploitation zombie movie *Sugar Hill* (1974), died on June 26, aged 77. A former radio broadcaster and TV news achor, he later worked as Devlopment Director at KTSU public radio and in 2011 was inducted into the Texas Radio Hall of Fame. Johnson's only other movie credit is 'The Clinic' segment of the 2004 horror film, *Street Tales of Terror*.

Don Jones

American low-budget filmmaker Don Jones (Donald Evan Jones, aka "Nod Senoj"/"Evan Jones") died of a stroke on August 10, aged 83. A former professional boxer (under the name "Irish Frankie Conway"), he moved to Hollywood in the late 1960s and started out as a stunt player and working on the special effects for Peter Bogdanovich's "fix-up" movie *Voyage to the Planet of Prehistoric Women*. Jones was the key grip on Ted V. Mikels' *The Astro-Zombies* (starring John Carradine) and the lighting director on David L. Hewitt's *The Mighty Gorga*. In 1970 he recorded sound on *The Psycho Lover* and that same year was the boom operator on *Is This Trip Really Necessary?* (aka *Blood of the Iron Maiden*), again featuring Carradine. Jones also worked with the actor four years later, this time as director of photography on *The House of Seven Corpses*. He wrote, produced and directed *Schoolgirls in Chains*; directed *The Love Butcher*; wrote, edited, produced and directed *The Forest*, and edited, produced and directed *Molly and the Ghost*. Jones' 2011 novel, *Alma's Daughter: A Child Possessed*, was about a teenage poltergeist.

Langdon Jones

British writer, editor, poet and composer Langdon Jones died in September, aged 79. During the 1960s he was Assistant Editor of Michael Moorcock's *New Worlds* magazine, and the pair also co-edited the anthologies *The Nature of the Catastrophe* and *The New Nature of the Catastrophe*. Jones' stories and poems appeared in *New Worlds*, *Science Fantasy* and *Orbit 5*, and his only collection, *The Eye of the Lens*, was published in 1972. He also edited the 1969 "New Wave" anthology *The New S.F.: An Original Anthology of Modern Speculative Fiction* and was responsible for reconstructing Mervyn Peake's *Titus Alone* (1959) for the definitive edition of the book in 1970.

Rick Jones

Canadian-born actor Rick Jones (Frederick Jones), who played "Luther Whately" in *The Shuttered Room* (1967, loosely based on the story by August Derleth and H.P. Lovecraft), died of cancer in America on October 8, aged 84. Probably best known to British audiences as "Yoffy", the presenter of the BBC children's show *Fingerbobs*

(1972), he also had small roles in *How to Stuff a Wild Bikini* and an episode of TV's *The Avengers*. Jones was subsequently the frontman and songwriter for the British country rock band Meal Ticket, whose song 'You'd Better Believe it, Babe' was used as the theme for the BBC *Play for Today* episode 'The Flipside of Dominick Hide' (1980) and its sequel, 'Another Flip for Dominick' (1982). After the band broke up, he co-wrote the music and appeared in the flop 1981 stage musical *Captain Crash Versus The Zzorg Women Chapters Five and Six* in Los Angeles.

Robert C. Jones

Oscar-winning American film editor Robert C. Jones, whose credits include *Heaven Can Wait* (1978), died after a long illness on February 1, aged 84. He also wrote a couple of episodes of TV's *Faerie Tale Theatre* in 1984.

Fred Jordan

Austrian-born Fred Jordan (Alfred Rotblatt), a former business manager and editor at Grove Press, died in New York City on April 19, aged 95. While at Grove he oversaw the imprint's legal battles to publish uncensored versions of D.H. Lawrence's *Lady Chatterley's Lover*, Henry Miller's *Tropic of Cancer* and William S. Burroughs' *Naked Lunch*. As an editor, he also published J.G. Ballard's *The Atrocity Exhibition* (as *Love and Napalm: Export USA*). Jordan later worked at Grosset & Dunlap (founding the Fred Jordan Books imprint), the American division of Methuen Publishing and at Pantheon Books, a division of Random House, where he was publisher and editor-in-chief. He retired in 1993.

Rémy Julienne

Veteran French stuntman and stunt co-ordinator Rémy Julienne died of complications from COVID-19 on January 21, aged 90. He began his

career in 1964 doing stunts on *Fantomas*, and his other credits include *Who?* (based on the novel by Algis Budrys), Disney's *Condorman*, *Sheena*, *Solarbabies*, *Mr. Stitch*, *A Witch's Way of Love*, *A Sound of Thunder* (based on the story by Ray Bradbury) and *The Da Vinci Code*. Julienne was also the driving stunt arranger on the James Bond films *For Your Eyes Only*, *Octopussy*, *A View to a Kill*, *The Living Daylights*, *Licence to Kill* and *Goldeneye*.

Nathan Jung

Asian-American character actor Nathan Jung died on April 24, aged 74. He was featured in John Carpenter's *Big Trouble in Little China*, *Darkman*, *The Shadow* (1994), *Ghoulies IV* and *Galaxis*. On TV, Jung was in episodes of *Star Trek* ('The Savage Curtain', as "Gengis Khan"), *Monster Squad*, *The Amazing Spider-Man*, *Manimal*, *Highway to Heaven* and *Lois & Clark: The New Adventures of Superman*. He was one of the few actors to have worked with both Bruce Lee and his son, Brandon Lee.

Norton Juster

Award-winning American author Norton Juster died of complications from a stroke on March 8, aged 91. His classic 1961 children's fantasy *The Phantom Tollbooth* (illustrated by Jules Feiffer) was adapted as a stage musical and turned into an animated movie in 1970.

Bernie Kahn

American TV scriptwriter Bernie Kahn (Bernard M. Kahn) died on April 21, aged 90. He wrote for such series as *My Favorite Martian*, *My Brother the Angel*, *My Mother the Car*, *The Addams Family*, *Get Smart*, *Bewitched*, *Dr. Shrinker*, *Tabitha* (he was also the executive story consultant), *The New Addams Family* and the animated *Super Friends* and *Valley of the Dinosaurs*.

Irma Kalish

American TV writer and producer Irma Kalish (Irma May Ginsberg) died of complications from pneumonia on September 3, aged 96. In collaboration with her husband Austin "Rocky" Kalish (who died in 2016) she co-scripted episodes of *I Dream of Jeannie*, *My Favorite Martian*, *F Troop* (including 'V is for Vampire' with Vincent Price), *The Flying Nun* and *Good Heavens*, along with the pilot shows *America 2100* and *Ghost of a Chance*. Kalish additionally wrote the 1985 reunion TV movie *I Dream of Jeannie . . . Fifteen Years Later*.

Alan R. Kalter

Alan R. (Robert) Kalter, best known as the announcer on *Late Show with David Letterman* (1995–2015), died on October 4, aged 78. He was also the announcer for the USA Network's non-hosted horror and science fiction movie series *USA Saturday Nightmares* (1986) and the companion show, *Commander USA's Groovie Movies* (1985–89).

Lorina Kamburova

30-year-old Bulgarian-born actress and singer Lorina Kamburova died in a Moscow hospital from bilateral pneumonia due to COVID-19 on May 26. She co-starred with Robert Englund in *Nightworld*, but slipped further down the cast in *Leatherface* (2017), *Day of the Dead: Bloodline*, *Death Race: Beyond Anarchy*, *Doom: Annihilation*, *Love and Monsters* and the Russian post-apocalyptic mini-series *The Young and the Strong Survive*.

Sayaka Kanda

35-year-old Japanese actress and singer Sayaka Kanda, best known for dubbing the voice of "Princess Anna" in the Japanese version of Disney's *Frozen*, apparently committed suicide by jumping from a hotel in Sapporo

on December 18. Her other credits include *Dragon Head*, *Farewell Kamen Rider Den-O: Final Countdown* and voice work for various *anime* TV series.

Marvin Kaye

American author, editor and actor Marvin [Nathan] Kaye died on May 13, aged 83. He collaborated with Parke Godwin on *The Masters of Solitude* and its sequel, *Wintermind*, along with the stand-alone *A Cold Blue Light*. His other novels include *The Incredible Umbrella*, *The Amorous*

Edward Gorey did the cover for the Doubleday anthology
Masterpieces of Terror and the Supernatural
edited Marvin Kaye (1938–2021).

Umbrella, Ghosts of Night and Morning, Fantastique, The Last Christmas of Ebenezer Scrooge (which was performed annually on stage in New York City for many years) and *The Passion of Frankenstein*, while some of his short fiction is collected in *The Possession of Immanuel Wolf and Other Improbable Tales*. Kaye edited the anthologies *Fiends and Creatures, Brother Theodore's Chamber of Horrors, Ghosts: A Treasury of Chilling Tales Old and New, Masterpieces of Terror & the Supernatural, Devils and Demons: A Treasury of Fiendish Tales Old and New, Weird Tales: The Magazine That Never Dies, Witches and Warlocks: Tales of Black Magic Old and New, 13 Plays of Ghosts and the Supernatural, Haunted America, Lovers and Other Monsters, Masterpieces of Terror and the Unknown, Angels of Darkness, The Resurrected Holmes, The Confidential Casebook of Sherlock Holmes, The Vampire Sextette, The Ultimate Halloween, The Dragon Quintet, The Fair Folk* (winner of the World Fantasy Award), *Forbidden Planets, A Book of Wizards* and *The Ghost Quartet*. He also edited the short-run *H.P. Lovecraft's Magazine of Horror* (2004-09), *Sherlock Holmes Mystery Magazine* (2008-21) and a later incarnation of *Weird Tales* (2011-19).

Ira Keeler

Ira Keeler, a former special effects model-maker for Industrial Light & Magic (ILM), died in the UK on April 15, aged 80. His numerous credits include *Return of the Jedi, Indiana Jones and the Temple of Doom, Star Trek III: The Search for Spock, Cocoon, Back to the Future, Captain EO, The Golden Child, The Witches of Eastwick, Innerspace, *batteries not included, Who Framed Roger Rabbit, Indiana Jones and the Last Crusade, Back to the Future II, Back to the Future Part III, The Rocketeer, Jurassic Park, Star Trek: Generations, Congo, James and the Giant Peach, Star Trek: First Contact, Mars Attacks!, The Lost World: Jurassic Park, Men in Black, Starship Troopers, Deep Impact, The Mummy* (1999), *Star Wars Episode I–The Phantom Menace, A.I. Artificial Intelligence, Jurassic Park III* and *Star Wars Episode II–Attack of the Clones*. Keeler also appears as the technician who ducks under his desk at the end of the *Star Tours* attraction at Disney theme parks.

Patricia Kennealy

American SF and mystery author and music critic Patricia Kennealy (Patricia Kennely, aka "Patricia Kennealy-Morrison") died of complications from heart disease on July 21, aged 75. Her "Keltiad" sequence of Arthurian space operas includes *The Copper Crown*, *The Throne of Scone*, *The Silver Branch* and several other titles. As editor-in-chief of *Jazz & Pop* magazine, she first interviewed Doors singer Jim Morrison in January 1969. The following year they were apparently "married" in a Celtic handfasting ceremony. Kennealy served as a consultant on Oliver Stone's movie *The Doors* (1991), even appearing onscreen as the Wicca priestess who spiritually linked Val Kilmer's Morrison with her own character, played by Kathleen Quinlan. However, her subsequent dissatisfaction with the film resulted in Kennealy writing her own memoir of the experience, *Strange Days: My Life with and Without Jim Morrison* (1992).

Mamat Khalid

Prolific Malaysian scriptwriter, director and occasional actor Mamat Khalid (Mohamad Mohamad Khalid) died on October 24 of a heart attack while playing keyboards during a live performance at a café he owned. He was 58. Khalid's films include the "first Malaysian zombie movie" *Zombi kampung pisang* (2007) and its sequel *Zombi Kilang Biskut*; the werewolf comedies *Kala malam bulan mengambang* and *Usop Wilcha dalam Werewolf dari Bangladesh*; the comedy ghost films *Hantu Kak Limah Balik Rumah*, *Hantu Kak Limah 2: Husin Mon dan Jin Pakai Toncit*, *Usop Wilcha Meghonjang Makhluk Muzium* (featuring Mason R. Walker as Count Dracula) and *Hantu Kak Limah*; the post-apocalyptic *Apokalips X*; the old dark house comedy *Rumah Pusaka di Simpang Jalan*; the supernatural action movie *Lebuhraya Ke Neraka*; the demonic *18 Puasa Di Kampong Pisang*, and the possession thriller *Rajawali*. He was the younger brother of comics artist "Lat" (Datuk Mohammad Nor Khalid).

Shunsuke Kikuchi

Prolific Japanese composer Shunsuke Kikuchi died of aspiration pneumonia on April 24, aged 89. His music can be heard in such movies as *House of Terrors* (1965), *The Terror Beneath the Sea*, *The Golden Bat*, *The Snake Girl and the Silver-Haired Witch*, *Snake Woman's Curse*, *Goke, Body Snatcher from Hell*, *Genocide*, *Gamera vs. Guiron*, *Gamera vs. Jiger*, *Gamera vs. Zigra* and *Gamera: Super Monster*. Kikuchi also worked on such *tokusatsu* TV series as *Kamen Rider* (1971-73) and its various spin-offs, and the poular *anime* shows *Dragon Ball* and *Dragon Ball Z*.

Larry King

American broadcasting legend Larry King (Lawrence Harvey Zeiger) died of complications from COVID-19 on January 23, aged 87. His *Larry King Live* interview show ran for more than 7,000 episodes on CNN from 1985-2010, and he turned up in cameos (usually as himself) in such movies as *Ghostbusters* (1984), *The Exorcist III*, *Contact*, *The Stepford Wives* (2004) and *Dude Bro Party Massacre III*. King was also the voice of "Doris" in the animated *Shrek 2*, *Shrek the Third*, and *Shrek Forever After*. He was married seven times.

Bruce Kirby

Italian-American character actor Bruce Kirby (Bruno Giovanni Quidaciolu, Sr.), who played "Capt. Harry Sedford" on the SF comedy series *Holmes and Yoyo* (1976-77) and was a regular on the short-lived 1979 show *Turnabout*, died complications related to leukemia on January 23, aged 95. He made his screen debut in a TV

adaptation of Gore Vidal's 'Visit to a Small Planet' on a 1955 episode of *Goodyear Playhouse*, and his other credits include *Night Gallery* (1969), *The Muppet Movie*, *Stand by Me*, *Lady in White* and episodes of *I Dream of Jeannie*, *The Greatest American Hero*, *Tucker's Witch* and *The Sentinel*. His son, actor Bruno Kirby, died in 2006.

Tommy Kirk

Former child star Tommy Kirk (Thomas Harvey Kirk) died on September 28, aged 79. Signed to a long-term contract in the mid-1950s by Walt Disney, the all-American Mickey Mouse Club member appeared in *The Shaggy Dog* (1959), *The Absent Minded Professor*, *Babes in Toyland* (1961), *Moon Pilot*, *Son of Flubber*, *The Misadaventures of Merlin Jones*, *The Monkey's Uncle* and other movies for the studio. However, Disney released Kirk from his contract in the mid-1960s after allegations (later dropped) of a gay relationship with an underage boy and marijuana use. His career never recovered, but he went on to appear in AIP's *Pajama Party*, *The Ghost in the Invisible Bikini* (with Basil Rathbone and Boris Karloff) and the 1965 TV special *The Wild Weird World of Dr. Goldfoot* (with Vincent Price), Bert I. Gordon's *Village of the Giants*, Al Adamson's *Blood of Ghastly Horror* (with John Carradine) and Larry Buchanan's *Mars Needs Women* and *It's Alive!*. After overcoming drug addiction, Kirk ran a successful carpet and upholstery cleaning company in California for two decades, before returning to the screen in Fred Olen Ray's *Attack of the 60 Foot Centerfolds*, *Little Miss Magic* and *Billy Frankenstein*, along with *Club Dead* and *The Education of a Vampire*. Despite his previous problems with the studio, he was named a "Disney Legend" in 2006.

Gray Morrow's one-sheet poster for Blood of Ghastly Horror (1973), which top-billed former child star Tommy Kirk (1941–2021) with old-timers John Carradine and Kent Taylor.

Tawny Kitaen

American actress and music video star Tawny Kitaen (Julie Kitaen) died on May 7, aged 59. She had struggled with substance abuse in the past. Kitaen appeared in *Witchboard* and played Hercules' wife "Deianeria" in the 1990s TV series *Hercules: The Legendary Journeys* and the spin-off movies *Hercules and the Circle of Fire*, *Hercules in the Underworld* and *Hercules in the Maze of the Minotaur*. She was also in episodes of *They Came from Outer Space* and *Shades of LA*. Kitaen's first husband (1989–91) was Whitesnake frontman David Coverdale.

Reuben B. Klamer

American toy inventor and props designer Reuben B. [Benjamin] Klamer died on September 14, aged 99. Klamer is not only credited with designing the distinctive gun used by Robert Vaughn's *The Man from U.N.C.L.E.* (along with the spin-off toy) and the Starfleet phaser rifle

from the original *Star Trek* series, but in 1960 he also created the board game The Game of Life for the Milton Bradley toy company, which sold an estimated 70 million units worldwide. Klamer additionally invented Magic Moon Rocks, the Art Linkletter Hula Hoop and Fisher-Price Preschool Trainer Skates, amongst many other toys.

Vladimir Korenev

Russian actor Vladimir [Borisovich] Korenev, who starred in the 1962 Soviet science fiction movie *Chelovek-Amfibiya* (aka *Amphibian Man*), died of complications from COVID-19 on January 2, aged 80.

Erle M. Korshak

Legendary American publisher, editor and collector Erle M. [Melvin] Korshak, one of the last two surviving attendees of the first Worldcon in 1939, died after a short illness on August 25, aged 97. With Mark Reinsberg and Wilson "Bob" Tucker he co-organised the second World Science Fiction Convention, Chicon I, in 1940, helping to ensure that Worldcon would become an annual event. In 1947, Korshak co-founded Shasta Publishers, one of the earliest SF specialty presses, with Reinsberg and T.E. ("Ted") Dikty. Their first book was the landmark reference work *The Checklist of Fantastic Literature* by Everett F. Bleiler (1948), which quickly sold out of its first printing, and they continued with such volumes as *Who Goes There?* (1948) and *Cloak of Aesir* (1952) both by John W. Campbell, Jr., *Slaves of Sleep* by L. Ron Hubbard (1948), *The Wheels of If* by L. Sprague de Camp (1949), *The Man Who Sold the Moon* (1950) and *The Green Hills of Earth* (1951) both by Robert A. Heinlein, *Kinsmen of the Dragon* by Stanley Mullen (1951), *Space on My Hands* by Fredric Brown (1951) and *This Island Earth* by Raymond F. Jones (1952). The final title, *Empire of the Atom* by A.E. van Vogt, was published in 1957, when the press closed under some controversy. Korshak spent the following three decades focusing on his career as a lawyer and businessman, before returning to conventions in the 1980s. With his son Stephen D. Korshak, he owned one of the largest collections of original SF and fantasy artwork in the world, and in 2009 they co-founded Shasta-Phoenix to publish the art books *From the Pen of Paul: The Fantastic Images of Frank R. Paul* and *The Alluring Art of Margaret Brundage Queen of Pulp Pin-Up Art* (with Vanguard Productions). Erle Korshak was inducted into the First Fandom Hall of Fame in 1996, and he was scheduled to be a Guest of Honour at Chicon 8, the 80th World Science Fiction Convention, to be held September 2022.

Yaphet Kotto

American character actor Yaphet [Frederick] Kotto, who played the ill-fated engineer "Parker" in *Alien* (1979), died in the Philippines on

March 14, aged 81. He was in *5 Card Stud*, the James Bond movie *Live and Let Die*, *Warning Sign*, *The Running Man* (1987, based on the novel by "Richard Bachman"/Stephen King), *Freddy's Dead: The Final Nightmare* and *The Puppet Masters* (based on the novel by Robert A. Heinlein). On TV, Kotto appeared in episodes of *Tarzan* (1967), *Rod Serling's Night Gallery*, *Fantasy Island*, *Alfred Hitchcock Presents* (1985) and *Seaquest 2032*.

David Anthony Kraft

American writer and publisher David Anthony Kraft (aka "DAK"), who published and edited *OAK Leaves* (1970–82), the official journal of pulp author Otis Adelbert Kline and his works, died of complications from COVID-related pneumonia on May 19, aged 69. A former rock and roll journalist, he was the editor of Marvel's fan magazine *FOOM* (1976–78) and scripted various comic books, including *Creatures on the Loose* ('Man-Wolf'), *Demon Hunter*, *Swamp Thing*, *Haunt of Horror*, *Logan's Run*, *Tales of the Zombie* and *Giant-Sized Dracula*.

Kraft also wrote the gaming novels *Micro Adventure No.6: Robot Race* and *Wizards Warriors & You Book 4: Ghost Knights of Camelot*, along with a number of children's books based on Marvel characters. His short fiction appeared in *Weirdbook*, *Amazing Science Fiction* and *Always Comes Twilight*. In 1974 Kraft founded the Fictioneer Books imprint which, amongst other titles, published 150 issues of *David Anthony Kraft's Comics Interview* (1983–95).

Willy Kurant

Belgian-born cinematographer Willy Kurant died in Paris, France, on May 1, aged 87. Having received a scholarship from the British Council in the late 1950s, he worked as a camera assistant at Pinewood Studios with Geoffrey Unsworth, Harry Waxman and Jack Hildyard. Kurant's credits include *The Creatures* (1966), *The Incredible Melting Man* (as "Willy Curtis"), *Mama Dracula*, *Under the Sun of Satan* and *Delivering Milo*.

Fred Ladd

American animation writer and producer Fred Ladd (Fred Laderman) died on August 3, aged 94. He was the voice director on the English-language versions of the 1960s Japanese TV series *Astro Boy* and *Gigantor*, and his other credits include *Pinocchio in Outer Space*, *Journey Back to Oz* (1972) and episodes of *The Incredible Hulk* (1982) and *Ghostbusters* ('Shades of Dracula').

Art LaFleur

American character actor Art LaFleur died of Parkinson's disease on November 17, aged 78. He appeared in *Jekyll and Hyde . . . Together Again*, *The Invisible Woman* (1983), *WarGames*, *Trancers* and *Trancers II*, *Zone Troopers*, *The Fifth Missile*, William Friedkin's *Rampage*, *The Blob* (1988), *Pulse Pounders*, *Field of Dreams*, *Forever Young*, *Tycus*, *The Santa Clause 2* and *The Santa Clause 3: The Escape Clause* (as the "Tooth Fairy"), *Speed Racer*, *The Rig*, *House Hunting* and *A Snow Globe Christmas*. On TV, LaFleur turned up in episodes of *The Incredible Hulk*, *Wizards and Warriors*, *Tales from the Crypt*, *Space Rangers*, *Strange Luck*, *A.J.'s Time Travelers*, *Angel* and *Night Stalker* (2005).

Jackie Lane

British actress Jackie Lane died on June 23, aged 73. In 1963 she was offered the part of the Doctor's granddaughter "Susan" in the BBC's

Doctor Who, but turned the role down. Lane did join the show three years later as companion Dorothea "Dodo" Chaplet, a role that lasted for four months. She subsequently gave up acting, but later headed up a talent agency's voice-over department.

Timothy Lane

Conservative American SF fan Timothy [Brian] Lane died after a long illness on January 15, aged 69. As co-editor of the fanzine *FOSFAX*, which started out as the clubzine of FOSFA, the Falls of the Ohio Science Fiction and Fantasy Association, he was nominated for the Best Fanzine Hugo seven times between 1988-96. Lane was Fan Guest of Honour at WindyCon XXIV (1997).

Tommy Lane

American character actor and jazz musician Tommy Lane (Tommy Lee Jones) died of COPD (chronic obstructive pulmonary disease) on November 29, aged 83. He had supporting roles in *Ganja & Hess*, the James Bond film *Live and Let Die*, and *Island Claws*.

Gil Lane-Young

Gil Lane-Young who, with Tony Edwards and Harry Nadler, co-founded Manchester's annual Festival of Fantastic Films in 1990, died in his sleep on September 5, aged 75.

Joe Lara

"Tarzan" actor Joe Lara (William Joseph Lara) died in a small plane crash near Nashville on May 29, aged 58. The private jet crashed into Percy Priest Lake shortly after take-off, killing Lara, his wife – Christian dietitian and church founder Gwen Shamblin Lara – and five other passengers. Having played the King of the Jungle in the 1989 TV movie *Tarzan in Manhattan*, Lara later recreated the character in the syndicated fantasy series *Tarzan: The Epic Adventures* (1996–97), which he also co-produced. The actor's other credits include *Night Wars*, *Danger Island* (aka *The Presence*), *American Cyborg: Steel Warrior*, *Steel Frontier*, *Hologram Man*, *Live Wire 2: Human Timebomb*, *Final Equinox*, *Starfire Mutiny* and an episode of the 1990s *Conan* TV series.

Milan Lasica

Slovakian humourist, actor, singer and director Milan Lasica died on July 18, aged 81. He appeared in the SF comedy *Srdecný pozdrav ze zemekoule*, *Falosny princ* (The False Prince) and the 1987 TV series *Frankenstein's Aunt* (and the spin-off movie *Freckled Max and the Spooks*) starring Viveca Lindfors as "Hannah Von Frankenstein" and Ferdy Mayne as "Count Dracula".

Silvio Laurenzi

Italian costume designer Silvio Laurenzi died on November 5, aged 85. He worked on *Orgasmo*, *Seven*

Blood-Stained Orchids, All the Colors of the Dark, The Case of the Bloody Iris, Knife of Ice, Torso, Spasmo, The Torment, The Invincible Barbarian, The Throne of Fire, The Red Monks, Fatal Frames and *Quel pranzo della domencia* (aka *Night of the Living Lasagna*).

Cloris Leachman

Oscar-winning American actress Cloris Leachman died on January 26, aged 94. She appeared in *Kiss Me Deadly* (1955), *Haunts of the Very Rich*, Disney's *Charlie and the Angel* and *Herbie Goes Bananas*, *Dying Room Only* (scripted by Richard Matheson), Mel Brooks' *Young Frankenstein* (as the memorable "Frau Blücher") and *High Anxiety*, *The New Original Wonder Woman* (as "Queen Hippolyta"), *It Happened One Christmas*, *The Muppet Movie*, *The Demon Murder Case*, *Shadow Play*, *Hansel and Gretel* (1987), *My Boyfriend's Back*, *Double Double Toil and Trouble*, *Scary Movie 4*, *Lake Placid 2* and *Scouts Guide to the Zombie Apocalypse*. On TV, Leachman was in episodes of *The Ford Theatre Hour* ('Night Must Fall'), *Tales of Tomorrow* (Fredric Brown's 'The Last Man on Earth'), *One Step Beyond*, *The Twilight Zone* (Jerome Bixby's 'It's a Good Life' and the 2003 sequel), *Alfred Hitchcock Presents*, *Rod Serling's Night Gallery*, *The Sixth Sense*, *Touched by an Angel*, *Joan of Arcadia* and Neil Gaiman's *American Gods*.

Libertad Leblanc

1960s Argentinean sex symbol Libertad Leblanc (Libertad María de los Ángeles Vichich Blanco) died of pneumonia on April 29, aged 85. She starred in *El satánico* (1968), *La endemoniada* and *Siege of Terror*.

Denise Lee

In September it was reported that American author Denise Lee (Denise Tyler) had died of COVID-19, a month after testing positive and being intentionally unprotected. A Clarion graduate, during the 1990s her short fiction appeared in *Pulphouse: A Fiction Magazine* and *Realms of Fantasy*, and the anthologies *Between the Darkness and the Fire: 23 Tales of Imaginative Fiction from the Internet* (with Kevin O'Donnell, Jr.) and *The Year's Best Fantasy & Horror: Thirteenth Annual Collection*. Lee also co-edited the Hugo Award-nominated online writers' resource *Speculations* with Kent Brewster and Susan Fry.

Peter A. Lees

American film producer Peter A. Lees died on August 6, aged 51. His credits include the low budget movies *The Lost Tree*, *An Accidental Zombie (Named Ted)*, *Living Among Us*, *The Little Mermaid* (2018), *Trico Tri Happy Halloween*, *Rapunzel: A Princess Frozen in Time*, *Purge of Kingdoms*, *Art of the Dead*, *A Christmas Carol* (2019), *Santa in Training*, *Anastasia* (2020), *Attack of the Unknown*, *The Mad Hatter* and *Bridge of the Doomed*. Lees also made cameo appearances in some of his films.

Richard Lee-Sung

American-Asian character actor Richard Lee-Sung (Lee Wan Sung) died on August 16, aged 91. Following an uncredited role in the remake of *Lost Horizon* (1973), he

appeared in *Slapstick of Another Kind*, *Inspector Gadget*, *Forbidden Warrior* and episodes of TV's *Kung Fu* ('The Devil's Champion', 1974), *The Incredible Hulk*, *Salvage 1*, *Fantasy Island*, *Voyagers!* and *Manimal*.

John Paul Leon

American comic book artist John Paul Leon died of colorectal cancer on May 1, aged 49. He began his career at the age of sixteen with a series of black and white illustrations in *Dragon and Dungeon* magazine. After studying under artists such as Will Eisner and Walt Simonson, Leon got his first professional comics job illustrating the Dark Horse Comics mini-series *RoboCop: Prime Suspect* (1992). He then moved over to DC Comics/Milestone for *Static*, and went on to work for both DC and Marvel on such titles as *Challengers of the Unknown*, *Batman: Creature of the Night*, *Logan: Path of the Warlord*, *The Further Adventures of Cyclops and Phoenix* and *New X-Men*. Leon also illustrated *Superman Returns: Be a Hero*, a children's book tie-in to the 2006 movie *Superman Returns*.

Larry Levine

American TV actor Larry Levine (Lawrence Lester Levine), who portrayed the "Wolfman" in the second part of *Hardy Boys and Nancy Drew Meet Dracula* (1978), died on

November 23, aged 90. During the 1970s and '80s he also turned up in small roles in *The Eyes of Charles Sands* and episodes of *The Six Million Dollar Man*, *The Amazing Spider-Man*, *Beyond Westworld* and the 1981 mini-series *Goliath Awaits* (with Christopher Lee and John Carradine). He seems to have retired from the screen in 1986.

Reg Lewis

American bodybuilder and actor Reg Lewis died on February 11, aged 85. In 1962 he starred as "Maciste"/"Maxus" in the Italian *peplum Colossus of the Stone Age* (aka *Land of the Monsters*/*Fire Monsters Against the Son of Hercules*). Lewis also turned up (uncredited) two years later as a slave in *The Brass Bottle* (the inspiration for the TV series *I Dream of Jeannie*). A former Mr. Olympics, Mr. Universe, Mr. America and Mr. America Over Forty, he often accompanied ageing actress Mae West as her escort.

David Lightfoot

Australian film producer David Lightfoot, who founded Ultrafilms in 1997, died of a heart attack on June 13, aged 61. A former production/location manager on such films as *Babe* and *Selkie*, his producing credits include *Bodyjackers*, *Cyber Wars*, *Wolf Creek* (2005) and *Rogue*.

Steve Lightle

61-year-old American comics artist Steve Lightle died of cardiac arrest on January 8, just three days after showing COVID-19 symptoms, which he had dismissed as just a head cold.

Lightle began his career in 1984, working for both DC and Marvel—most notably on such titles as *The Legion of Super-Heroes*, *Doom Patrol* and *Classic X-Men*.

Gunnel Lindblom

Swedish actress Gunnel Lindblom, who worked with director Ingmar Bergman on a number of films, died on January 24, aged 89. Her credits include Bergman's *The Seventh Seal* (1957).

Steve Lines

British editor, artist, writer and musician Steve Lines, publisher of small press imprint Rainfall Records & Books, died from complications of COVID-19 and pneumonia on March 23, aged 63. With John B. Ford he co-edited such magazine and chapbook series as *Lovecraft's Disciples* (2005–18), *Weird Worlds* (2006–12), *Thrilling Tales of Fantastic Adventure* (2006–16), *E'ch Pi El* (2006–18), *Strange Sorcery* (2006–18), *Tales of the Weird West* (2014–18), *Terror Tales* (2014–18), *Tales of the Weird & Uncanny* (2016–17), *Terrifying Tales* (2016–18), *Tales of Horror* (2016–18), *Chilling Tales* (2016–19), *Descent Into Darkness* (2018) and many other titles. Lines and Ford also co-edited the anthologies *The Derelict of Death & Other Stories*, *Inhabitants of Innsmouth* and *Tales of the Cthulhu Mythos: Cthulhu's Creatures*, and they collaborated on the serialised novel *The Night Eternal*. Starting in the late 1980s, Lines' short fiction and poetry (often in collaboration with others or under the pseudonyms "Lucy Francis", "Holly Hudson" and "Haydon Atwood Prescott") and artwork appeared in a wide variety of small press publications, and his short fiction was collected in *Dreams of a Diseased Mind*, *Nightmares from Infinity*, *Death Songs of Carcosa* and *Visions of*

Carcosa (both with Ford) and *Halloween Howlings*. He also produced a number of music albums, including the *Stormclouds* series, *Strange Aeons*, *Society of the Yellow Sign*, *The Doctor's Pond*, *Childe Roland* and *The Ungrateful Dead* series.

Joanne Linville

American actress [Beverly] Joanne Linville, the first female actor to portray a Romulan in the original *Star Trek* series, died on June 20, aged 93. She played the "Romulan Commander" in the 1968 episode 'The Enterprise Incident', and her other TV credits include episodes of *Dow Hour of Great Mysteries* (John Dickson Carr's 'The Burning Court'), *One Step Beyond*, *The Twilight Zone*, *The Invaders* and the 1989 movie *From the Dead of Night*. Linville was married to director Mark Rydell from 1962-73.

Christopher Little

British literary agent Christopher Little, who launched J.K. Rowling's career, died after a long illness on January 7, aged 79. He set up his own literary agency in 1979, and in 1995 he received the first three chapters of Rowling's *Harry Potter and the Philosopher's Stone*. Little went on to represent the author, although every UK publisher turned the book down, except for the fledgling children's imprint at Bloomsbury, which bought it for just £2,500 and the rest is history. Little was reportedly paid £10 million after he and Rowling acrimoniously parted ways in 2011.

Gary Littlejohn

American stuntman-actor Gary Littlejohn died on May 15, aged 75. He began his screen career in the late 1960s working on exploitation biker movies such as *Hells Angels on Wheels*, *Easy Rider*, *Angels Die Hard* and *Bury Me an Angel*, before moving on to such titles as *The Dark* (1979), *Howard*

the Duck, A Nightmare on Elm Street 3: Dream Warriors, Cyclone, Near Dark, Sundown: The Vampire in Retreat, Death Spa, Peacemaker, Pale Blood, Freaked, Witchboard 2, Phantasm III: Lord of the Dead, The Mask (1994), Leprechaun 3, Vampire in Brooklyn, Mulholland Falls, Crossworlds and Megiddo: The Omega Code 2. Littlejohn was inducted into the BMX Hall of Fame in 1998, for his outstanding contributions to the sport of BMX.

Douglas Livingstone

British actor and scriptwriter Douglas [Ian] Livingstone died of heart failure on April 19, aged 86. He had small roles in The Night Caller (aka Blood Beast from Outer Space), a 1980 TV adaptation of Maria Marten or Murder in the Red Barn (which he also scripted), and was semi-regular on the BBC series The Indian Tales of Rudyard Kipling (1964). Livingstone voiced "Gimli the Dwarf" in BBC Radio 4's epic dramatisation of J.R.R. Tolkien's The Lord of the Rings. He also wrote episodes of TV's The Frighteners and Chillers, and adapted the 1981 series The Day of the Triffids.

Norman Lloyd

Veteran Hollywood character actor, producer and director Norman Lloyd (Norman Perlmutter) died on May 10, aged an incredible 106. A member of the original company of the Orson Welles-John Houseman Mercury Theatre, he made his movie debut in

1939. Lloyd's many screen credits include *The Unseen* (1945), Alfred Hitchcock's *Spellbound*, *M* (1951), *Audrey Rose*, *The Dark Secret of Harvest Home*, *The Nude Bomb*, *Jaws of Satan*, *Amityville Horror: The Evil Escapes*, *The Omen* (1995), *Fail Safe* (2000) and *The Adventures of Rocky & Bullwinkle*. On TV, he played "Dr. Isaac Mentnor" on the UPN time-travel series *Seven Days* (1998-2001), and he was in episodes of *One Step Beyond*, *Alfred Hitchcock Presents*, *Rod Serling's Night Gallery*, *The Twilight Zone* (George R.R. Martin's adaptation of Roger Zelazny's 'The Last Defender of Camelot', 1986) and *Star Trek: The Next Generation*. LLoyd also produced and directed episodes of *Alfred Hitchcock Presents* (including Roald Dahl's 'Man from the South' with Peter Lorre), *The Alfred Hitchcock Hour* (including Ray Bradbury's 'The Jar') and *Tales of the Unexpected*, and he was an executive producer on the 1968-69 Hammer TV series *Journey to the Unknown*.

Dimension, *The Goonies*, *The Midnight Hour*, *Howard the Duck*, *Captain EO*, *Teen Wolf Too*, *Scrooged*, *Meet the Hollowheads*, *The Exorcist III*, *Captain America* (1990), *Adventures in Dinosaur City*, *Star Trek VI: The Undiscovered Country*, *Hook*, *Batman Returns*, *Wolf*, *The Puppet Masters*, *The Shadow* (1994), *The Mask* and *The Arrival*. On TV, he worked on episodes of *The Twilight Zone* (1985), *Amazing Stories* and *Tales from the Crypt*, and Logan was the make-up department head on the 1994-95 NBC series *Earth 2*.

John Logan

American special effects make-up artist John "Johnny" Logan died in 2021, following a long battle with cancer. He began his career The Burman Studio, Inc. in the early 1980s, and went on to work at Cannom Creations. Logan's credits include *My Bloody Valentine* (1981), *One Dark Night*, *Cat People* (1982), *Halloween III: Season of the Witch*, *Spacehunter: Adventures in the Forbidden Zone*, *Metalstorm: The Destruction of Jared-Syn*, *The Adventures of Buckaroo Banzai Across the 8th*

Phil Lonergan

Irish stuntman-actor Phil Lonergan died on October 28. He worked on *Frankenstein* (1992), *The Wind in the Willows* (1996), *The Fifth Element*, *The Borrowers* (1997), *Ella Enchanted*, *Stormbreaker*, *The Golden Compass*, *Neverland*, *Wrath of the Titans*, *Avengers: Age of Ultron*, *Paddington 2*, *Black Widow* and the James Bond films *GoldenEye*, *Tomorrow Never Dies* and *The World is Not Enough*. Lonergan's TV credits include episodes of *The Tomorrow People* (1995), *Penny Dreadful*, *Game of Thrones* and *War of the Worlds* (2019).

William Lucking

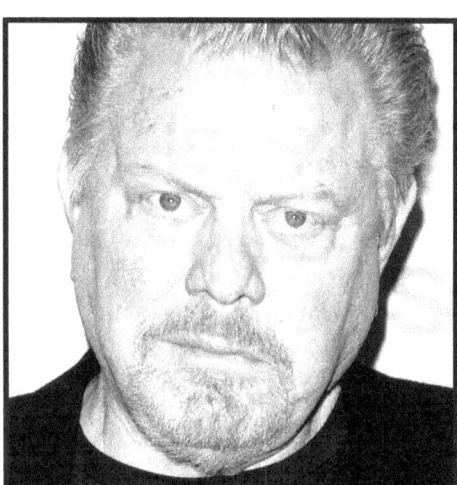

American character actor William Lucking died on October 18, aged 80. The busy actor appeared in *Doc Savage: The Man of Bronze* (as "Renny"), *Dr. Scorpion*, *Captain America II: Death Too Soon*, *The Ninth Configuration*, *Duplicates*, *The Man Who Wouldn't Die*, *Sleepstalker*, *K-PAX*, *Red Dragon* and *Slipstream* (2007). Often cast as detectives or sheriffs, on TV Lucking turned up in episodes of *The Incredible Hulk*, *The Greatest American Hero*, *Voyagers!*, *Knight Rider*, *Outlaws*, *The X Files*, *The Pretender*, *Millennium*, *Star Trek: Deep Space Nine*, *Star Trek: Enterprise* and *Night Stalker* (2005).

Hugh Lund

British actor Hugh Lund, who worked inside a Zarbi "larvae gun" in the second *Doctor Who* serial 'The Web Planet' (1965) and later turned up in a supporting role in 'The Android Invasion' (1975), died on December 29. He was also in episodes of the 1960s TV science fiction series *A for Andromeda* and *R3*.

Frank Lupo

American TV writer and producer Frank Lupo, who created such hit TV series as *The A-Team*, *Wiseguy* and *Hunter*, died on February 18, aged 66.

He produced and wrote for such shows as *Galactica 1980* (and the spin-off movie *Conquest of Earth*), *The Greatest American Hero*, *Something is Out There*, *The Last Precinct* and *Werewolf* (also creating the last two). Lupo additionally scripted the 1990 TV movie *Dark Avenger* and an episode of *Battlestar Galactica* (1978), and contributed an original story to the 2007 series *Painkiller Jane*.

Betty Lynn

American supporting actress Betty [Ann] Lynn, who had a recurring role as "Thelma Lou" in the CBS-TV sitcom *The Andy Griffith Show* (1961-66), died on October 16, aged 95. She also appeared in episodes of *Matinee Theatre* ('The Hex'), *My Brother the Angel* and *Shades of LA*.

Norm MacDonald

Canadian stand-up comedian, comedy writer and actor Norm MacDonald (Norman Gene MacDonald) died on cancer on September 14, aged 61. Best known for being a regular on *Saturday Night Live* (1993-98), before he was fired by NBC, MacDonald was a prolific voice actor in such films and TV shows as the *Doctor Dolittle* movies (as "Lucky", 1998-2009), *Vampire Dog*, *The Seventh Dwarf*, *Treasure Hounds*, *Skylanders Academy*, *Klaus*, *Mike Tyson Mysteries* and *The Orville* (as "Yaphit", the sarcastic green blob). He also had a small role in *Casper Meets Wendy* (1998).

Ray MacDonnell

American actor Ray MacDonnell, best known for starring as "Dr. Joe Martin" in the long-running soap opera *All My Children*, died on June 10, aged 93. In 1967 he portrayed the title character in an unsold TV pilot for *Dick Tracy*, which also featured Victor Buono as the villainous "Mr. Memory".

Joyce Mackenzie

1950s American actress Joyce [Elaine] Mackenzie died on June 10, aged 95. Best known for playing "Jane" opposite Lex Barker's Ape Man in *Tarzan and the She-Devil* (1953), she also appeared in an episode of TV's *Topper* (1954) before retiring from the screen in the early 1960s and later becoming a high school English teacher.

Doug MacLeod

Australian scriptwriter, children's author and playwright Doug MacLeod died after a long illness on November 22, aged 62. He had been suffering from the autoimmune disease discoid lupus since 2014. MacLeod's TV credits include an episode of the live-action *Time Trackers* and the animated *Monster Auditions*, *Dogstar* (2007–11) and *Dogstar: Christmas in Space*.

Gavin MacLeod

American actor Gavin MacLeod (Allan George See), who set sail as "Captain Merrill Stubing" on ABC-TV's *The Love Boat* for ten seasons (1977–87), died after a short illness on May 29, aged 90. His other credits

include the 2002 Christian SF movie *Time Changer* and episodes of *World of Giants*, *Men Into Space*, *The Munsters*, *The Man from U.N.C.L.E.*, *My Favorite Martian*, *The Flying Nun*, *Wonder Woman* and *Touched by an Angel*. MacLeod was apparently the only star of *The Love Boat* not to appear in *Fantasy Island*.

Catherine MacPhail

Scottish author Catherine MacPhail died on August 28, aged 75. Her supernatural novels for children and young adults include *Dark Waters*, *Another Me* (filmed in 2013), *Underworld* and *The Evil Within*, along with the "Tyler Lawless" series (*Out of the Depths*, *Secret of the Shadows*, *The Disappeared* and *Scarred to Death*) and "Nemesis" series (*Into the Shadows*, *The Beast Within*, *Sinister Intent* and *Ride of Death*).

Wes Magee

Scottish poet and children's author Wes Magee (Wesley Leonard Johnston Magee) died on October 21, aged 82. His verse was collected in *The Phantom's Fang-Tastic Show*, illustrated by Leo Broadley and published in 2000 by Oxford University Press. Magee also had two poems included in *Spaceways: An Anthology of Space Poetry* edited by John Foster.

Ugo Malaguti

Italian author, translator, editor and publisher Ugo Malaguti died after a long illness on September 26, aged 76. His career began in 1965 when, at the age of 20, he took over the SF magazine *Galassia* and the SFBC series from Roberta Rambelli. He continued to edit *Galassia*, which published original fiction by Italian authors and American reprints, until 1970. In 1967, Malaguti founded the publishing house Libra Editrice, which published the "Slan" and "Classics of Science Fiction" series (often with introductions by Malaguti himself) and the magazine *Nova SF**. When Libra closed in 1985, Malguti continued the latter title at his new imprint, Perseo Libri. As a translator he worked for Mondadori, Nord and other publishers. Malaguti also wrote a dozen novels (some as "Hugh Maylon") and around sixty short stories (four in collaboration with future film director Luigi Cozzi), some of which were collected in *Storie di ordinario infinito* and *Millennium*.

George Mandel

American Golden Age comics artist George [Mikali] Mandel died on February 13, two days after celebrating his 101st birthday. As part of the Funnies, Inc. shop in the early 1940s he worked on several titles for Better Publications, including 'The Woman in Red' series, about a masked female crime-fighter, in *Thrilling Comics*. He also illustrated such strips as 'Doc Strange' for Better, 'Voodoo Man' for Fox, 'Black Marvel' for Timley and 'Blue Bolt' for Novelty. After being severely wounded during World War II, he had to stop drawing and became a novelist. His 1985 horror novel *Crocodile Blood* was published by Arbor House.

Isidore Mankofsky

American cinematographer Isidore Mankofsky died on March 11, aged 89. His credits include *Werewolves on Wheels*, *Scream Blacula Scream*, *Homebodies*, *The Muppet Movie*, *Somewhere in Time*, *Midnight Lace* (1981), *Ewoks: The Battle for Endor*, Disney's *The Absent-Minded Professor* (1988) and the pilot episodes of TV's

Misfits of Science and *Nowhere Man*. Mankofsky also worked on *The Arrival* and (uncredited) on *Carrie* (1976) and *Evil Town*.

Lisa Mannetti

American horror writer Lisa Mannetti died of lung cancer on August 19. She was in her late sixties. Mannetti's 2008 debut novel *The Gentling Box* won the Bram Stoker Award, and her other publications include *The New Adventures of Tom Sawyer and Huck Finn* (published in both "YA" and "Adult" editions), the novella *The Box Jumper*, and *51 Fiendish Ways to Leave Your Lover* (illustrated by Glenn Chadbourne). She also won the Stoker Award in 2017 for her story 'Apocalypse Then' and was nominated another five times in the Short and Long Fiction categories. Some of Mannetti's stories are collected in *Deathwatch* (2011), while Paul Leyden's short film *Bye Bye Sally* (2009) was based on her story 'Everybody Wins'.

Biz Markie

American rapper Biz Markie (Marcel Theo Hall) died of complications from diabetes on July 16, aged 57. He had small roles (mostly as himself) in a number of movies, including *The Meteor Man*, *Men in Black II* and *Sharknado 2: The Second One*.

Alan Marques

Irish-born digital effects supervisor Alan Marques died on March 26, aged 60. His credits include *Hardware*, *GoldenEye*, *20,000 Leagues Under the Sea* (1997), *The Borrowers* (1997), *Lost in Space* (1998), Dave McKean's *Luna* and the TV series *Space Precinct*, *Strange* and *Outcasts*.

Simon Marshall-Jones

58-year-old British author, editor and independent publisher Simon Marshall-Jones died in hospital on November 9, following double bypass surgery four days earlier. He had suffered a heart attack on October 1, possibly due to complications caused by type 2 diabetes. Marshall-Jones (known as "Moon" to his family and friends) created Spectral Press in 2011 and published work by such authors as Paul Kane, Gary McMahon, Gary Fry, Alison Littlewood, John Llewellyn Probert, Stephen Volk, Terry Grimwood, Tim Lebbon, Angela Slatter and others, along with

Tony Earnshaw's *The Christmas Ghost Stories of Lawrence Gordon Clark*, two volumes of *The Spectral Book of Horror Stories* edited by Mark Morris, and *Darker Terrors* edited by Stephen Jones and David A. Sutton, until the imprint controversially collapsed in 2016. He also edited the 2012 anthology *The 13 Ghosts of Christmas* under the Spectral banner, and his short story collection, *Biblia Longcrofta*, appeared from Tickety Boo Press three years later.

George Martin

Spanish-born leading man, screenwriter and director George Martin (Francisco Martínez Celeiro, aka "Jorge Martín"), who co-starred with Cameron Mitchell in *Island of the Doomed* (aka *Maneater of Hydra*, 1967), died in Miami, Florida, on September 1, aged 84. Best known for his Western roles, he also starred in *Electra One*, *3 Supermen a Tokio*, *Three Supermen in the Jungle* (aka *Supermen*), *Three Supermen of the West* (which he co-scripted), *Escalofrío diabólico* (which he produced, co-scripted and directed) and *Passi di danza su una lama di rasoio* (which he also co-wrote).

Elizabeth I. McCann

Broadway theatre producer Elizabeth I. (Ireland) McCann died of cancer on September 9, aged 90. In 1976 she co-founded the producing and management company McCann & Nugent Productions, Inc. with Nelle Nugent, and they won the Tony Award for either best play or best revival every year from 1978 to 1982. Her productions include the stage revival of *Dracula* (1977) starring Frank Langella, which ran for two-and-a-half years, and *The Elephant Man* (1980).

Helen McCrory

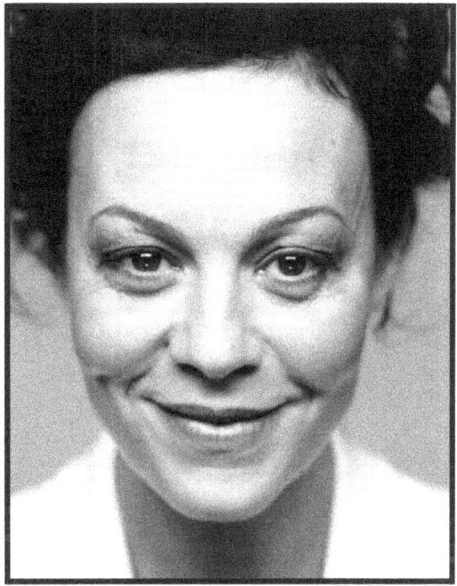

British stage and screen actress Helen [Elizabeth] McCrory OBE died of cancer on April 16, aged 52. Perhaps best known for portraying "Narcissa Malfoy" in *Harry Potter and the Half-Blood Prince* and *Harry Potter and the Deadly Hallows Part 1* and *Part 2*, her other credits include *Interview with the Vampire: The Vampire Chronicles*, *Sherlock Holmes and the Case of the Silk Stocking*, *Frankenstein* (2007), *Hugo*, the James Bond film *Skyfall* and Hammer's *The Woman in Black 2: Angel of Death*. On TV, McCrory brought a lot of class to her role as the sinister "Madame Kali" in the second season of *Penny Dreadful* (2014

–15), she appeared in episodes of *Doctor Who* ('The Vampires of Venice') and *Inside No.9* ('The Harrowing'), and supplied the voice of "Stelmaria" in *His Dark Materials* (2019–20). McCrory was married to actor Damian Lewis from 2007 until her death.

John A. McGlashan

New Zealand-born British cinematographer John A. McGlashan died on April 1, aged 86. He worked at the BBC for thirty-five years on such shows as the M.R. James adaptations *The Stalls of Barchester* (1971), *A Warning to the Curious* (1972) and *The Ash Tree* (1975), the 1984 *Play for Today* 'Z for Zachariah' and the 1990 mini-series *The Green Man* (based on the book by Kinsley Amis). He also shot all six episodes of *The Infinite Worlds of H.G. Wells* (2001). McGlashan was a camera operator on *The Monsters* (1962) and James' *Lost Hearts* (1973) and *The Treasure of Abbot Thomas* (1974), and he worked as the film cameraman on episodes of *Doomwatch* and *Doctor Who* ('Pyramids of Mars' and 'The Face of Evil').

Biff McGuire

Veteran American character actor Biff McGuire (William Joseph McGuire, Jr.) died on April 3, aged 94. He made his screen debut in 1950 and was in *Destination Space* and *The Werewolf of Washington* (as the "President"). On TV, McGuire appeared in episodes of *The Ford Theatre Hour* ('Alice in Wonderland', 1950) and *Kraft Theatre* ('A Christmas Carol', 1952; 'Flying Object at Three O'Clock High'). On stage, he co-starred with his wife, British actress Jeannie Carson, in the 1960 Broadway production of *Finian's Rainbow*.

Joe McKinney

Double Bram Stoker Award-winning American horror author Joe McKinney (Joe Clayton McKinney, Jr.)

died in his sleep on July 13, aged 52. McKinney, who also worked as a San Antonio Police Department sergeant, published around twenty books, including the "Dead World" zombie quartet (*Dead City*, *Apocalypse of the Dead*, *Flesh Eaters* and *Mutated*) and the "Deadlands" duology (*Plague of the Undead* and *The Dead Won't Die*), along with the novels *Quarantined*, *The Red Empire*, *Inheritance*, *Crooked House*, *The Savage Dead*, the young adult *Dog Days* and the four-book "The Retreat" series (*The Pandemic*, *Slaughterhouse*, *Die Laughing* and *Alamo*) with Craig DiLouie and Stephen Knight. Some of his short fiction is collected in *The Red Empire and Other Stories* and *Speculations*, and he co-edited the anthologies *Dead Set: A Zombie Anthology* (with Michelle McCrary) and *The Forsaken: Stories of Abandoned Places* (with Mark Onspaugh). In recent years McKinney was forced to withdraw from the writing community over his conservative views.

Frank McRae

Former NFL player-turned-character actor Frank McRae, often cast as angry police captains, died of a heart attack on April 29, aged 77. He appeared in

Red Dawn, **batteries not included*, *Last Action Hero*, *The Killing Jar*, *Asteroid*, *One Hell of a Guy* and *G-Men from Hell*, along with episodes of TV's *Wonder Woman* and *The Twilight Zone* (1985).

Eddie Mekka

American character actor and dancer Eddie Mekka (Edward Rudolph Mekjian), who played "Carmine 'The Big Ragoo' Ragusa" on the TV sitcom *Laverne & Shirley* (1976–83), died on November 27, aged 69. His other

credits include episodes of *Fantasy Island*, *The Munsters Today*, *Weird Science* and *Power Rangers Wild Force*.

Ed Meskys

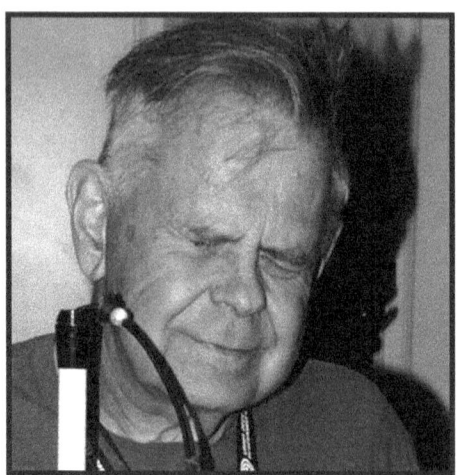

American science fiction and fantasy fan Ed Meskys (Edmund R. Meskys) died of a heart attack on July 25, aged 85. He had been in declining health for some time. In 1953 Meskys lost the sight in one eye as a result of juvenile diabetes, and he became fully blind in 1971 from a detached and torn retina in his remaining eye. His J.R.R. Tolkien-themed fanzine *Niekas* (co-edited with Felice Rolfe) won the Hugo Award for Best Amateur Magazine in 1967, and the following year he helped Charles N. Brown and Dave Vanderwerf found *Locus*. Meskys was also one of the organisers of Tolkien fandom in the US, and he edited such publications as *The Tolkien Journal*, *Valinorian Times* and *Green Dragon*, and he was president of the Tolkien Society of America from 1967–72. In 1972, the Tolkien Society of America merged with the Mythopoeic Society, and Meskys was a guest of honour at the 1975 Mythcon.

Art Metrano

American character actor Art Metrano (Harpo Mesistrano, aka "Arthur Metrano"), probably best known for his portrayal of "Mauser" in the second and third *Police Academy* movies, died on September 8, aged 84. He was also in Disney's *The Strongest Man in the World*, *Linda Lovelace for President* and *Beverly Hills Bodysnatchers*. On TV, Metrano appeared in episodes of *Bewitched*, *Kolchak: The Night Stalker*, *Wonder Woman*, *The Incredible Hulk* and *Fantasy Island*. The actor also voiced "Spike" in the Marvel animated TV series *The Thing* and spin-offs *Fred and Barney Meet the Thing* and *Fred and Barney Meet the Shmoo* (all 1979). In 1989, Metrano fell from a ladder while working on a house and broke his neck in six places. After extensive rehabilitation he continued to use a wheelchair but still raised around

$300,000 for Project Support for Spinal Cord Injury through his one-man stage show entitled *The Accidental Comedy*.

Curt Meyer

Wisconsin cable TV horror host Curt (Curtis) Meyer died of complications from COVID-19 on December 18, aged 56. Since 2009, he hosted *Deadgar's Dark Coffin Classics* as "Deadgar Winter", assisted by "Deadgar's Deadgirls", on Kenosha's KCM Channel 14.

Diana Millay

American actress Diana [Claire] Millay, who played "Laura Collins" in sixty-two episodes of TV's Gothic soap opera *Dark Shadows* (1966-69) and the 1971 spin-off movie, *Night of Dark Shadows*, died on January 8, aged 85. A

former swimsuit model, her other credits include *Tarzan and the Great River* and an episode of *The Man from U.N.C.L.E.* Millay retired from the screen in the early 1970s and became an author. Her books include the non-fiction study *The Power of Halloween*.

Frank Mills

Busy British character actor [Albert] Frank Mills, who played "Billy Williams" in the TV soap opera *Coronation Street* (1995-97), died on

February 11, aged 93. Mills made an early appearance in the BBC's *Quatermass and the Pit* serial (1958-59) and he was also in the 1974 adaptation of M.R. James' *The Treasure of Abbott Thomas*, along with episodes of *The Avengers*, *Doctor Who*, *The Rivals of Sherlock Holmes*, *The Frightners*, *Rentaghost*, *1990* and *The Adventures of Sherlock Holmes*.

Mike Mitchell

Scottish bodybuilder and actor Mike Mitchell died of a heart attack in Turkey on July 23, aged 65. A former Mr. Universe, he appeared in *The Planet*, *Zombie Massacre* (aka *Apocalypse Z*), *Legend of the Red Reaper*, *Morning Star*, *Dark Highlands*, *The Dark Kingdom* (aka *Dragon Kingdom*) and *The Legend of Mordred*.

Kentaro Miura

Japanese *manga* writer and artist Kentaro Miura died of an acute aortic dissection on May 6, aged 54. He is best known for his best-selling dark fantasy series *Berserk*, which he created in 1989 and reportedly has 50 million copies in print. It has also been adapted into *anime* TV series, films and video games.

Sharyn Moffett

Former child actress [Patricia] Sharyn Moffett (aka Sharon Moffett Forrest) died on December 23, aged 85. In 1945 she appeared as the crippled

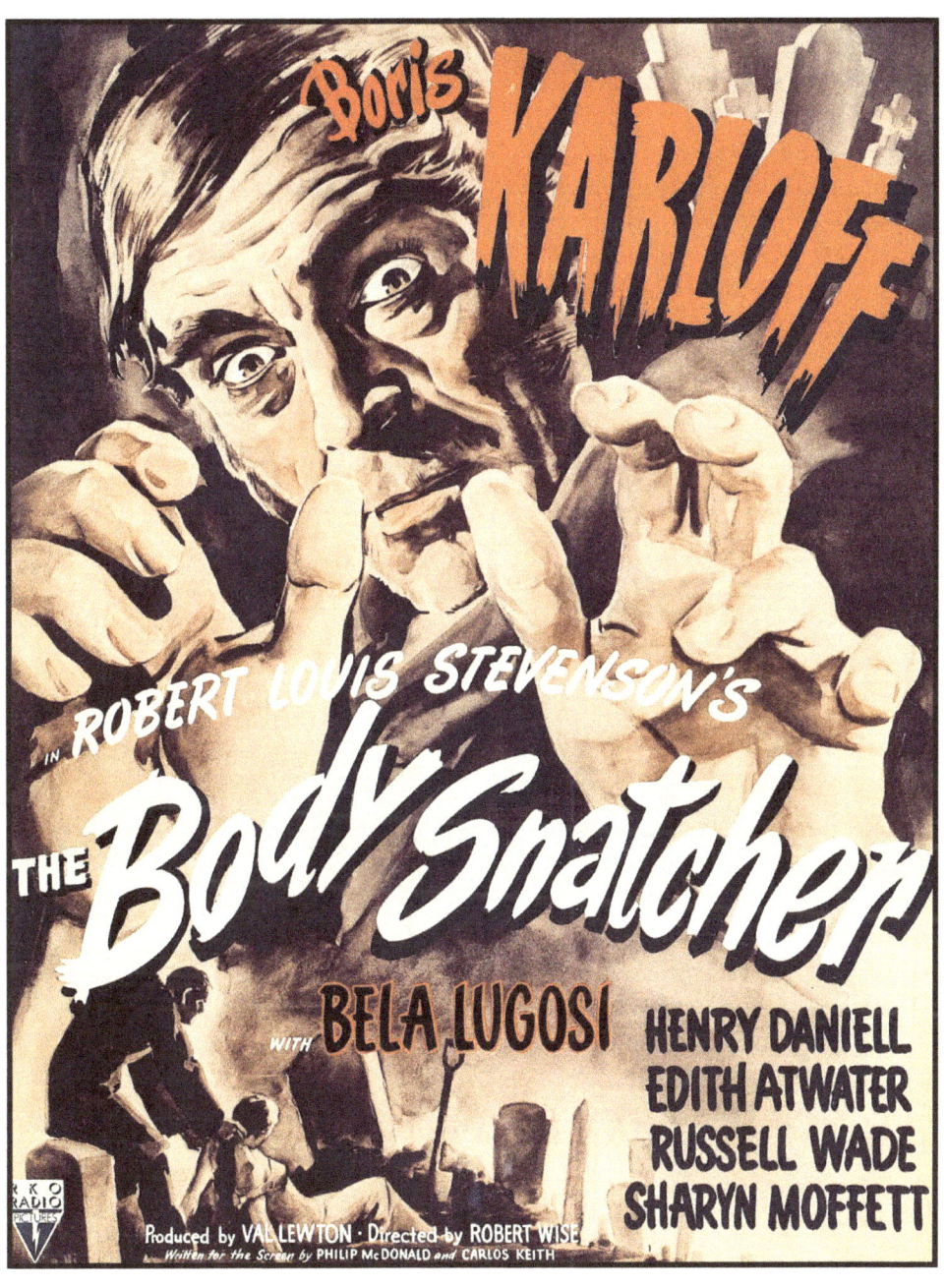

Sharyn Moffett (1936–2021) co-starred alongside Boris Karloff and Bela Lugosi in their last on-screen pairing in Robert Wise's The Body Snatcher (1945).

"Georgina Marsh" in the classic Val Lewton horror film *The Body Snatcher*, alongside Boris Karloff. She also had memorable supporting roles in *The Falcon in San Francisco* and *The Locket* before retiring from the screen in the mid-1950s, after making just eleven movies. Moffett eventually married and moved to Pennsylvania, where she and her husband became Episcopalian ministers.

Alec Monteath

Scottish character actor Alec Monteath (Alexander Monteath), who played "Dougal Lachlan" in the STV soap opera *Take the High Road* (1980-91), died on November 9, aged 80. He also appeared in episodes of *Witch Wood*, *The Omega Factor* and *Doom Castle*.

Inés Morales

Spanish supporting actress Inés Morales [Iglesias] (aka "Inés Skorpio") died on December 5, aged 69. During the 1970s she appeared in the horror films *The Feast of Satan* (aka *Feast for the Devil/Night of the Devils*),

Necrophagus, *La llamada del vampiro*, *Curse of the Devil* (with Paul Naschy), *The Witches Mountain* and *Blue Eyes of the Broken Doll*. Morales later became a TV soap opera actress in Mexico and Spain.

Joey Morgan

American actor Joey Morgan died on November 21, aged 28. He made his movie debut in 2015, co-starring in *Scouts Guide to the Zombie Apocalypse*. Morgan also appeared in *Max Reload and the Nether Blasters* and he starred in Shudder's eight-episode TV series *Critters: A New Binge* (2019).

Jane Morpeth

British publisher Jane Morpeth died of complications from motor neurone disease (MND) on July 17, aged 61. After joining the company as a commissioning editor in 1986, Morpeth went on to become Managing Director at Headline Publishing Group in 2009 and eventually chair of the group in 2016. Amongst the authors she published were Neil Gaiman, Ramsey Campbell, Martina Cole, James Patterson and Dean Koontz.

Rowena Morrill

American artist Rowena A. Morrill died of cardiac arrest on February 11, aged 76. She had been in poor health for some time. She started producing book covers in 1977, most notably for authors such as H.P. Lovecraft, Anne McCaffrey, Piers Anthony and others. Her art appeared in numerous magazines, including *Playboy*, *Heavy Metal*, *Omni* and the revived *Weird Tales*, and was collected in the Hugo Award-nominated *The Fantastic Art of*

Rowena and *The Art of Rowena*. She received the British Fantasy Award in 1984 and the World Fantasy Life Achievement Award in 2020. In 2003, following the fall of Saddam Hussein in Iraq, copies of Rowena's art were discovered in one of the president's palaces.

Christine Morrison

American actress Christine [Louise] Morrison died of injuries sustained in a car accident on February 10, aged

Airbrush cover by Rowena Morrill (1944–2021) for the 1978 paperback edition of H.P. Lovecraft's The Dunwich Horror and Others, published in the US by Jove/HBJ.

55. She was killed when another vehicle crossed over into her lane and struck her car head-on. Morrison appeared in *Humanoids from Atlantis*, *Galaxy of Dinosaurs* and *Ozone*, all directed by J.R. Bookwalter, along with the short film *First Date* which is included in the anthology *Brimstone Incorporated*. Morrison also worked behind the camera in various capacities on some of the above movies, along with *Skinned Alive*, *Ghoul School*, *Zombie Cop* and the short film *Scars at the Spook House*.

Dean Morrissey

American fantasy artist Dean [Walter] Morrissey died on March 4, aged 70. Self-taught, he began painting covers on *Dragon* magazine in the late 1970s before going on to illustrate Robert E. Howard's *Jewels of Gwahlur* for Donald M. Grant and produce covers for a wide selection of books, including Jack Dann and Gardner Dozois' anthology *Sorcerers!*, John Morressy's five volume *Kedrigern* series, Kevin J. Anderson's *Gamearth* trilogy, and a 1988 reissue of Richard Matheson's *The Incredible Shrinking Man*. In 1994, Morrissey wrote and illustrated the children's book *Ship of Dreams*, and he went on to create *The Moon Robber* and *The Winter King* (both with Stephen Krensky), *The Monster Trap*, *The Crimson Comet* and *The Wizard Mouse*.

Gerardo Moscoso

Mexican supporting actor and gynaecologist Gerardo Moscoso died on May 23, aged 76. He had small roles in *México 2000*, Guillermo del Toro's *Cronos*, and *All of them Witches*. Moscoso and his partner were the first gay couple in the city of Torreón, in the Mexican State of Coahuila, to sign a Solidarity Civil Pact (the equivalent to a civil union).

Jill Murphy

British children's author and illustrator Jill Murphy died of cancer on August 18, aged 72. Her popular eight-volume series of "The Worst Witch" books (1974–2018) was made

into a 1989 movie starring Diana Rigg, Tim Curry and Fairuza Balk, and have been adapted twice into series on TV, in 1999–2001 and 2017–2020. They were also turned into a hit stage show. In 2019, Murphy acknowledged the similarities between "The Worst Witch" and author J.K. Rowling's subsequent "Harry Potter" series.

Alan Robert Murray

Oscar-winning American sound editor Alan Robert Murray, who worked with Clint Eastwood for more than thirty years, died on February 24, aged 66. His credits include *The Clone Master*, *Star Trek: The Motion Picture*, *Firefox*, *Ladyhawke*, *Pale Rider*, *Ratboy*, *The Dead Pool*, *Scrooged*, *The 13th Warrior*, *Lara Croft: Tomb Raider*, *Star Trek X: Nemesis* and *Joker*.

Guillermo Murray

Argentinean-born Mexican leading man Guillermo Murray [Muttis Bird Sayi] died of septic shock in Mexico City on May 6, aged 93. Best known for starring as the undead "Count Sergio Subotai" in *The World of the Vampires* (1961), his other credits include starring as another vampire in *La huella macabra*, *Los murciélagos*, *Neutron Traps the Invisible Killers*, *Gigantes planetarios* and its sequel *Planet of the Female Invaders*, *The Chinese Room*, *Six Tickets to Hell* and the 1962 TV series *Las momias de Guanajuato*.

Italian poster for the Mexican movie The World of the Vampires (1960), starring Guillermo Murray (1927–2021) as the undead "Count Sergio Subotai".

Michael Nader

American character actor Michael [Robert] Nader, the nephew of actor George Nader, died of cancer on August 23, aged 76. Best known for his recurring roles in the soap operas *Dynasty* (as "Dex Dexter", 1983–89) and *All My Children* (as "Dimitri Marick", 1991–2001/2013), he began his career in the 1960s (as "Mike Nader") appearing in AIP's *Beach Party*, *Muscle Beach Party*, *Bikini Beach*, *Pajama Party*, *Beach Blanket Bingo*, *Ski Party* and *How to Stuff a Wild Bikini*. Nader's other credits include *Sergeant Dead Head*, Roger Corman's *The Trip*, *Nick Knight* and a couple of episodes of TV's *The Flash* (1990–91).

Kichiemon Nakamura II

Japanese actor, kabuki performer and costume designer Kichiemon Nakamura II (Tatsujiro Namino), who starred in the 1968 horror movie *The*

Black Cat (*Yabu no naka no kuroneko*), died of heart failure on November 28, aged 77.

Peggy Neal

American-born actress and former model Peggy Neal died on December 5, aged 74. While attending university in Tokyo, Japan, she made her screen debut at the age of 17 co-starring with Shin'ichi ("Sonny") Chiba in *Terror Beneath the Sea* (1966). Neal went on to appear in *The X from Outer Space* (1967) and had an uncredited role in

French affiche by Constantin Belinsky for the Japanese kaiju, The X from Outer Space (1967), *which co-starred American-born Peggy Neal (1947–2021).*

Latitude Zero (1969). After thirty years away from the screen, she turned up in the 2018 *tokusatsu kaiju* film *The Great Buddha Arrival*, a crowdfunded remake of a lost 1934 movie of the same name.

Salman A. Nensi

Canadian publisher Salman "Sal" A. Nensi, who took over the ChiZine imprint from Sandra Kasturi and Brett Savory after its controversial collapse in 2019, committed suicide on August 19, aged 53. He started out in the 1990s writing articles and reviews for *Star Trek* fan magazines. In 2001 Nensi created Bakka Books, publishing titles by Fredrick Philip Grove, Phyllis Gotlieb, James De Mille, Sandra Kasturi and Dave Duncan, along with John Rose's *The Bakka Anthology*, which featured employees of Toronto's Bakka Books store who had gone on to become professional writers.

Michael Nesmith

American singer, songwriter and actor [Robert] Michael Nesmith died of heart failure on December 10, aged 78. A member of the 1960s music group The Monkees, he co-starred in the eponymous NBC-TV series *The Monkees* (1966–68) and the surreal spin-off movie, *Head* (1968, co-scripted by Jack Nicholson). As a movie producer, Nesmith's credits include *Timerider: The Adventure of Lyle Swann* (1982) and *Repo Man* (1984). His mother, legal secretary Bette Nesmith, invented Liquid Paper typing correction fluid and made a $35 million fortune, while Nesmith himself came up with the concept for what became MTV. Former child actor Micky Dolenz is now the only surviving member of The Monkees, after Davy Jones died in 2012 and Peter Tork in 2019.

Leslie Newman

American food columnist and screenwriter Leslie Newman who, with her husband David (who died in 2003) co-scripted *Superman* (1978), *Superman II* and *Superman III*, and

came up with the story for *Santa Claus: The Movie*, died in on January 26, aged 68.

Ivo Niederle

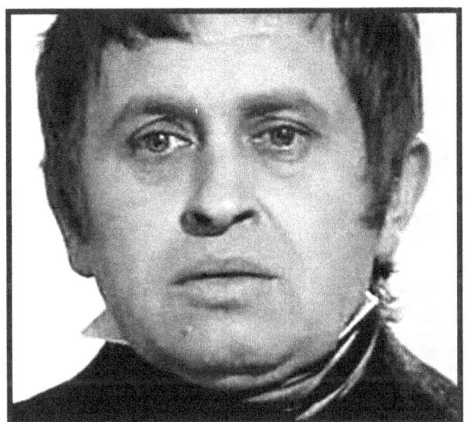

Czech character actor Ivo Niederle died on January 8, aged 91. He appeared in *Howling II . . . Your Sister is a Werewolf* (aka *Howling II: Stirba – Werewolf Bitch*, with Christopher Lee).

Masanari Nihei

Japanese actor Masanari Nihei (Masanori Nihei, aka "Masaya Nihei"), who co-starred as "Mitsuhiro Ide" in

the original *Ultraman* TV series (1966–67) and various compilation movies, died of aspiration pneumonia on August 21, aged 80. He also appeared in *Mothra* (uncredited), *Gorath*, *The Lost World of Sinbad*, *Urutoraman Zeasu*, *Ultraman Zearth 2*, *Ultraman Cosmos: The First Contact* and *Superior Ultraman 8 Brothers*. Nihei's other TV credits include episodes of *Ultra Q*, *Space Ironmen Kyodain*, *Ultraman Max* and *The Ultraman* animated series.

William F. Nolan

American author, poet, cartoonist and screenwriter William ("Bill") F. (Francis) Nolan died in hospital of complications from COVID-19 and an infection on July 15, aged 93. In the early 1950s he was a member of "The Group", a collection of Southern California writers that included Charles Beaumont, Richard Matheson, George Clayton Johnson, Chad Oliver, John Tomerlin, Charles E. Fritch and several others, who would hang out together. Best known

for co-authoring the classic SF novel *Logan's Run* (with George Clayton Johnson) and the sequels *Logan's World* and *Logan's Search*, Nolan's other novels include *Space for Hire* and *Helltracks*. He started publishing short fiction in the early 1950s, and much of it is collected in *Impact-20, Alien Horizons, Wonderworlds, Things Beyond Midnight, Night Shapes, Dark Universe: Stories 1951–2001, Nightworlds, Wild Galaxy: Selected Science Fiction Stories, Ill Met by Moonlight, Nightshadows, Dark Dimensions* and *Like a Dead Man Walking*. In 1952 Nolan edited *Ray Bradbury Review*, which contained the first bibliography of the author, and as an anthologist he edited a number of books, including *The Pseudo-People: Androids in Science Fiction, Man Against Tomorrow, 3 to the Highest Power, A Wilderness of Stars: Stories of Man in Conflict with Space, A Sea of Space, The Future is Now* and *The Human Equation*. With Martin H. Greenberg he co-edited *Science Fiction Origins, Urban Horrors* and *The Bradbury Chronicles: Stories in Honor of Ray Bradbury; California Sorcery* was co-compiled with William Schafer, and *The Bleeding Edge: Dark Barriers Dark Frontiers* and *The Devil's Coattails: More Dispatches From the Dark Frontier* were both edited with Jason V. Brock. His non-fiction titles include *The Ray Bradbury Companion, The Work of Charles Beaumont: An Annotated Bibliography, How to Write Horror Fiction* and *Nolan on Bradbury. Logan's Run* was filmed in 1976 and turned into a short-lived TV series the following year. Nolan scripted *The Norliss Tapes, The Turn of the Screw* (1974), *Trilogy of Terror* (three segments), *Burnt Offerings, Terror at London Bridge* and *Trilogy of Terror II* (one segment), while an episode of *Darkroom* ('The Partnership') was based on his story. A proposed third "Kolchak" TV movie, *The Night Killers*, was scripted by Richard Matheson and Nolan in the early 1970s, but never filmed. Nolan also acted alongside his friends Charles Beaumont and George Clayton Johnson in Roger Corman's 1962 social drama *The Intruder*. He won three Bram Stoker Awards, including one for Lifetime Achievement; the International Horror Guild Living Legend Award, and a Special World Fantasy Award.

Scott Allen Nollen

Prolific American writer Scott Allen Nollen died in Indonesia after a long illness on August 12, aged 58. Beginning in the late 1980s, he wrote

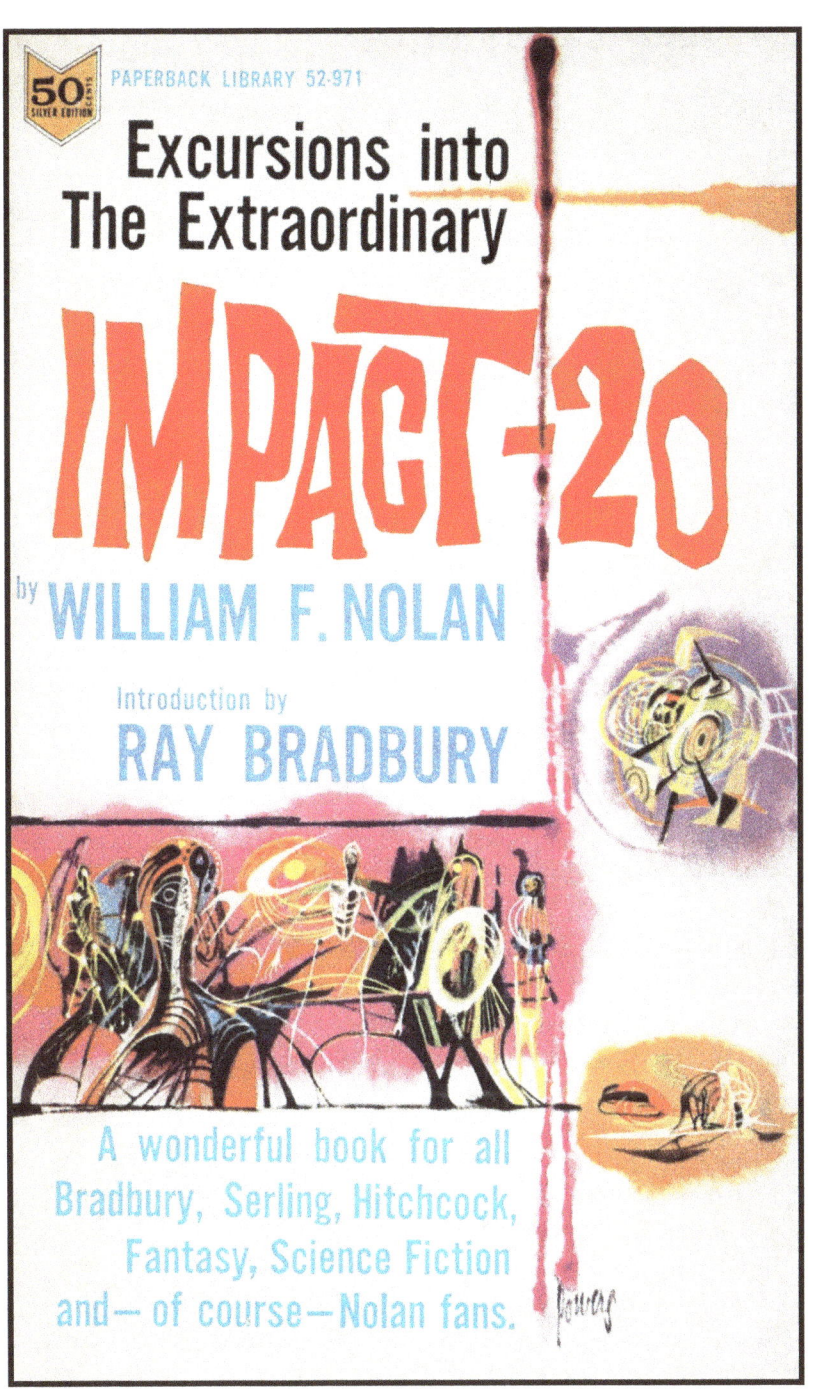

Richard Powers' cover for Impact-20 *(1963), the debut collection from William F. Nolan (1928–2021), which came with an Introduction by the author's old friend, Ray Bradbury..*

around thirty movie reference books, usually for McFarland, Midnight Marquee or BearManor Media, including *Boris Karloff: A Critical Account of His Screen Stage Radio Television and Recording Work* (with a Foreword by Ray Bradbury), *Midnight Marquee Actors Series: Vincent Price*, *Boris Karloff: A Gentleman's Life: The Authorized Biography* (with a Foreword by Sarah Jane Karloff), *Midnight Marquee Actors Series: Peter Lorre*, *Midnight Marquee Actors Series: Peter Cushing*, *Karloff and the East: Asian Indian Middle Eastern and Oceanian Characters and Subjects in His Screen Career* and *The Body Snatcher: Cold-Blooded Murder Robert Louis Stevenson and the Making of a Horror Film Classic* (both with his wife, Yuyun Yuningsih Nollen). Nollen, who was a member of the prog-folk group The Bramwell Fletcher Band, also authored books about Robert Louis Stevenson, Sir Arthur Conan Doyle, Chester Morris, Henry Brandon and the "Sons of Charlie Chan": actors Keye Luke, Sen Yung and Benson Fong. In 2019, he contributed a commentary track to Universal's first-ever Blu-ray set of Abbott and Costello films.

Denis O'Brien

American-born film producer Denis [James] O'Brien died in England from intra-abdominal sepsis on December 3, aged 80. O'Brien co-founded Handmade Films with former Beatle George Harrison, and his credits as an executive producer include *Monty Python's Life of Brian* and *Time Bandits*.

Denis O'Dell

British-born film producer Denis O'Dell, a director of the Beatles' Apple Corps organisation and the head of Apple Films, died in Spain on December 30, aged 98. He started out as an assistant director in the early

1940s, working on such movies as *The Perfect Woman*, *A Christmas Carol* (1951), *Mother Riley Meets the Vampire* (starring Bela Lugosi) and *Svengali* (1954). Around the mid-1950s, O'Dell turned to producing, and his credits include *A Midsummer Night's Dream* (1959), *The Bedford Incident*, *Kiss the Girls and Make Them Die* and the Beatles' *Magical Mystery Tour*. In his 2002 memoir (with Bob Neaverson), *At the Apple's Core, the Beatles from The Inside*, O'Dell recalled how he raised funding from United Artists to make *The Lord of the Rings* with John Lennon as "Gandalf", before Stanley Kubrick persuaded the Beatles that the books were "unmakeable".

Gavan O'Herlihy

Irish supporting actor Gavan [John] O'Herlihy, the son of veteran actor Dan O'Herlihy, died on November 9, aged 70. He appeared in *Superman III*, the James Bond film *Never Say Never Again*, *Willow*, *Prince Valiant* (1997), *Cruise of the Gods* and *The Descent Part 2*. On TV, O'Herlihy guest starred in episodes of *The Six Million Dollar Man*, *The Bionic Woman*, *The Amazing Spider-Man*, *Tales from the Crypt*, *Twin Peaks* (1990-91), *Tarzan* (1991-92), *The Memoirs of Sherlock Holmes*, *Star Trek: Voyager* and *Jonathan Creek* ('Danse Macabre').

Walter Olkewicz

American character actor Walter Olkewicz (aka "Ray Holland" and "Walter Oklewicz"), who played "Marko" in the TV series *Wizards and Warriors* (1983) and "Jacques Renault" in *Twin Peaks* (1990) and *Twin Peaks: Fire Walk with Me*, died of an infection on April 6, aged 72. His other credits include *Futureworld*, *Stillwatch* and *The Surgeon*, along with episodes of *Tall Tales & Legends* ('The Legend of Sleepy Hollow'), *The Charmings*, *The Flash* (1990), *The Visitor*, *Sliders*, *Beyond Belief: Fact or Fiction*, *Good vs Evil* and the 2017 revival of *Twin Peaks* (as "Jean-Michel Renault"). Olkewicz was also the voice of "Carmine Falcone" in two episodes of *Batman: The Animated Series*.

Colette O'Neil

Scottish-born character actress Colette O'Neil (Mary Irene Colette McCrossan) died on July 11, aged 85. She appeared in Hammer's *Frankenstein Must Be Destroyed*, *Dreams Lost Dreams Found* and episodes of TV's *Adam Adamant Lives!* ('The Village of Evil'), *Mystery and Imagination* (Algernon Blackwood's 'The Listener'), *Thriller* (1974) and *Doctor Who* ('Snakedance'). In 1963, while appearing in the Jean-Paul Sartre play *Huis Clos* in Edinburgh, O'Neil was accidentally stabbed in the abdomen by a fellow actor but still managed to deliver her final line and take a bow before collapsing in a pool of blood in her dressing room. She spent three weeks recovering in hospital following emergency surgery.

Henry Orenstein

Polish-born entrepreneur and toy designer Henry Orenstein (Henryk Orenstein) died of complications from COVID-19 in New Jersey on

December 14, aged 98. In the 1950s he founded Topper Toys, which at one time was said to be the fourth-largest toy company in the United States. After Topper went bankrupt in 1973, Orenstein put together a deal between Hasbro, Inc. and the Japanese manufacturer Takara that led the creation in 1984 of the Transformers action-figures—toy robots that could turn into vehicles or beasts—and *The Transformers* animated TV series (1984-87). A Holocaust survivor who immigrated to the US as a refugee, the multi-millionaire held more than 100 patents, including one for the Transformers toy line.

Ota

67-year-old Brazilian cartoonist and magazine editor Ota (Otacílio Costa d'Assunção Barros) was found dead in his apartment in Rio de Janeiro on September 24. He was the uncredited art director for the Brazilian edition of *Asimov's Science Fiction* (1990-93)

and edited that country's version of MAD magazine from the 1970s until 2008 and the horror comic *Spektro* from 1977–83.

Scott Page-Pagter

American TV voice director, actor and producer Scott Page-Pagter died of cancer on December 5, aged 52. He worked on such shows as *V.R. Troopers*, *Mighty Morphin Power Rangers*, *Masked Rider*, *BeetleBorgs*, *Power Rangers Zeo*, *Power Rangers Turbo*, *Power Rangers in Space*, *Power Rangers Lost Galaxy*, *Power Rangers Lightspeed Rescue*, *Power Rangers Time Force*, *Power Rangers Wild Force*, *Nowhere Man* and *Ju-on: Origins*. Page-Pagter was the voice of "Porto" in *Power Rangers Turbo*, as well as other characters in the *Power Rangers* series.

Nicola Pagett

Egyptian-born British actress Nicola Pagett (Nicola Mary Pagett Scott) died of complications from a brain tumour on March 3, aged 75. For many years she had been living with acute mental depression. Pagett appeared in Hammer's *The Viking Queen* and *Frankenstein: The True Story* (as "Elizabeth"), along with episodes of TV's *The Avengers* and *The Rivals of Sherlock Holmes*. In 1976 she co-starred with Anton Rodgers and Peter Vaughan in the Patrick Hamilton play *Gaslight* at London's Criterion Theatre.

Peter Palmer

American actor Peter [Webster] Palmer died on September 21, aged 90. He made his debut co-starring as "Li'l Abner Yokum" in the Broadway and 1959 movie versions of the comedy/musical *Li'l Abner*, based on the comic strip by Al Capp. His other credits include Fred Olen Ray's *Deep Space*, *Edward Scissorhands*, and episodes of TV's *Tabitha*, *Fantasy Island*, *Super Force*, *Superboy* and *Swamp Thing* (1991–92). He retired from the screen in 1994.

John Paragon

American actor, scriptwriter and director John [Dixon] Paragon, who got his start in the Los Angeles-based improv comedy group The Groundlings alongside Paul Reubens and Phil Hartman, died on April 3, aged 66. Best known for playing the blue-faced "Jambi the Genie" in *Pee-wee's Playhouse* (1986–90), he also voiced "Pterri-Dactyl" on the CBS-TV show. Paragon's other acting credits include *Eating Raoul*, *Pandemonium*, *Pee-wee's Big Adventure*, *The Frog Prince* (1986), *Spaceballs*, *Christmas at Pee-wee's Playhouse*, *UHF*, *Honey I Blew Up the Kid*, *Red Riding Hood* (2006), *Pee-wee's Big Holiday* and episodes of TV's *Harry and the Hendersons* and *Star Trek: Deep Space Nine*. He also worked with fellow Groundling Cassandra Peterson in various capacities on *Elvira's Movie Macabre*, *Elvira's MTV Halloween Party*, *Elvira: Mistress of the Dark*, *The Elvira Show*, *Elvira's Haunted Hills* and *13 Nights of Elvira*. Paragon scripted *The Pee-wee Herman Show* and he and star Paul Reubens were nominated for an Emmy Award for writing *Christmas at Pee-wee's Playhouse* (1988). He reprised his role as "Jambi the Genie" for the 2010 Broadway stage adaptation of *The Pee-wee Herman Show* and, more recently, he worked with Walt Disney Imagineering on ideas for improv performances at Disney theme parks.

Darroll Pardoe

British SF and fantasy writer, reviewer and fan [W.] Darroll Pardoe, the husband of writer and editor Rosemary Pardoe, died of complications from COVID-19 on January 28, aged 77. Amongst the fanzines he edited were single issues of the British Science Fiction Association's *Vector* (1967) and the British Fantasy Society's *Dark Horizons* (1974), and with his wife he wrote the non-fiction study *The Female Pope: The Mystery of Pope Joan* (1988).

Victoria Paris

American adult film actress Victoria Paris (Sheila Young) died of breast cancer on August 10, aged 60. Her career began in the late 1980s, and Paris' credits include *Voodoo Lust: The Possession*, *The Chameleon*, *Mystery of the Golden Lotus*, *The New Barbarians* (1990), *Ghostlusters*, *Beauty and the Beast: Part II*, *Will and Ed's Excellent

Boner Christmas*, *Snatched to the Future*, *Miracle on 69th Street* and *Rocket Girls* ("In Space No-one Can Hear You Cream"), along with an uncredited appearance in the non-porn *Time Barbarians* (1991).

Eddie Paskey

Eddie Paskey (Edward J. Paskey), who was William Shatner's stand-in and

occasional body-double on the original *Star Trek* TV series (1966-68), died on August 17, aged 81. Paskey also played various (mostly uncredited) crew members and U.S.S. *Enterprise* bridge officer "Lieutenant Leslie" on the show, and he portrayed the latter character's father – "Admiral Leslie" – in a 2004 episode of the fan-produced online series *Star Trek: New Voyages*.

Gary Paulsen

Gary [James] Paulsen, an American author of coming of age stories set in the wilderness, died of cardiac arrest on October 13, aged 82. His more than 200 books include *The Implosion Effect*, *Meteorite Track 291*, *Compkill*, *Canyons*, *The Night White Deer Died*, *The Transall Saga*, *The White Fox Chronicles* and *The Time Hackers*. Paulsen won the Margaret Edwards Award from the American Library Association in 1997 for his "significant and lasting contribution to young adult literature".

Allen Payne

American make-up artist [Norbert] Allen Payne, who worked with actor David Hasselhoff on various projects, died on October 26, aged 82. His credits include *Jennifer*, *The Golden Child*, *Back to the Future Part II*, *Avalon: Beyond the Abyss*, *Fail Safe* (2000) and *Anaconda 3: Offspring*. On TV, Payne was the hair stylist on *Knight Rider* (1983–86), *Highway to Heaven* (1987–89), *Baywatch* (1989–99) and *Baywatch Nights* (1995–97), along with the pilot for *The Flash* (1990).

Trevor Peacock

British character actor, scriptwriter and songwriter Trevor [Edward] Peacock died from complications of vascular dementia and Alzheimer's disease on March 8, aged 89. His performing credits include the 1961 Loch Ness Monster comedy *What a Whopper* (which was based on an idea of his), *Hamlet* (1990), *A Christmas Carol* (1990) and *Fred Claus*, along with episodes of TV's *The Storyteller: Greek Myths*, *Merlin of the Crystal Cave*, *Highlander* ('The Vampire'), *Neverwhere* (based on the novel by Neil Gaiman) and *Dinotopia*. Peacock's most famous song is perhaps 'Mrs. Brown, You've Got a Lovely Daughter', a 1960s hit single for Herman's Hermits.

John C. Pelan

Bram Stoker Award-wining American editor, author and publisher John C. Pelan died of a heart attack on April 12, aged 63. His original anthologies include the Bram Stoker Award-winning *Darkside: Horror for the Next Millennium*, *The Darker Side: Generations of Horror*, *A Walk on the Darkside: Visions of Horror*, *Lost on the Darkside: Voices from the Edge of Horror* and *Alone on the Darkside: Echoes from the Shadows of Horror*, along with *The Last Continent: New Tales of Zothique*, *The Children of Cthulhu: Chilling New Tales Inspired by H.P. Lovecraft* (with Benjamin Adams), *Shadows Over Baker Street* (with Michael Reaves) and *Dark Arts*. An expert on horror fiction, he edited *The Century's Best Horror Fiction 1901–1950* and *The Century's Best Horror Fiction 1951–2000* for Cemetery Dance Publications and *Tales of Terror and Torment: Stories from the Pulps, Volume 1* from his own Dancing Tuatara Press. Pelan also founded the independent publishing imprints Axolotl Press, Darkside Press and Silver Salamander Press and co-founded Midnight House. With Edward Lee he co-authored the books *Goon*, *Shifters*, *Splatterpunk: The Micah Hayes Stories* and *Family Tradition*, and Pelan's short fiction appeared in such small press magazines as *Palace Corbie*, *Carpe Noctem*, *The Urbanite* and *Enigmatic Tales*, and was collected by Fedogan & Bremer in *Darkness, My Old Friend*.

Christopher Pennock

American actor and comic-book writer Christopher Pennock, who played "Gabriel Collins" (and various other characters) in the TV soap opera *Dark Shadows* (1970–71) and

the second spin-off movie, *Night of Sark Shadows*, died of complications from melanoma on February 12, aged 76. His other credits include *Savages* (1972), *Doctor Mabuse: Etiopomar* and *The Night-Time Winds*, along with episodes of TV's *Tucker's Witch* and *Theatre Fantastique*. Pennock also created a series of comic books based upon his *Dark Shadows* experiences.

Clare Peploe

78-year-old British East African-born screenwriter and director Clare Peploe, who co-scripted Michelangelo Antonioni's iconic *Zabriskie Point* (1970), died of lung cancer in Rome, Italy, on June 24. Best known for her 1995 movie *Rough Magic*, starring Bridget Fonda and Russell Crowe, she also directed an episode of the 1990 French TV series *Chillers* ('Sauce for the Goose'), based on the short stories of Patricia Highsmith. She was married to Bernardo Bertolucci from 1978 until his death in 2018.

Morris Perry

Veteran British TV character actor [Frank] Morris Perry died on September 19, aged 96. He appared in episodes of *Out of This World* (John Wyndham's 'Dumb Martian'), *City Beneath the Sea*, *Turn Out the Lights*, *Witch Hunt*, *Haunted*, *The Champions*, *Counterstrike*, *Doctor Who* ('Colony in Space'), *Doomwatch*, *Jack the Ripper* (1973), *Survivors*, *The Hound of the Baskervilles* (1982, with Tom Baker as Holmes) and *The Dark Side of the Sun*. A rare film credit for Perry was

Nothing But the Night (1973, with Christopher Lee and Peter Cushing), and he starred in the 1974 *The Price of Fear* radio production, 'Come as You Are'.

Pierre Philippe

French writer and director Pierre Philippe, whose credits include the experimental 1970 horror film *Midi minuit*, died on December 20, aged 90.

Jay Pickett

American daytime soap opera actor Jay [Harris] Pickett, who was a regular in *Days of Our Lives* (1991-92), *Port Charles* (1997-2003) and *General Hospital* (2006-08), died on July 30, aged 60. He apparently suffered a heart attack while sitting on a horse, waiting to shoot a scene on location in Idaho for a Western. Pickett also appeared in *Eve of Destruction*, *Rumpelstiltskin* (1995) and an episode of TV's *Dexter*.

Ronald Pickup

British character actor Ronald [Alfred] Pickup died after a long illness on February 24, aged 80. He appeared in the alternate James Bond film *Never Say Never Again*, *The Hound of the Baskervilles* (1988), *Jekyll & Hyde* (1990), *Supernova*, *Dark Floors* and *Prince of Persia: The Sands of Time*. Pickup made his TV debut in a 1964 episode of the BBC's *Doctor Who* (for which he was paid £30), and his other credits include episodes of *Sea of Souls*, *Young Dracula* and *Atlantis*. He was also the voice of "Aslan" in the BBC productions of C.S. Lewis' *The Lion the Witch and the Wardrobe* (1988), *Prince Caspian and the Voyage of the Dawn Treader* (1989) and *The Silver Chair* (1990).

Paolo Pietrangeli

Italian protest singer-songwriter and filmmaker Paolo Pietrangeli, who was the assistant director on Andy Warhol's *Flesh for Frankenstein* (1973) and *Blood for Dracula* (1974), died after a long illness on November 22, aged 76.

Marc Pilcher

53-year-old British hair stylist and make-up designer Marc Pilcher died on October 3 of complications from COVID-19, even though he had been double vaccinated and reportedly had no underlying health problems. The Creative Emmy Award winner's

credits include *Sherlock Holmes* (2009), *Clash of the Titans* (2010), *Prince of Persia: The Sands of Time*, *The Great Ghost Rescue*, *Sherlock Holmes: A Game of Shadows*, *John Carter*, *Wrath of the Titans*, *Dark Shadows* (2012), *Thor: The Dark World*, *47 Ronin*, *Vampire Academy*, *Maleficent*, *Macbeth* (2015), *Star Wars Episode VII–The Force Awakens*, *Rogue One: A Star Wars Story*, *Beauty and the Beast* (2017), *Solo: A Star Wars Story*, *The Nutcracker and the Four Realms*, *Star Wars Episode IX–The Rise of Skywalker* and *The King's Man*.

Jerry Pinkney

Caldecott Medal-winning children's illustrator Jerry Pinkney died of a heart attack on October 20, aged 81. Amongst the more than 100 picture-books he worked on were *Oz: The Hundredth Anniversary Celebration* and the Franklin Library's limited edition of Jonathan Swift's *Gulliver's Travels*.

Pinkney was appointed by President George W. Bush to serve as a member of the National Council on the Arts in 2003, and in 2016 he was the recipient of both the Laura Ingalls Wilder Award for lifetime achievement (now known as the Children's Literature Legacy Award) and the Coretta Scott King Virginia Hamilton Award for lifetime achievement.

Doris Piserchia

American science fiction author Doris [Elaine Summers] Piserchia died on September 15, aged 92. She made her SF debut in a 1966 issue of *Fantastic*, and her novels include *Mister Justice*, *Star Rider*, *A Billion Days of Earth*, *Earthchild*, *Spaceling*, *The Spinner*, *The Fluger*, *Doomtime*, *Earth in Twilight*, *The Dimensioneers* and *The Deadly Sky*. In the early 1980s, Piserchia also wrote two horror novels for DAW Books, *Blood County* and *I, Zombie*, under the pseudonym "Curt Selby". She stopped writing in 1983, shortly before her adult daughter died, leaving her with a three-year-old granddaughter to raise.

Gian Filippo Pizzo

Italian science fiction writer, critic and anthologist Gian Filippo Pizzo died on December 31, aged 70. He published a number of short stories and (most often in collaboration with with Roberto Chiavini and Michele Tetro) the non-fiction books *Dictionary of Fantastic Characters: The Protagonists of Science Fiction, Fantasy and Horror in Cinema, Comics and Literature*; *The Great Science Fiction Cinema: From "2001" to 2001*, *The*

Great Science Fiction Cinema: Waiting for the Black Monolith (1902–1967), The Great Fantasy Cinema, Contact!: All the Films About UFOs and Aliens, Parallel Worlds: Science Fiction Stories from Book to Film, Guide to Science Fiction Cinema, Guide to Horror Literature, Guide to Horror Cinema and *Guide to Fantasy Cinema*. Pizzo also edited (again, often in collaboration with Chiavini, Walter Catalano, Vittorio Catani or Luca Ortino) such anthologies as *Ambiguous Utopias: 19 Tales of Fantasy Resistance, Alien Night: 22 Fantanoir Tales, Sinister Presences: 17 Committed Horror Stories, The Price of the Future: Fairy Tales, The Bad Road: 18 Stories of Assorted Cruelty, The Gernsback Variations: Tales of Fantasy Music, Crimes from the Future, Continuum Hopper: Fantastic Tales About Art, Our Lady of the Aliens* and *Futura Lex*.

Edward L. Plumb

American independent movie producer, writer, director and actor Edward L. Plumb died of cancer on March 5, aged 64. His many low-budget credits include *The Erotic Rites of Countess Dracula* (with William Smith as the Count and Del Howison as Renfield), *The Low Budget Time Machine* (with Patrick Macnee), *Boogie with the Undead* (with Bobby "Boris" Pickett), *The Devil's Due at Midnight* (with George Kennedy, Brad Dourif and Peter Atkins), *Her Morbid Desires* (with Tippi Hedren, Kevin McCarthy, Barbara Steele and Ray Harryhausen), *The Boneyard Collection* (with Forrest J Ackerman), *Crustacean* (with Atkins again), *The Dead Undead* (with Luke Goss), *Feed Me, Dances with Werewolves, The Pod* (aka *Alien Hunger*), *Deadly Crush* (with William Sadler) and *Tales of Frankenstein* (with Ann Robinson).

Christopher Plummer

Canadian-born actor Christopher Plummer (Arthur Christopher Orme Plummer), who portrayed "Sherlock Holmes" in *Murder by Decree* (1979) and a half-hour TV adaptation of

Christopher Plummer (1929–2021) donned the famous deerstalker to track down Jack the Ripper in Murder by Decree (1979), which featured an impressive supporting cast.

Silver Blaze (1977), died of complications from a fall in Weston, Connecticut, on February 5, aged 91. The Oscar-winner began his career in television in 1953, and his movie credits include *The Night of the Generals*, *The Pyx*, *The Spiral Staircase* (1975), *The Man Who Would Be King*, Luigi Cozzi's *Starcrash*, *Somewhere in Time* (based on the novel by Richard Matheson), *Prototype*, *Dreamscape*, *Vampire in Venice*, *Red Blooded American Girl*, *Firehead*, *Star Trek VI: The Undiscovered Country* (as "General Chang"), *Wolf*, *Dolores Claiborne* (based on the novel by Stephen King), *12 Monkeys*, *The Clown at Midnight*, *Possessed*, *Dracula 2000* (as "Abraham Van Helsing"), *Blizzard* (as "Santa Claus"), *Cold Creek Manor*, *The Lake House*, *The Imaginarium of Doctor Parnassus*, *The Tempest* (2010), *Priest* and *The Man Who Invented Christmas* (as "Scrooge"). Plummer also voiced characters in many animated movies and TV shows, including *Kali the Little Vampire*, *Howard Lovecraft and the Frozen Kingdom*, *Howard Lovecraft & the Undersea Kingdom* and *Howard Lovecraft and the Kingdom of Madness*.

Markie Post

American actress Markie Post (Marjorie Armstrong Post) died of cancer on August 7, aged 70. Her credits include *Massarati and the Brain* (with Christopher Lee), *Visitors of the Night*, *I've Been Waiting for You* and the 2018 short film *Keep the Gaslight Burning*, based on a story by R.

Chetwynd-Hayes. On TV, Post appeared in episodes of *The Incredible Hulk*, *Buck Rogers in the 25th Century*, *The Greatest American Hero*, *Fantasy Island*, *VR.5*, *Twice in a Lifetime*, *Ghost Whisperer* and *Santa Clarita Diet*, and she appeared as "Electra Woman" in a 2001 pilot for a revival of *Electra Woman and Dyna Girl*.

Anthony Powell

Oscar-winning British costume designer Anthony Powell died on April 16, aged 85. His credits include *Indiana Jones and the Temple of Doom*,

Markie Post (1950–2021) starred in the award-winning short film Keep the Gaslight Burning *(2018), which was based on a 1976 short story by R. Chetwynd-Hayes.*

Indiana Jones and the Last Crusade, *Hook*, *101 Dalmations* (1996), *The Avengers* (1998), *The Ninth Gate* and *102 Dalmations*.

Jane Powell

Hollywood leading lady Jane Powell (Suzanne Lorraine Burce) died on September 16, aged 92. Although best remembered for appearing in such classic MGM musicals as *Royal Wedding* (1951) and *Seven Brides for Seven Brothers* (1954), her screen career never really took off. In the late 1970s and early '80s she turned up in three episodes of TV's *Fantasy Island*.

Norman S. Powell

American producer and director Norman S. Powell (Norman Scott Barnes) died of respiratory failure on June 16, aged 86. The son of actress Joan Blondell, he was adopted by his

mother's second husband, Dick Powell. Powell's credits include the 1971 movie *The Night Digger*, scripted by Roald Dahl. As senior vice president of CBS Entertainment Productions he supervised the development and production of TV movies and series, including *The New Twilight Zone*.

Don Poynter

American inventor Don Poynter (Donald Byron Poynter), who came up with such ideas as a Rye whiskey-flavoured toothpaste, the talking toilet and a Jane Mansfield-shaped hot water bottle, died of cancer on August 13, aged 96. One of his most successful inventions was The Little Black Box, created in 1959. When switched on, the box vibrated and a hand emerged and switched it off. In 1964 his company, Poynter Products Inc., struck a deal with *The Addams Family* TV show to produce a coin-grabbing money box variation on the idea featuring the show's disembodied hand, "The Thing". It reportedly sold 14 million units. The following year, Poynter also marketed another tie-in toy to the ABC show, Uncle Fester's (Unbreakable) Mystery Light Bulb.

Joe Praml

American stage and screen actor Joe Praml (Joseph Patrick Pramrl) June 18, aged 85. He appeared in small roles in *Superman II* (uncredited), *Demonwarp*, Fred Olen Ray's *Deep Space* and the TV movie *From the Dead of Night*. During the 1970s and early '80s Praml lived and worked in London. He retired from the screen in the late 1980s to become a community organiser and tenants' rights advocate.

Zdenka Procházková

Czechoslovakian actress Zdenka Procházková (aka "Zdena Procházková") August 25, aged 95. Her film career began in 1947 and she appeared in *The Lost Face* and *Ferat Vampire* (both based on a stories by Josef Nesvadba), *Lady Dracula*, and episodes of the comedy SF TV series *The Visitors*.

Al Pugliese

American character actor Al Pugliese (Albert Pasquale Pugliese) died of complications from COVID-19 on July 24, aged 74. Often cast as police detectives, he was in *Annihilator*, *Satan's Princess* and *Philadelphia*

Experiment II, along with episodes of TV's *Something is Out There*, *The Adventures of Brisco County Jr.*, *Firefly* and *American Horror Story*.

Timothy Patrick Quill

American supporting actor Timothy Patrick Quill (Timothy Joseph Quill), a long-time friend of Bruce Campbell and Sam Raimi, died on April 14. He appeared in *Army of Darkness*, *The Sender* (1998), *The Darwin Conspiracy*, *From Dusk Till Dawn 2: Texas Blood Money*, *Spider-Man*, *Spider-Man 2*, *My Name is Bruce*, *Mutant Swinger from Mars*, *Count Ghastly's Cinema Crypt*, *Oz the Great and Powerful*, *Hobbes & Phil vs Zombies*, *Elder Island*, *Last American Horror Show* ('Homewrecked' segment), *Dick Johnson & Tommygun vs. The Cannibal Cop: Based on a True Story*, *The Trees Have Eyes*, *The Blood Hunter*, *Thursday the 12th* and *Cemetery Stories* ('Bloodfire of the Satanic Warlock Ritual' segment), along with episodes of TV's *Beyond Belief: Fact or Fiction* and *Paranormal Burbank*.

Rosita Quintana

Argentinean-born Mexican movie star Rosita Quintana (Trinidad Quintana Nuñez de Kogan) died in Mexico City on August 23, aged 96. In a film career that began in the late 1940s, she appeared in the episodic horror movie *El demonio en la sangre* (Demon in the Blood) and *Hasta que la muerte nos separe* (Until Death Do Us Part).

Kumar Ramsay

Screenwriter and producer Kumar Ramsay, the eldest member of India's seven-brother Ramsay filmmaking

dynasty, died of cardiac arrest on July 8, aged 85. During the 1970s and '80s he wrote such low-budget cult horror hits as *Darwaza*, *Aur Kaun?*, *Guest House*, *Dahshat*, *Hotel*, *Purana Mandir*, *3D Saamri*, *Om*, *Dak Bangla*, *Saaya* and *Khoj*.

Marion Ramsay

American actress Marion Ramsay, best known as the squeaky-voiced "Officer Laverne Hooks" in six of the *Police Academy* films, died on January 7, aged 73. She also appeared in the Syfy movie *Lavalantula* and its sequel *2 Lava 2 Lantula*, as well as an episode of TV's *3rd Eye*. Ramsay was the voice of "D.I. Holler" in Hanna-Barbera's animated TV series *The Addams Family* (1992–93).

Joel Rapp

American TV scriptwriter Joel [Malcolm] Rapp died on September 15, aged 87. He wrote for such shows as *Topper* (1954), *Science Fiction Theatre*, *It's About Time*, *The Flying Nun* and *Bewitched*. Rapp later authored fourteen books on indoor gardening and cooking and spent more than a decade on TV's *Live with Regis and Kathie Lee* as their regular gardening expert. Roger Corman wrote the Foreword to his 2004 autobiography, *Radio, TV, Mother Earth & Me: Memories of a Hollywood Life*.

Alex Rebar

American supporting actor and scriptwriter Alex Rebar (Alexander John Rebar, aka "A.J. Rebar"), whose rare starring role was as astronaut "Steve West", who was transformed

into *The Incredible Melting Man* (1977), died on November 19, aged 81. He also appeared in Don Edmonds' *Terror on Tour*, *Amityville Horror: The Evil Escapes* and episodes of TV's *The Incredible Hulk* and *Voyagers!*. As executive producer, Rebar's credits include *To All Goodnight*, *Demented*, *Terror on Tour* and *Home Sweet Home*. He also scripted *To All Goodnight*, *Demented* and *Terror on Tour* (as "Dell Lekus"), and collaborated on the 1974 Italian horror movie *The Devil Within Her* (aka *Beyond the Door*).

Juli Reding

American actress and cover model Juli Reding (Julie Otis, aka "Julie Redding"), who memorably co-starred as the vengeful ghost of "Vi Mason" in Bert I. Gordon's *Tormented* (1961), died on September 16, aged 85. Voted "Miss Hollywood Stars" in 1957, she appeared in a number of films and TV shows from the late 1950s onwards. In 1969, she married wealthy financial consultant Herbert L. Hutner, who was almost twice her age, and moved to Beverly Hills to become a society matron.

John Reilly

American soap opera actor John Reilly, who was a regular on *General Hospital* (1984-95) and *Passions* (2000-08), died on January 9, aged 86. He also appeared in episodes of *The Bionic Woman*, *Wonder Woman*, *The Incredible Hulk*, *The Powers of Matthew Star*, *Mortal Kombat: Conquest* and the 1983 pilot *Wishman*. Reilly was the voice of "Hawkeye" in the 1994-96 animated TV series of Marvel's *Iron Man*.

Jonathan Reynolds

American screenwriter and playwright Jonathan [Randolph] Reynolds died of organ failure on October 27, aged 79.

Juli Reading (1935–2021) co-starred as a vengeful ghost haunting her former boyfriend (Richard Carlson) in Bert I. Gordon's Tormented *(1960).*

He scripted the 1980s comedies *Leonard Part 6* and *My Stepmother is an Alien*.

Anne Rice

American author Anne Rice (Howard Allen Frances O'Brien Rice, aka "Anne Rampling" and "A.N. Roquelaure") died of complications from a stroke on December 11, aged 80. Her first novel, the Gothic romance *Interview with the Vampire*, was published in 1976 and became an instant bestseller. It was filmed in 1994, and Rice went on to publish a further twelve volumes in "The Vampire Chronicles", including *The Vampire Lestat*, *The Queen of the Damned* (filmed in 2002) and *The Tale of the Body Thief*, with the thirteenth book (*Blood Communion: A Tale of Prince Lestat*) appearing in 2018. Her other novels include and *The Mummy*, *Servant of the Bones*, *Violin*, *Pandora*, *Vittorio the Vampire*, *The Wolf Gift*, *The Wolves of Midwinter*, *Ramses the Damned: The Passion of Cleopatra* (with her son, Christopher Rice) and the "Lives of the Mayfair Witches" trilogy (*The Witching Hour*, *Lasher* and *Taltos*). An atheist for decades, Rice returned to her childhood faith of Catholicism in 1998, but reversed her decision in 2010 because of the religion's attitude to birth control, homosexuality and science. She had more than 150 million books published worldwide and received the 1994 World Horror Convention Grand Master Award and the 2003 HWA Bram Stoker Award for Life Achievement.

John Richardson

British leading man John Richardson, who portrayed "Leo Vincey"/"Killicrates" in Hammer's *She* (with Christopher Lee and Peter Cushing) and the sequel *Vengeance of She*, died of complications from COVID-19 on January 5, aged 86. He also co-starred with Raquel Welch in Hammer's *One Million Years B.C.* (with dinosaur

Giuliano Nistri's 2-foglio *for Mario Bava's* Black Sunday *(1960), which co-starred Barbara Steele and John Richardson (1934–2021) and was banned in the UK until 1968.*

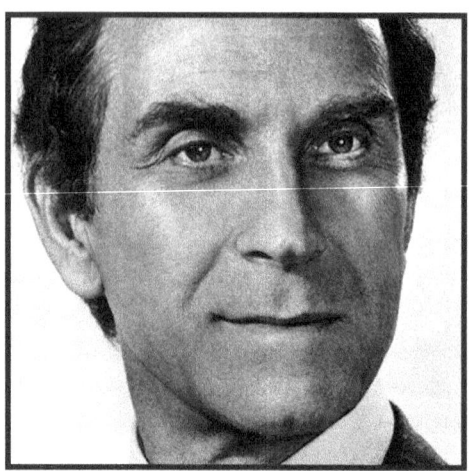

effects by Ray Harryhausen), and his other credits include Mario Bava's *Black Sunday* (aka *Revenge of the Vampire*, with Barbara Steele), *On a Clear Day You Can See Forever*, *Frankenstein '80*, Sergio Martino's *Torso*, *Eyeball*, *Reflections in Black*, *Nine Guests for a Crime*, *War of the Planets*, *Battle of the Stars*, Riccardo Freda's *Murder Syndrome* and Michele Soavi's *The Church*. Richardson retired from acting in the early 1990s and became a photographer. He was married to actress Martine Beswick from 1967–73.

Peter Mark Richman

American actor, playwright and novelist Peter Mark Richman (Marvin Jack Richman), who starred in the 1961-62 NBC-TV series *Cain's Hundred*, died on January 14, aged 93. He appeared in the underrated *Dark Intruder* (a busted TV psychic detective pilot released theatrically), *Agent for H.A.R.M.*, *PSI Factor*, *Judgement Day*, *Friday the 13th Part VIII: Jason Takes Manhattan* and *After the Wizard*. On TV, Richman was a familiar face in episodes of *Alfred Hitchcock Presents* ('The Cure' by Robert Bloch), *Moment of Fear*, *The Twilight Zone*, *The Outer Limits*, *The Wild Wild West*, *The Man from U.N.C.L.E.*, *Voyage to the Bottom of the Sea*, *The Invaders*, *Land of the Giants*, *Search*, *Electra Woman and Dyna Girl* (as "The Pharaoh"), *The Bionic Woman*, *The Six Million Dollar Man*, *Wonder Woman* ('Gault's Brain' with John Carradine), *BJ and the Bear* ('BJ and the Witch'), *Galactica 1980*, *The Incredible Hulk*, *Fantasy Island*, *Knight Rider*, *Star Trek: The Next Generation* and *Swamp Thing* (1990). Richman was also the voice of "Kit Walker"/"The Phantom" on the 1986 animated series *Defenders of the Earth*.

J.W. Rinzler

American author J.W. (Jonathan) Rinzler died of pancreatic cancer on July 28, aged 58. Having joined the company in 2001, he was the executive editor at Lucasfilm for fifteen years, eventually rising to senior editor at LucasBooks. During

Peter Mark Richman (1927–2021) co-starred in the occult detective movie Dark Intruder (1965), which was intended to be a pilot for a TV series called The Black Cloak.

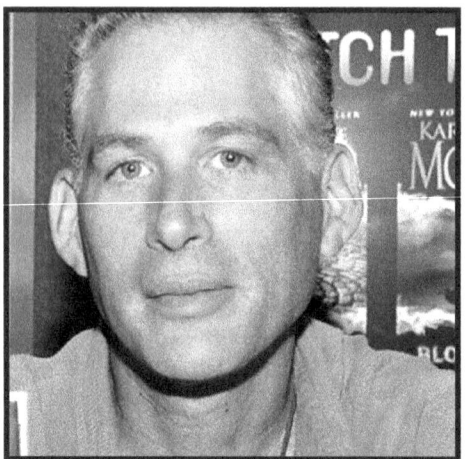

Busy British character actor Paul Ritter (Simon Paul Adams) died of a brain tumour on April 5, aged 55. He appeared in *Nostradamus* (2006), *Hannibal Rising*, the James Bond movie *Quantum of Solace*, *Harry Potter and the Half-Blood Prince* (as "Eldred Worple"), *The Limehouse Golem*, *Inferno* (2016) and episodes of TV's *Dirk Gently*, *Houdini and Doyle* (as "Bram Stoker"), *Neil Gaiman's Likely Stories* and *Electric Dreams*.

that time he wrote such non-fiction guides as *The Making of Star Wars: The Definitive Story Behind the Original Film*, *The Making of Star Wars: The Empire Strikes Back*, *Star Wars Art: Visions*, *Star Wars: The Blueprints* and *Star Wars Storyboards*. Along with *The Complete Making of Indiana Jones: The Definitive Story Behind All Four Films*, he also authored "making of" books about *Alien*, *Planet of the Apes* and *Monster House*. *Riddle of the Black Cat!* (2014) is an illustrated interpretation of Edgar Allan Poe's story based on his short animated movie.

Paul Ritter

Tanya Roberts

65-year-old American actress and former *Playboy* model Tanya Roberts (Victoria Leigh Blum) died on January 4 from a urinary tract infection that developed into sepsis. She collapsed after taking her dogs for a walk on Christmas Eve and never recovered. Her death was erroneously announced a day early by her boyfriend and management. Roberts' movie credits include *The Last Victim*, *Tourist Trap*, *The Beastmaster*, *Hearts*

and *Armour*, *Sheena* (as the titular "Queen of the Jungle"), the James Bond film *A View to a Kill* and *Inner Sanctum* (1991). On TV she was a regular (as final Angel "Julie Rogers") on *Charlie's Angels* (1980–81) and she appeared in an episode of *Fantasy Island* ('The Ghost's Story').

Charles Robinson

75-year-old African-American singer and character actor Charles Robinson died on July 12 from cardiac arrest with multisystem organ failure due to septic shock and metastatic adenocarcinoma, a type of glandular cancer. Although probably best remembered as court clerk "Mac Robinson" on the NBC sitcom *Night Court* (1984–92), he also appeared in AIP's zombies vs. gangsters movie *Sugar Hill* (Robinson also did the casting), *Apocalypse Now*, *Project: ALF*, *Beowulf* (1999), *Santa Jr.*, *Heaven Sent* (aka *How Sarah Got Her Wings*) and *Pee-wee's Big Holiday*, along with episodes of *Touched by an Angel*, *Carnivàle* and *Charmed* (2005) on TV.

Robinson began his career as a theater actor and singer for R&B groups Archie Bell and the Drells and Southern Clouds of Joy.

Doug Robinson

Veteran British stuntman-actor Doug Robinson (Douglas Bowbank Robinson) died on December 16, aged 91. He began his career in the mid-1950s and, amongst the numerous films he worked on are Hammer's *The Two Faces of Dr. Jekyll* (aka *Jekyll's Inferno*), *Jason and the Argonauts*, *2001: A Space Odyssey*, *Warlords of Atlantis*, *Superman*, *The Empire Strikes Back*, *Superman II*, *Outland*, *An American Werewolf in London*, *Superman III*, *Prisoners of the Lost Universe*, *The Keep*, *Indiana Jones and the Temple of Doom*, *Lifeforce*, *Enemy Mine*, *Jane and the Lost City*, *Willow*, *Without a Clue*, *Batman* (1989), Clive Barker's *Nightbreed*, and the James Bond movies *Casino Royale*

Charles Robinson (1945–2021) was featured in American International Pictures' "blaxploitation" zombie movie Sugar Hill (1974).

(1965), *You Only Live Twice, Diamonds Are Forever, Live and Let Die, The Man with the Golden Gun, The Spy Who Loved Me, For Your Eyes Only, Never Say Never Again, A View to a Kill* and *The Living Daylights*. Robinson's TV work included episodes of *The Avengers* and *Space: 1999*. His older brother, Joe Robinson (who died in 2017), was a fellow stuntman-actor and, with actress Honor Blackman, they co-authored the book *Honor Blackman's Book of Self-Defence* (1965).

Richard Robinson

American publisher Richard Robinson (Maurice Richard Robinson, Jr.) died on June 5, aged 84. Having started a career as a high school teacher, in 1962 he joined his father's publishing imprint, Scholastic, first as an editor, and then becoming President in 1974, CEO in 1975 and Chairman of the Board when his father died in 1982. Robinson acquired the American rights for J.K. Rowling's *Harry Potter* series for $105,000, and the franchise is now worth an estimated $15 billion. Scholastic became the world's largest publisher and distributor of children's books, which include *The Hunger Games* and *Goosebumps* series. Robinson was awarded the Publishers Weekly Publishing Innovator of the Year award in 2011, and PEN America honoured him for his contributions to free expression in literature and publishing in 2019.

Enrique Rocha

Mexican leading man Enrique [Miguel] Rocha [Ruiz] died on November 7, aged 81. His credits include *La endemoniada, El club de los suicidas* (1970, based on a story by Robert Louis Stevenson), *Muñeca reina, Satanás de todos los horrores* (based on Edgar Allan Poe's 'The Fall of the House of Usher'), *Satanico Pandemonium: La Sexorcista* (as "Lucifer"), *Historias violentas* and *Serafín: La película*, along with numerous *telenovelas*.

Robson Rocha

41-year-old Brazilian comics artist Robson Rocha died on July 11, two weeks after he was hospitalised for COVID-19. Having signed an exclusive contract with DC Comics, he worked on multiple "New 52" titles, including *Birds of Prey*, *Batman/Superman*, *Lobo*, *Superboy* and *Earth 2: World's End*, such "Rebirth" titles as *Aquaman* and *Green Lanterns*, along with issues of *Supergirl*, *Justice League*, *Teen Titans*, *Demon Knights* and *World's Finest*.

Robert Rodan

American actor Robert Rodan (Robert Trimas), who portrayed the Frankenstein Monster-like "Adam" in the 1968 season of ABC-TV's *Dark Shadows*, died of heart failure on March 25, aged 83. He later turned

up in some documentaries and podcasts about the show. After retiring from acting, Rodan went into real estate.

Jean-Claude Romer

French film critic and historian Jean-Claude Romer, who, with Michel Caen, was co-editor (1963–71) of *Midi-Minuit Fantastique* magazine, died of heart failure on May 8, aged 88. He contributed to a number of books and TV shows about the cinema and was also the head of the selection committee for works screened at the Avoriaz Fantastic Film Festival. As an

Co-edited by Jean-Claude Romer (1933–2021) and Michel Caen, the third issue of the French magazine Midi-Minuit Fantastique (November, 1962) was a King Kong Special.

actor, Romer also turned up in (often uncredited) small roles in such films as *Je t'aime je t'aime*, *Sexyrella*, *Threshold of the Void*, *Celine and Julie Go Boating*, *Seven Women for Satan*, *Baby Blood* and *Time Demon*. He also played the Frankenstein Monster in the 1978 short *Cinémania*.

Jeanine Ann Roose

Jeanine Ann Roose, whose only movie credit was playing "Little Violet Bick" in the classic Christmas fantasy *It's a Wonderful Life* (1946), died from an infection of the abdomen on December 31, aged 84. As a child actor, she appeared on a number of TV and radio shows, before enrolling at UCLA and later became a Jungian psychoanalyst.

Ronald Roose

American sound and film editor Ronald Roose died of Parkinson's disease on September 15, aged 75. His

credits include *The Wiz*, *The Princess Bride*, *My Demon Lover* and *Star Trek VI: The Undiscovered Country*.

Clifford Rose

British character actor [John] Clifford Rose died on November 6, aged 92. His credits include *Marat/Sade*, *The Cold Room*, *Pirates of the Caribbean: On Stranger Tides* and episodes of TV's *Mystery and Imagination* (Algernon Blackwood's 'The Listener'), *The Rivals of Sherlock Holmes*, *Doctor Who* ('Warriors' Gate') and *Hammer House of Mystery and Suspense*. A member of the Royal Shakespeare Company,

Rose appeared on stage in Peter Brook's 1965 production of *The Persecution and Assassination of Marat as Performed by the Inmates of the Asylum of Charenton Under the Direction of Marquis De Sade*, along with Glenda Jackson, Clive Revill, Patrick Magee and Freddie Jones.

Giuseppe Rotunno

Italian cinematographer Giuseppe "Peppino" Rotunno died on February 7, aged 97. His credits include *On the Beach* (1959), *Phantom Lovers*, *The Witches* (1967), *Spirits of the Dead* (Federico Fellini's 'Toby Dammit'), *Fellini Satyricon*, *All That Jazz*, *Popeye*, *Red Sonja*, *Julia and Julia*, *Haunted Summer*, *The Adventures of Baron Munchausen* (1988), *Wolf* and Dario Argento's *The Stendhal Syndrome*.

Yvonne Rousseau

Australian SF Fan, editor, writer and critic Yvonne Rousseau died of Parkinson's disease on February 13,

aged 75. From 1986–91 she co-edited the Ditmar Award-winning *Australian Science Fiction Review: Second Series* with Jenny Blackford, Russell Blackford, John Foyster and Janeen Webb. Rousseau also published *The Murders at Hanging Rock* and *Minmers Marooned* and *Planet of the Marsupials: The Science Fiction Novels of Cherry Wilder*. Her criticism appeared in *Foundation: The Review of Science Fiction*, *The Metaphysical Review*, *Science Fiction Eye* and *SF Commentary*.

Richard Rush

Oscar-nominated Richard Rush (1929–2021) directed American International's hippie thriller Psych-Out (1968), which starred former child actor Dean Stockwell.

American screenwriter, producer and director Richard Rush, best known for the Oscar-nominated *The Stunt Man* (1980), died after a long illness on April 8, aged 91. Early in his career, Rush directed exploitation movies as *Hells Angels on Wheels*, *A Man Called Dagger*, *Psych-Out* and *The Savage Seven*. Following the 1994 erotic thriller *Color of Night* he never made another movie.

Will Ryan

American musician and prolific voice actor Will Ryan (William Frank Ryan), who was "Willio" in the comedic singing group Willio & Phillio (with Phil Baron as "Phillio"), died of cancer on November 19, aged 82. He was the voice of "Rabbit" in the Walt Disney shorts *Winnie the Pooh and a Day for Eeyore* and *Pooh's Great School Bus Adventure*, along with the TV series *Welcome to Pooh Corner* (1983-86). Ryan's many other credits include *Mickey's Christmas Carol*, *An American Tail*, *Alice Through the Looking Glass* (1987), *The Land Before Time*, *The Wizard of Speed and Time*, *The Little Mermaid* (1989), *A Gnome Named Gnorm*, *Rock-A-Doodle*, *A Troll in Central Park*, *A Flintstones Christmas Carol*, *Looney Tunes: Back in Action* and such TV series as *G.I. Joe: The Revenge of Cobra*, *Teen Wolf* (as "Chubs") and *The Twisted Tales of Felix the Cat*.

Antonio Sabáto, Sr.

Italian-born actor Antonio Sabáto, Sr., the father of Antonio Sabáto, Jr., died in Los Angeles of complications from COVID-19 on January 6, aged 77. He appeared in *Barbarella*, *When Men Carried Clubs and Women Played Ding-Dong*, *Seven Blood-Stained Orchids*, *War of the Robots* and *Escape from the Bronx*.

Takao Saitô

Japanese *manga* writer and artist Takao Saitô, who created the iconic character of hired assassin "Golgo 13"/"Duke Togo" in 1968, died of

pancreatic cancer on September 24, aged 84. The *Golgo 13* comic book series has since sold more than 300 million copies and been adapted into *anime* movies, TV series and video games. Saitô also adapted the James Bond novels for serialisation in Shogakukan's *Boy's Life* magazine in 1963. He was awarded the Order of the Rising Sun from the Japanese government in 2010 for his contributions to the arts.

Don Sakers

Japanese-born American SF author Don Sakers died on May 17, aged 63. Perhaps best known for writing the review column, 'The Reference Library', in *Analog: Science Fiction & Fact* from 2009 until his death, he also authored the young adult novels *The Curse of the Zwilling* and (with Phil Meade) *At Risk* and *Bright Promise*, while his short fiction is collected in *Meat and Machine: Queer Writings* and *Elevenses*, all issued by the CoastLine SF Writers Consortium. Sakers also edited the anthology *Carmen Miranda's Ghost Is Haunting Space Station Three*.

Jay Sandrich

Emmy Award-winning American comedy TV producer and director Jay [Henry] Sandrich died of dementia on September 22, aged 89. Amongst the many shows he worked on were *Science Fiction Theatre*, *Get Smart*, *The Ghost & Mrs. Muir*, *Captain Nice* and the 1984 pilot *Earthlings*.

Sompote Sands

Thai film producer, director and special effects creator Sompote Sands (Sompote Saengduenchai) died of

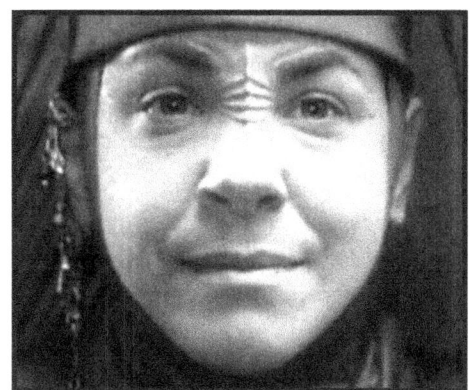

cancer in Bangkok on August 26, aged 80. Founder of the Thai film production company, Chaiyo Productions, between the early 1970s and mid-1980s he directed the mythological-inspired *tokusatsu* horror and SF movies *Tah Tien*, *Hanuman vs. 7 Ultraman* (with Shohei Tôjô), *Jumborg Ace & Giant*, *Hanuman and the 5 Kamen Riders*, *Computer Superman*, the international hit *Crocodile*, *Kraithong* (uncredited), *Phra Rot-Meri*, *The Noble War*, *Space Warriors 2000*, *Magic Lizard* and *Kraithong 2*. Sands reportedly owned the world's largest collection of Ultraman memorabilia (he claimed to have a paper that proved he owned the franchise, until a Los Angeles Federal Court ruled in 2017 that the document was not authentic).

Camille Saviola

American actress-singer Camille Saviola, who appeared as Bajoran spiritual leader "Kai Opaka" in four episodes (1993-96) of TV's *Star Trek: Deep Space Nine*, died of heart failure on October 28, aged 71. She was also in Woody Allen's *The Purple Rose of Cairo* and *Shadows and Fog*, *Nightlife* (1989), *Addams Family Values* and *Silent But Deadly*. On stage, Saviola appeared in the 1980 Off-Broadway science fiction musical *Starmites* and was also in a touring production of the rock opera *Tommy*.

Roy Scammell

British stunt arranger-actor Roy Scammell (Royston Edwin Scammell), who stunt-doubled such actors as Frank Sinatra, Steve McQueen, Deborah Kerr, Malcolm McDowell, Susan Hampshire, Kirk Douglas and Kenneth Williams, died following a short illness on May 15, aged 88. He worked on *Vice Versa* (1948), *Circus of*

Fear (aka *Psycho-Circus*), *Casino Royale* (1967), *A Clockwork Orange*, *Psychomania* (aka *The Death Wheelers*), *O Lucky Man!*, *Horror Hospital*, *The Sexplorer* (aka *The Girl from Starship Venus*), *Rollerball* (1975), *The Spy Who Loved Me*, *Alien*, *Flash Gordon* (1980), *Saturn 3*, *Venom* (1981), *Greystoke: The Legend of Tarzan Lord of the Apes*, *Sheena* and *Willow*. Scammell's TV credits include episodes of *The Champions*, *Into the Labyrinth*, *Space: 1999* and *Doctor Who* (performing the highest fall attempted up to then on the small screen—from the top of a 50ft gasometer in the 1970 episode 'Inferno').

Liam Scarlett

35-year-old British dancer and choreographer Liam Scarlett reportedly committed suicide on April 16, a day after an announcement by the Royal Danish Ballet that it had cancelled a production Scarlett's 2016 ballet *Frankenstein* following allegations of offensive behaviour towards members of the company's staff over 2018-19. He had already been suspended as the Royal Ballet's first artist-in-residence in August 2019 in the wake of unproven allegations of inappropriate sexual behaviour and bullying involving students. Scarlett's other narrative ballets include *Hansel and Gretel* (2013), *Sweet Violets* (2012, which dealt with the theory that the artist Walter Sickert may have committed Jack the Ripper's crimes), *A Midsummer Night's Dream* (2016) and *Queen of Spades* (2018).

Renato Scarpa

Italian supporting actor Renato Scarpa, who appeared as "Inspector Longhi" in *Don't Look Now* (1973) and "Prof. Verdegast" in Dario Argento's *Suspiria*, died on December 30, aged 82. His other credits include *Julia and Julia*, *Tale of Tales* and an episode of TV's *The Young Indiana Jones Chronicles*.

Walter Schneiderman

Veteran British make-up artist Walter Schneiderman, who should have been nominated for an Oscar for his application of John Hurt's monstrous make-up on *The Elephant Man* (1980), died on April 8, aged 98. His lack of recognition caused an outcry, which led the following year to a new Oscar category for Best Make-up. Schneiderman also worked on Powell and Pressburger's *The Tales of Hoffman* (1951), *Corridors of Blood* (with Boris Karloff and Christopher Lee), *Where Has Poor Mickey Gone?*, *Catacombs* (aka *The Woman Who Wouldn't Die*), Hammer's *One Million Years B.C.*, *Prehistoric Women* and *Scars of Dracula*, *The Magus*, *Rollerball* (1975), *Lisztomania*, *Beauty and the Beast* (1976), *The Shout* and *Labyrinth*. He retired in 1992.

Enzo Sciotti

Acclaimed Italian poster artist Enzo Sciotti died on April 11, aged 76. He created more than 300 posters and

VHS covers for such films as *The Mountain of the Cannibal God*, *Army of Darkness*, *Beetlejuice*, *Interview with a Vampire*, Dario Argento's *Phenomena* and Lucio Fulci's *The Beyond*, *The House by the Cemetery*, *Manhattan Baby* and *A Cat in the Brain*.

Peter Scolari

Emmy Award-winning American character actor and director Peter Scolari died of cancer on October 22, aged 66. On TV, he starred as "Wayne Szalinski" in the 1997-2000 series *Honey, I Shrunk the Kids: The TV Show* and appeared in episodes of *The Twilight Zone* (1988), *Lois & Clark:*

Original 4-foglio poster by Italian artist Enzo Sciotti (1944–2021) for Lucio Fulci's The House by the Cemetery (1981).

The New Adventures of Superman, *Touched by an Angel* and *Sabrina the Teenage Witch*, with recurring roles in *Gotham* (as "Commissioner Loeb") and *Evil* (as "Bishop Thomas Marx"). Scolari's movie credits include *Amazons* (1984) and *Ticks*.

Clive Scott

South African supporting actor Clive Scott (Robert Clive Cleghorn) died on July 28, aged 84. He appeared in episodes of TV's *Doctor Who* ('The Mind of Evil'), *Tales of Mystery and Imagination* ('The Masque of the Red Death', introduced by Christopher Lee) and *The Adventures of Sinbad*. Scott's movie credits include the 2003 version of *Sumuru* (co-scripted by Harry Alan Towers).

Geoffrey Scott

American supporting actor Geoffrey [Chase] Scott, a former Marlboro and Camel man in cigarette ads, died of Parkinson's disease on February 23, aged 79. Although probably best

known for playing the ultimately murdered "Mark Jennings" on TV's *Dynysty* (1982–84), he also portrayed "Sky Rumson" on thirteen episodes of the Gothic soap opera *Dark Shadows* in 1970. Scott's other credits include *Hulk* (2003, as the President) and an episode of *Fantasy Island*.

George Segal

Hollywood leading man George Segal [Jr.] died on Match 23 of complications from heart bypass surgery. He was 87. Equally skilled in light comedy or dramatic roles, Segal's credits include *No Way to Treat a Lady*, *The Terminal Man* (based on the novel by Robert Crichton), *The Cold Room*, *The Cable Guy* and *2012*. On TV, he was the voice of "Dr. Benton C. Quest" in the 1996-97 animated series *The Real Adventures of Jonny Quest* and appeared in episodes of *The Alfred Hitchcock Hour* and *Pushing Daises*.

Tony Selby

British character actor Tony Selby (Anthony Samuel Selby) died on September 5, aged 83. A former child actor, he appeared in *City in the Sea* (aka *War-Gods of the Deep*) and *Witchfinder General*—both with Vincent Price, *Superman* (1978), *The Secret Garden* (1987) and *Cockneys vs Zombies*. On TV, Selby co-starred as sidekick "Sam Maxstead" in the first two seasons of *Ace of Wands* (1970-71), and he also turned up in episodes of *The Avengers*, *Catweazle* (1971), *Thriller* (1974), *Doctor Who* (as "Sabalom Glitz" in 'The Trial of the Time Lord' and 'Dragonfire'), *The Vanishing Man* and *Lucky Man*.

Lee Server

American author Lee Server died on December 28, aged 68. A graduate of New York University Film School, his books include *Danger is My Business: An Illustrated History of the Fabulous Pulp Magazines: 1896-1953*, *Over My Dead Body: The Sensational Age of the American Paperback: 1945-1955*, *The Big Book of Noir*, *Encyclopedia of Pulp Fiction Writers* and *Asian Pop Cinema: Bombay to Tokyo*, along with acclaimed biographies of Sam Fuller, Robert Mitchum and Ava Gardner.

Barbara Shelley

Hammer horror star Barbara Shelley (Barbara T. Kowin) died on January 4, aged 88. Although she contracted COVID-19 in hospital before Christmas, she had reportedly recovered from the virus and passed away from underlying health issues. A former fashion model, her first horror film was the Val Lewton-influenced *Cat Girl* (1957), although she is best known for her co-starring roles in

Barbara Shelley (1932–2021) co-starred alongside Sir Donald Wolfit's undead scientist in the Hammer-inspired Blood of the Vampire (1958).

Hammer's *The Camp on Blood Island*, *The Shadow of the Cat*, *The Gorgon* (with Christopher Lee and Peter Cushing), *The Secret of Blood Island*, *Dracula Prince of Darkness* and *Rasputin: The Mad Monk* (both with Lee again), and *Quatermass and the Pit* (aka *Five Million Years to Earth*). Shelley's other credits include *Blood of the Vampire*, *Village of the Damned* (1960) and *Ghost Story* (1974), while on TV she appeared in episodes of *The Invisible Man* (1959), *The Man from U.N.C.L.E.*, *The Avengers* ('From Venus with Love'), *Blakes 7*, *Doctor Who* ('Planet of Fire') and the 1989 mini-series *Uncle Silas* (aka *The Dark Angel*, based on the novel by J. Sheridan Le Fanu).

Antony Sher

South African-born British stage and screen actor Sir Antony Sher died on December 3, aged 72. It was revealed in September that he had terminal cancer. Although best known as one of the great modern Shakespearean stage actors, Sher also appeared in *Superman II*, *Erik the Viking* (as "Loki"), *The Young Poisoner's Handbook*, *Mr. Toad's Wild Ride*, *The Moonstone* (1996), *Macbeth* (2001), *Home* (2003, based on a story by J.G. Ballard), *The Wolfman* (2010) and *The Hobbit: The Desolation of Smaug* (uncredited).

Steve Sherman

American comic book writer Steve Sherman (Steven William Sherman), who was an assistant to artist Jack Kirby in the 1970s, died on June 24, aged 72. He collaborated with Kirby on some of the artist's later projects for DC Comics and Pacific, including *New Gods*, *Forever People*, *Mister Miracle*, *Silver Star* and *Captain Victory*. Sherman then moved to Filmation, where he contributed to the *Star Trek* animated series and the live-action *Shazam!* show. As a puppeteer he

worked for Sid and Marty Krofft Productions and on *Pee-wee's Playhouse*, *Men in Black* and *Men in Black II*, and the 1998 remake of *Mighty Joe Young*.

Ina Shorrock

British science fiction fan and popular fannish hostess Ina [Margaret] Shorrock died of a heart attack on February 10, aged 92. She discovered fandom in 1950 and became a member of the "Liverpool Group", attending her first convention two years later (the London Eastercon). Shorrock was also one of the few surviving attendees of the 1957 London Worldcon. A former chair of the British Science Fiction Association, she received a number of awards, including Lady of St. Fantony (1957), Doc Weir Award (1976), the Nova Award for Best Fan (2003) and the Big Heart Award for services to fandom (2005). Ina Shorrock was married to fellow fan Norman Shorrock, who died in 1999.

Jan Shutan

American actress Jan Shutan [Levinson] (Janice Dottenheim) died on October 7, aged 88. She appeared in the TV movies *Dracula's Dog* and *This House Possessed*, along with episodes of *The Outer Limits*, *Star Trek* ('The Lights of Zetar'), *Rod Serling's Night Gallery* and a 1967 pilot for *Dick Tracy* (featuring Victor Buono). Shutan retired from acting in 1988. Her second husband was the Emmy Award-winning writer/producer David Levinson (who died in 2019).

Gregory Sierra

American character actor Gregory Sierra, who was a regular as "Det. Sgt. Chano Amenguale" on TV's *Barney Miller* (1975-76), died of cancer on January 4, aged 83. His other credits include *Beneath the Planet of the Apes*, *The Clones*, *Honey I Blew Up the Kid*, Ray Bradbury's *The Wonderful Ice Cream Suit* and John Carpenter's *Vampires*, along with episodes of *The Flying Nun*, *The Greatest American Hero*, *Blue Thunder*, *The Munsters Today*, *The Ray Bradbury Theater*, *The X Files*, *Star Trek: Deep Space Nine*, *Beyond Belief: Fact or Fiction* and the 1988 mini-series and subsequent spin-off show *Something Is Out There*.

Felix Silla

Three-foot, eleven-inch Italian-born American actor Felix [Anthony] Silla died of pancreatic cancer on April 16, aged 84. A trained circus performer, he is best remembered for playing "Cousin Itt" on TV's *The Addams Family* (1965-66), "Lucifer" on *Battlestar Galactica* (1978-79) and

"Twiki" on *Buck Rodgers in the 25th Century* (1979-81). Silla appeared in *She Freak*, *Planet of the Apes* (1968), *Pufnstuff*, *Ssssss* (aka *Sssnake*), *Don't Be Afraid of the Dark* (1973), *Demon Seed*, *Halloween with the New Addams Family* (as "Cousin Itt" again), *The Manitou*, David Cronenberg's *The Brood*, *Return of the Jedi*, *The Dungeonmaster*, *House*, *Spaceballs*, *Batman Returns* and *The Legend of Galgameth*. On TV, his other credits include episodes of *The Girl from U.N.C.L.E.*, *Star Trek*, *H.R. Pufnstuff*, *Bewitched*, *Rod Serling's Night Gallery*, *Lidsville* and *Mork & Mindy*. Silla also worked (mostly uncredited) as a stunt performer on many movies, including *Battle for the Planet of the Apes*, *Earthquake*, *E.T. the Extra-Terrestrial*, *Poltergeist*, *Indiana Jones and the Temple of Doom*, *Howard the Duck*, *The Golden Child*, *The Monster Squad* and *Phantasm II*.

Cliff Simon

58-year-old South African-born actor and voice artist Cliff [Mark] Simon was killed in a kite-boarding accident in California on March 9. Best known for his role as the Goa'uld System's

"Lord Ba'al" in fifteen episodes of TV's *Stargate SG-1* (2001–07) and the 2008 spin-off film *Stargate: Continuum*, the former model's other credits include the 2017 movie *Project Eden*. Simon was also hosted and executive produced the Travel Channel's paranormal documentary series *Into the Unknown* (aka *Uncharted Mysteries*).

L. Neil Smith

American libertarian SF author L. Neil Smith (Lester Neil Smith III) died on August 27, aged 75. Best known for his 1980s trilogy of "Lando Calrissian" *Star Wars* expanded universe novels (*Lando Calrissian and the Mindharp of Sharu*, *Lando Calrissian and the Flamewind of Oseon* and *Lando Calrissian and the Starcave of ThonBoka*), he also wrote the "North American/Galactic Confederacy" and "Forge of the Elders" series and Smith's other books include *The Wardove*, *The Crystal Empire*, *Hope* (Aaron Zelman), *Sweeter Than Wine*, *Blade of P'na* and the graphic novel *Roswell, Texas* (with Rex F. May). In 1979 he created the Prometheus Awards to honour libertarian science fiction, and he received a Special Award for Lifetime Achievement from the Libertarian Futurist Society in 2016.

Wilbur Smith

International bestselling South African author Wilbur [Addison] Smith, described as the "best historical novelist" by Stephen King, died on November 13, aged 88. His many action-adventure books include the lost city novel, *The Sunbird* (1972), and a series of historical fantasy titles set in Ancient Egypt—*River God*, *The Seventh Scroll*, *Warlock*, *The Quest*, *Desert God* and *Pharaoh* (1993-2016). Since his debut novel appeared in 1964, Smith sold more than 140 million copies worldwide in more than thirty languages.

William Smith

American tough-guy actor William Smith (aka "Bill Smith") died on July 5, aged 88. Although he made his screen debut as an uncredited child actor in Universal's *The Ghost of Frankenstein* (1942), he came to prominence in the late 1960s and early '70s in a trio of violent biker movies: *Run Angel Run!*, *The Losers* and *Angels Die Hard*. Smith's other movie appearances include *The Boy with Green Hair*, George Pal's *Atlantis: The Lost Continent*, *Crowhaven Farm* (with John Carradine), *The Thing with Two Heads*, *Grave of the Vampire*, *Piranha* (1972), *Invasion of the Bee Girls*, *The Ultimate Warrior*, *Twilight's Last Gleaming*, *Conan the Barbarian* (as "Conan's Father"), *Red Dawn*, *Moon in Scorpio*, *Hell Comes to Frogtown*, *Maniac Cop*, *Evil Altar*, *Empire of Ash III*, *Memorial Valley Massacre*, *B.O.R.N.*, *The Final Sanction*, *The Roller Blade Seven*, *Cybernator*, *Feast*, *Legend of the Roller Blade Seven*, *Kiss and Be Killed*, *Return of the Roller Blade Seven*, *Big Sister 2000* (aka *Girls from Another World*), *Uncle Sam*, *Debbie Does Damnation*, *The Eritic Rites of Countess Dracula* (as "Count Dracula"), *Body Shop* (aka *Deadly Memories*), *Zombiegeddon*, *Grave Tales* (aka *Killer Story*), *Voices from the Graves*, *Rapturious*, *The Boneyard Collection* ('Her Morbid Desires' segment), *Island of Witches* and the short, *The Vampire Hunters Club*. On TV he appeared in episodes of *The Alfred Hitchcock Hour*, *Batman* (1968), *I Dream of Jeannie*, *Search*, *The Six Million Dollar Man*, *Planet of the Apes*, *Kolchak: The Night Stalker* (1974), *Logan's Run*, *Buck Rogers in the 25th Century*, *Fantasy Island* (as Frankenstein's Monster in 'The Lady and the Monster'), *Knight Rider*, *The Twilight Zone* (1986), *Shades of LA* and *Beyond Belief: Fact or Fiction*. Smith was the "Marlboro Man" in the final televised Marlboro cigarettes commercial.

Invasion of the Bee Girls (1973), scripted by Hollywood newcomer Nicholas Meyer, was a rare starring vehicle for tough-guy character actor William Smith (1933–2021).

Paul Soles

Canadian actor Paul Soles, the voice of ABC-TV's animated "Spider-Man"/"Peter Parker" from 1967-70, died on May 26, aged 90. He also voiced "Hermey", the misfit elf in Rankin/Bass' stop-motion special *Rudolph the Red-Nosed Reindeer* (1964), and his other cartoon credits include *Willy McBean and His Magic Machine*, *The Trolls and the Christmas Express* and episodes of *King Kong*, *Iron Man*, *Captain America* and *Hulk* (all 1966) and *Spider-Woman* (1979). Soles also appeared in *Really Weird Tales*, *Shadow Builder* (based on a story by Bram Stoker), *Teen Knight*, *The Incredible Hulk* (2008) and episodes of the TV's *Alfred Hitchcock Presents* (1987), *The Hidden Room* and *F/X: The Series*.

Stephen Sondheim

Legendary American composer and lyricist Stephen [Joshua] Sondheim died on November 26, aged 91. One of the most important figures in 20th-century musical theatre, he created such stage productions as *Sweeney Todd: The Demon Barber of Fleet Street* (1979, filmed in 1982, 2001 and 2007) and *Into the Woods* with James Lapine (1987, filmed in 1987, 2011 and 2014). The multiple award-winning Sondheim also wrote five songs for Warren Beatty's 1990 movie *Dick Tracy*, including the Academy Award-winning 'Sooner or Later (I Always Get My Man)', sung by Madonna. At the age of 19, while studying at the Williams College in Massachusetts, he received permission from August Derleth at Arkham House to broadcast his thirty-minute adaptation of H.P. Lovecraft's story 'The Rats in the Walls' on the college radio station. Sondheim's first job after graduating from Williams was to work as an assistant writer (with George Oppenheimer) on eleven episodes of the supernatural comedy TV series *Topper* (1953-54), starring Leo G. Carroll. With actor Anthony Perkins, he also co-scripted the murder-mystery movie *The Last of Sheila* (1973).

Si Spencer

British comics writer and TV scriptwriter Si Spencer (Simon J. Spencer) died on February 16, aged 59. His work appeared in *Crisis*, *Judge Dredd Megazine*, *Books of Magick: Life During Wartime* and *Hellblazer: City of Demons*.

Peggy Spirito

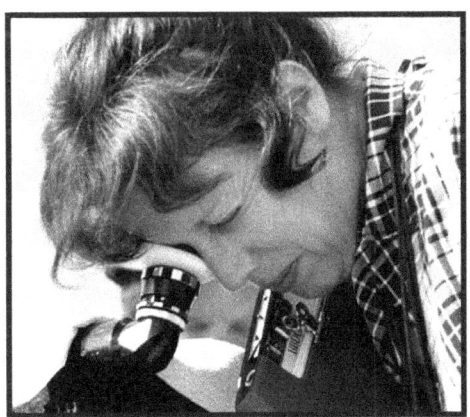

British film and TV continuity and script editor Peggy Spirito (Maggie Spirito Perkins) died in May, aged 92. She began working with Freddie Yong's camera department at MGM British Studios in the 1940s, and her credits include Hammer's *One Million Years B.C.* (1966) and such TV series as *The Avengers* (1967-69) and *Randall & Hopkirk (Deceased)*.

Anne Stallybrass

British actress [Jacqueline] Anne Stallybrass, probably best known for playing "Anne Onedin" on the first two seasons (1971-72) of BBC-TV's *The Onedin Line* (which starred her future husband, Peter Gilmore), died on July 3, aged 82. She also had a small role in Hammer's *Countess Dracula* and turned up in episodes of *Orson Welles Great Mysteries* and the near-future series *Knights of God*.

Lynn Stalmaster

Veteran Hollywood casting director Lynn (Arlen) Stalmaster died on February 12, aged 93. He started out as an actor in the early 1950s before

Bill Starr

American author Bill Starr (Billie Joe Starr), whose linked space operas *The Way to Dawnworld* and *The Treasure of Wonderwhat* were published by Ballantine/Del Rey in the late 1970s, died on May 8, aged 87.

working on such movies and TV shows as *The Invisible Boy, The Pied Piper of Hamelin, Half Human, Lady in a Cage, The Satan Bug, What Ever Happened to Aunt Alice?, Castle Keep, Sweet Sweet Rachel, The Resurrection of Zachary Wheeler, Isn't It Shocking?, Sleeper, Rhinoceros, Rollerball* (1975), *Beyond the Bermuda Triangle, Audrey Rose, Good Against Evil, The Fury, Damien: Omen II, Superman* (1978), *Prophecy, Nightwing, The Two Worlds of Jennie Logan, Wholly Moses!, Superman II, Caveman, Blow Out, Dark Night of the Scarecrow, Looker, Starflight: The Plane That Couldn't Land, Brainstorm* (1983), *Supergirl, Creator, Santa Claus: The Movie, Lady in White, Get Smart Again!, Teenage Mutant Ninja Turtles II: The Secret of the Ooze, Fluke, Battlefield Earth, The Adventures of Hiram Holliday, My Living Doll, My Favorite Martian, The Sixth Sense* and *Fantasy Island*. In 2017, Stalmaster was presented with a Honarary Academy Award.

Dorothy Steel

American character actress Dorothy Steel, who played tribal leaders in *Jumanji: The Next Level, Black Panther* and *Black Panther: Wakanda Forever*, died on October 14, aged 95. She also appeared in the 2016 short films *Black Majick* and *The Refuge*. Steel began acting at the age of 88.

the Vampires, which opened in October 2002 and closed just three months later. He also produced the 2003 TV movie of *Wuthering Heights*.

Jim Steinman

Grammy Award-winning American songwriter a record producer Jim Steinman (James Richard Steinman) died of kidney failure on April 19, aged 73. Best known for his horror-themed rock albums *Bat Out of Hell* and *Bat Out of Hell II: Back to Hell*, both with singer Meat Loaf, he wrote and produced such hits as 'You Took the Words Right Out of My Mouth (Hot Summer Night)', 'I'd Do Anything For Love (But I Won't Do That)', 'Making Love Out of Nothing At All', 'Holding Out For a Hero' and 'Total Eclipse of the Heart'. Steinman also wrote the music for the biggest failure in Broadway history— the $12 million stage musical *Dance of*

Dr. Aaron Stern

American psychiatrist Dr. Aaron Stern, who in the early 1970s became the controversial head of Hollywood's movie rating board, died on April 13, aged 96. From 1971-74, Dr. Stern was the director of the self-policing Classification and Rating Administration of the Motion Picture Association of America (MPAA), which a few years earlier had replaced the infamous Production Code created in the early 1930s. The new ratings board graded films by letter to let moviegoers know much violence, sex and foul language to expect on the screen. He reclassified the "PG" rating (for "parental guidance") to include a warning that "some material might not be suitable for pre-teenagers." However, he failed to abolish the "X" rating, which banned films to anyone under seventeen-year-olds. "You can only rate the explicit elements on the screen—never the morality or the thought issues behind it," Dr. Stern said in 1972.

Jan Stirling

American SF fan and author Jan Stirling (Janet Cathryn Stirling, née Moore) died on May 8, aged 71. She had been rushed to hospital on April 23 and never recovered. She met author S.M. Stirling at a World Fantasy Convention in the mid-1980s and they were married in 1988. Her short stories (several written in collaboration with her husband) appeared in editor Esther M. Friesner's anthologies *Chicks in Chainmail*, *Did You Say Chicks?!*, *Chick 'n Chained Males* and *Turn the Other Chick*, along with *In Celebration of Lammas Night*, *Urban Nightmares*, *Packing Fraction and Other Tales of Science and Imagination*, *Space Inc.*, *Young Warriors: Stories of Strength*, *Witch Way to the Mall* and *Black Gate* magazine.

Dean Stockwell

Former Hollywood child star turned character actor [Robert] Dean Stockwell, who co-starred as "Al", the hologram of Admiral Al Calavicci, in NBC-TV's *Quantum Leap* (1989–93), died on November 7. He was 85. Stockwell made his screen debut in 1945, and his credits include *The Boy with Green Hair*, *The Secret Garden* (1949), *Psych-Out*, *The Dunwich Horror* (1970, as "Wilbur Whateley"), *Paper Man*, *The Werewolf of Washington*, David Lynch's *Dune* and *Blue Velvet*, *The Time Guardian*, *Limit Up*, *Naked Souls*, *The Shadow Men*, *Sinbad: The Battle of the Dark Knights*, *They Nest*, *The Manchurian Candidate* (2004), *The Dunwich Horror* (2008, as "Dr. Henry Armitage"), *Battlestar Galactica: The Plan* and *Deep in Darkness*. On TV, he was a regular on NBC's revival of

Dean Stockwell (1936–2021) starred as "Wilbur Whateley" in American International Pictures' The Dunwich Horror (1970), a psychedelic version of H.P. Lovecraft's short story.

Battlestar Galactica (2006–09, as "John Cavil") and also appeared in episodes of *Alfred Hitchcock Presents*, *The Twilight Zone* (1961 and 1989), *The Alfred Hitchcock Hour* (Robert Bloch's 'Annabel'), *Night Gallery*, *Orson Welles Great Mysteries*, *Tales of the Unexpected*, *Hammer House of Mystery and Suspense*, *Lois & Clark: The New Adventures of Superman*, *Nowhere Man*, *Star Trek: Enterprise*, *Stargate SG-1* and the two-part mini-series of Stephen King's *The Langoliers*. Stockwell's father, Broadway performer Harry Stockwell, was the uncredited voice of "Prince Charming" in Walt Disney's *Snow White and the Seven Dwarfs* (1937).

Matthew Strachan

British composer and songwriter Matthew Strachan, best known for comosing the theme music for the TV quiz show *Who Wants to Be a Millionaire*, died on September 8, aged 50. His other credits include the horror movies *Psychomanteum* and *Devil Witch Way*. In October 2020, Strachan appeared at Lavender Hill Magistrates Court in London, charged with one count of arson after setting fire to his home. He was given a suspended prison sentence. Strachan was married to novelist Bernadette Strachan (aka "Juliet Ashton"), and together they co-wrote two "Jess Castle Mysteries" under the pseudonym "M.B. Vincent".

Julie Strain

American actress and "Scream Queen" Julie [Ann] Strain died of complications from degenerative dementia (possibly caused by a fall from a horse when she was in her early twenties) on January 10, aged 58. As with Tanya Roberts the previous week, her death had been announced (originally in January 2019 and again in January 2020!), retracted, and eventually re-announced. In a career that was based more on looks than talent, the

6-foot 1-inch former "Penthouse Pet of the Year" appeared (often in various states of undress) in *Repossessed*, *Witchcraft IV: The Virgin Heart*, *The Unnamable II: The Statement of Randolph Carter* (inspired by the works of H.P. Lovecraft), *Soulmates*, *Love Bites* (with Adam Ant as a vampire), *Psycho Cop Returns*, *Future Shock*, *The Mosaic Project*, *The Devil's Pet*, *Sorceress*, *Big Sister 2000*, *Guns of El Chupacabra*, *Sorceress II: The Temptress*, *Crimes of the Chupacabra*, *Bloodthirsty*, *Ride with the Devil*, *The Bare Wench Project*, *Battle Queen 2020*, *How to Make a Monster* (2001), *The Bare Wench Project 2: Scared Topless*, *Bleed*, *Thirteen Erotic Ghosts*, *The Bare Wench Project 3: Nymphs of Mystery Mountain*, *Planet of the Erotic Ape*, *Baberellas*, *Birth Rite*, *Delta Delta Die!*, *Bare Wench Project: Uncensored*, *Horrortales.666*, *Tales from the Crapper*, *Blood Dancers* (aka *Bloodsucking Strippers*), *Blood Gnome*, *Exterminator City*, *Bare Wench: The Final Chapter*, *Evil Ever After*, *Azira: Blood from the Sand*, *Magus*, *Space Girls in Beverly Hills* and numerous direct-to-video "erotic thrillers". Strain was married to Kevin Eastman, editor-in-chief of *Heavy Metal* and the creator of Teenage Ninja Turtles, from 1995-2007.

Una Stubbs

British character actress Una Stubbs, who is probably best known to modern audiences as "Mrs. Hudson" in the BBC's *Sherlock* (2010-17), died in Scotland after a long illness on

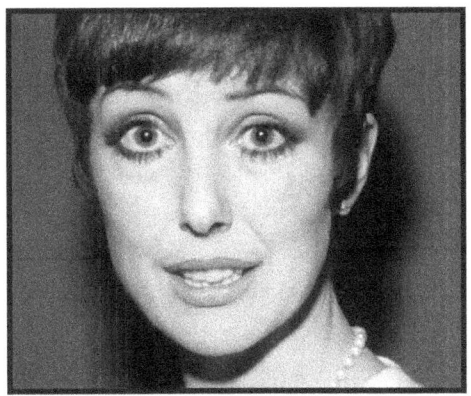

August 12, aged 84. She made her TV debut in 1958, and her first film was co-starring with Cliff Richard and The Shadows in the feel-good musical *Summer Holiday* (1963). Stubbs joined them again the following year in *Swingers' Paradise*. On TV, she portrayed "Aunt Sally" in ITV's 1979-81 series of *Worzel Gummidge* and the 1987-89 follow-up, *Worzel Gummidge Down Under*, "Miss Bat" in *The Worst Witch* (1998-2000), and "Miss Chambers" in Mark Gatiss' 2013 adaptation of M.R. James' *The Tractate Middoth*. In 1986 Stubbs acted in Clive Barker's stage play *The Secret Life of Cartoons* at the Aldwych Theatre in London. She was married to actors Peter Gilmore from 1958-69, and Nicky Henson from 1969-75.

Bertrand Tavernier

French writer, producer and director Bertrand Tavernier died complications from pancreatitis on March 25, aged 79. The former film critic's credits include the futuristic *Death Watch* (1980).

Bill Taylor

American visual effects supervisor Bill Taylor, who in 1983 co-founded vfx shop Illusion Arts with Syd Dutton, died on August 28, aged 77. His numerous movie credits include John Carpenter's *Dark Star* and *The Thing*, Alfred Hitchcock's *Family Plot*, *The Wiz* (1978), *Ghost Story* (1981), *Heartbeeps*, *Cat People* (1982), *Cloak & Dagger*, *Red Sonja*, *Maxie*, *Psycho III*, *The Gate*, *Spaceballs*, *The Running Man*, *Mac and Me*, *DeepStar Six*, *Millennium*, *The NeverEnding Story II: The Next Chapter*, *Graveyard Shift* (1990), Roger Corman's *Frankenstein Unbound*, *Mannequin: On the Move*, *The Addams Family* (1991), *Innocent Blood*, *Addams Family Values*, *The Shadow* (1994), *Batman Forever*, *DragonHeart*, *What Dreams May Come*, *Psycho* (1998), *Muppets from Space*, *Bicentennial Man*, *The Gift*, *From Hell*, *The Time Machine* (2002), *Star Trek: Nemesis*, *The Village*, *Serenity*, *Æon Flux*, *The Chronicles of Narnia: The Lion the Witch and the Wardrobe*, *Charlotte's Web* (2006), the 2007 "Final Cut" of *Blade Runner* and *The Mummy: Tomb of the Dragon Emperor*. Having started out as the Universal Studios matte shop, Illusion Arts finally closed its doors in 2009.

T. Mark Taylor

American artist and toy designer T. (Terrell) Mark Taylor died of congestive heart failure on December 23, aged 80. He began his career in 1976 as a package designer at Mattel, and went on to help develop the design for that company's He-Man and the Masters of the Universe and Playmates' Teenage Mutant Ninja Turtles franchises.

James R. Terry

American *Star Trek* and *Doctor Who* fan James R. "Jim" Terry, Jr., who helped start Los Angeles' *Doctor Who*-themed convention Gallifrey One,

died on December 1 from complications following heart bypass surgery.

Andreas Teuber

American actor and academic Andreas Teuber died on February 15, aged 78. As a young drama student at Oxford he portrayed "Mephistopheles" in a 1966 stage production of *Doctor Faustus*, a role he recreated in the 1967 film version opposite original stars Richard Burton and Elizabeth Taylor.

Mikis Theodorakis

Greek composer Mikis Theodorakis (Mihail Theodorakis) died of cardiac arrest on September 2, aged 96. Although best known for his score to *Zorba the Greek* (1964), he also created the music for Hammer's 1961 chiller *The Shadow of the Cat* and the nuclear comedy *The Day the Fish Came Out* (1967).

Frank Thorne

American comic book artist and writer Frank Thorne (Benjamin Franklin Thorne) died on March 7, the same day as his wife Marilyn, aged 90. He began his comics career in the late 1940s, and was soon working for Dell on such titles as *Flash Gordon*, *Jungle Jim*, *The Green Hornet*, *Tom Corbett Space Cadet*, *Mighty Samson* and *20,000 Leagues Under the Sea*. However, Thorne is perhaps best known from taking over as penciller from Dick Giordano on Marvel's *Red Sonja* title in the late 1970s, and he also stepped in to pencil for Jim Apro on DC's *The Spectre*. He went on to produce a number of erotic and fantasy strips, including 'Moonshine McJugs' in *Playboy* and 'Lann' in *Heavy Metal*.

Robert Thurston

American SF author Robert [Donald] Thurston died on October 20, aged 84. He started publishing short fiction in the early 1970s in *The Magazine of Fantasy and Science Fiction*, *Amazing Science Fiction* and various anthologies. Thurston wrote tie-in books for the *Battlestar Galactica* (including the original film), "Battletech" and "Isaac Asimov's Robot City" series, along with the movie tie in to *Robot Jox* and the stand-alone novels *Alicia II*, *Set of Wheels*, *Q Colony* and *Trial of Heroes*.

Kartal Tibet

Turkish leading man Kartal Tibet died on July 2, aged 83. During the late 1960s and early '70s he starred as the comic-book barbarian hero "Tarkan" in a series of popular films: *Tarkan*, *Tarkan and the Silver Saddle*, *Tarkan and the Blood of the Vikings*, *Tarkan: The Gold Medallion* and *Tarkan: Güçlü Kahraman*. Tibet turned to directing in the late 1970s, and his credits include the 2006 SF comedy *Turks in Space*.

Bill Titcombe

British comic strip artist Bill Titcombe (William Thomas Roland Titcombe) died in early February, aged 82. He worked on more than sixty-five franchised cartoon characters, many for such TV-related magazines as *Film Fun*, *TV Comic*, *TV*

Turkish actor Kartal Tibet (1939–2021) starred as the titular swords and sorcery hero in Tarkan: The Gold Medallion (1973), the fourth in the five-film series.

Century 21 and Look-In. Amongst the strips he drew were 'Jerry Lewis', 'Space Age Kit', 'The Telegoons', 'Adam Adamant', 'My Favourite Martian', 'Get Smart', 'Bewitched', 'The Tomorrow People', 'Charlie's Angels', 'Inspector Gadget', 'Scooby Doo', and the long-running 'Tom and Jerry'. Titcombe mostly retired from comic-strip work in the mid-1990s to concentrate on painting.

Stacy Title

American director Stacy Title died after a three-year battle with amyotrophic lateral sclerosis (ALS) on January 11, aged 56. Her credits include the hip-hop horror anthology movie *Snoop Dogg's Hood of Horror*, *The Bye Bye Man* and an episode of TV's *Freakish*. She was married to actor and writer Jonathan Penner.

Greta Tomlinson

British artist Greta Tomlinson (née Greta Edwards), an original member of Frank Hampson's studio from 1950–53, died on September 4, aged 94. With Harold Johns she worked on 'Dan Dare' and other characters for the weekly *Eagle* comic and was also the physical model for the SF strip's principle female character, "Professor Jocelyn Peabody". After Edwards and Johns were sacked from Hampson's team for taking on extra work, she became a fashion artist and created storyboards for the advertising industry.

Ruthie Tompson

Ruthie Tompson (Ruth Irene Tompson), a veteran animation ink-and-paint artist and scene planner for Walt Disney Studios, died peacefully in her sleep at her home at the Motion Picture and Television Fund in Woodland Hills, California, on October 10, aged 111. She worked for the studio on *Snow White and the Seven Dwarfs*, *Bambi*, *Pinocchio*, *Fantasia*, *Dumbo*, *Sleeping Beauty*, *Mary Poppins* (1964), *The Aristocats*, *Robin Hood*, *Winnie the Pooh and Tigger Too* and *The Rescuers*, before retiring in 1975. Thompson also worked on *Winds of Change* and *The Lord of the Rings* (both 1978). She was named a "Disney Legend" in 2000.

Lorna Toolis

Lorna Toolis, the former head of the Toronto Public Library's Merril Collection of Science Fiction, Speculation & Fantasy, died of heart failure on August 11, aged 68. She had been undergoing chemotherapy

treatment for cancer. The collection started out as the Spaced Out Library, seeded by a donation of writer and editor Judith Merril's personal collection of books in 1970. When Toolis retired in 2017, after more than three decades, under her direction the collection had grown to over 80,000 items. With her husband, Michael Skeet, she co-edited the Aurora Award-winning 1992 Canadian anthology *Tesseracts 4*.

Bill Tortolini

American graphic designer and comic-book lettering artist Bill Tortolini (William Tortolini) died of a heart attack on July 14, aged 46. He began working in comics in 1996, and his credits include comics such as *Anita Blake: Vampire Hunter*, *Army of Darkness*, *The Green Hornet*, *Robert Jordan's The Wheel of Time* and *Jim Butcher's The Dresden Files*. A GoFundMe page was set up to help his family.

Linda S. Touby

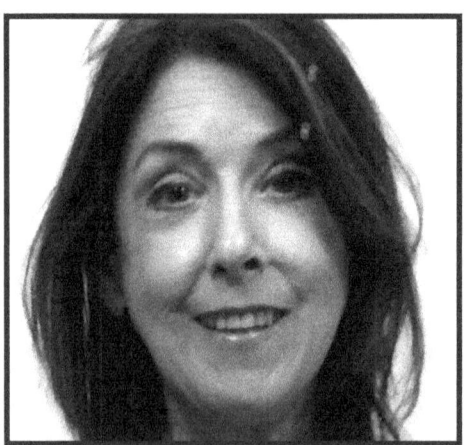

American fine artist Linda S. Touby, the widow of Basil Gogos, died on June 9, aged 78. They shared a studio, and worked and travelled together. Touby also compiled the 2020 volume *The Monster Art of Basil Gogos* for FantaCo Enterprises.

Michael Tylo

American soap opera actor Michael [Edward] Tylo died on September 29, aged 72. He appeared in the movies *They Are Among Us*, *Prototype* (2009)

and *Little Monsters*. Tylo was also the voice of Bob Lee Dysinger's "Deathstroke" in YouTube's five-part *Nightwing: The Series*.

Cicely Tyson

Former American fashion model and actress Cicely Tyson died on January 28, aged 92. She appeared in *The Blue Bird* (1976), *Duplicates*, *House of Secrets* (a version of Boileau and Narcejac's *Les diaboliques*), *Bridge of Time*, *Ms. Scrooge* and *The Haunting in Connecticut 2: Ghosts of Georgia*. On TV, Tyson's credits include episodes of *Touched by an Angel* and *The Outer Limits* ('The Final Appeal', based on George R.R. Martin's *Sandkings*,

2000), and the 1999 mini-series *Aftershock: Earthquake in New York*. She was awarded the Presidential Medal of Freedom by President Barack Obama in 2016 and received an Honorary Academy Award in 2019. Tyson was married to jazz musician Miles Davis from 1981–88.

Andrew Vachss

American child-protection attorney, social campaigner, author and comics writer Andrew [Henry] Vachss died on December 27, aged 79. Best known for his series of hardboiled "Burke" mysteries and the "Dell & Dolly" trilogy, he is also the author of *Batman: The Ultimate Evil* and the science fiction novel *Carbon*. Vachss' "Cross" trilogy (*Blackjack, Urban Renewal* and *Drawing Dead*) involves the supernatural, and his short fiction is collected in *Another Chance to Get it Right, Born Bad, Everybody Pays* and *Proving It*. 'Veil's Visit' is a "Hap and Leonard" short story collaboration with Joe R. Lansdale, and he also scripted the five-issue series *Predator: Race War* for Dark Horse Comics. When Vachss was seven years old, an older boy swung a chain at his right eye. The injuries he sustained resulted in him wearing an eye-patch for the rest of his life.

Nikki Van der Zyl

German dubbing artist Nikki Van der Zyl (Monica Van der Zyl) died on March 6, aged 85. She dubbed various "Bond Girls" in the German versions of *Dr. No, From Russia with Love, Goldfinger, Thunderball, Casino Royale* (1967), *You Only Live Twice, On Her Majesty's Secret Service, Live and Let Die, The Man with the Golden Gun* and *Moonraker*, along with Hammer's *She* (Ursula Andress' "Ayesha"), *One Million Years B.C., Prehistoric Women, Frankenstein Created Woman* and *Scars of Dracula, Deadlier Than the Male* and *Gawain and the Green Knight*. Van der

Zyl was also Gert Fröbe's dialogue coach on *Goldfinger*, and she later became a lawyer and artist.

"Buddy" Van Horn

Clint Eastwood's long-time stunt double and sometimes director, [Wayne] "Buddy" Van Horn, died on May 11, aged 92. He performed stunts or appeared in *Prince Valiant* (1954), *Around the World in 80 Days* (1956), *Our Man Flint*, *Chamber of Horrors*, *The Beguiled* (1971), *High Plains Drifter*, *The Sword and the Sorcerer*, *The Beastmaster*, *Pale Rider*, *The Night Stalker* (1986), *Ratboy*, *Outbreak* (1995) and episodes of TV's *The Green Hornet* and *The Six Million Dollar Man*. Van Horn also directed Eastwood in the 1988 "Dirty Harry" movie *The Dead Pool*.

Melvin Van Peebles

American writer, producer, director and actor Melvin Van Peebles, the father of actor Mario Van Peebles, died on September 22, aged 89. His directing credits include *Watermelon

Man*, *Identity Crisis* and a 1997 episode of TV's *The Outer Limits*, while as an actor he also turned up in *Jaws: The Revenge*, *Last Action Hero*, *Fist of the North Star* (1995) and Mick Garris' 1997 TV mini-series of Stephen King's *The Shining* (as "Richard Halloran").

Isela Vega

Mexican leading lady Isela Vega [Durazo] died of cancer on March 9, aged 81. She made her screen debut in 1960 and her credits include *Fear

Model and singer Isela Vega (1939–2021) starred alongside John Carradine's crazed scientist in Diabolical Pact (1969), a very loose Mexican version of Dr. Jekyll & Mr. Hyde.

Chamber (with Boris Karloff), *Diabolical Pact* (with John Carradine), *Enigma de muerte* (with luchador "Mil Mascaras"), *Madame Death* (with Carradine again), *Blood Screams* (aka *The Bloody Monks*), *Island of the Dolls*, *Dora and the Lost City of Gold* and episodes of TV's *The Greatest American Hero* and *Conan*. Vega also co-scripted, produced, directed and starred in the 1986 witchcraft thriller *Lovers of the Lord of the Night*. The former model appeared nude in a 1974 spread in *Playboy*.

Chick Vennera

American supporting actor Chick Vennera died of cancer on July 7, aged 74. He appeared in *The Milagro Beanfield War*, *The Terror Within II*, *Time Under Fire*, *Tycus*, and Fred Olen Ray's *Prophet* (with Barbara Steele), *Stranded* (aka *Black Horizon*) and *Glass Trap*, along with an episode of TV's *Beyond Belief: Fact or Fiction*. In 1999 Vennera co-directed the family fantasy *Angel in Training*.

Peter Vere-Jones

British-born New Zealand character actor Peter Vere-Jones died on January 26, aged 81. He appeared in Peter Jackson's *Braindead* (aka *Dead Alive*) and did voice work for Jackson's *Bad Taste*, *Meet the Feebles* and *The Hobbit: The Desolation of Smaug*. Jones also turned up in episodes of TV's *Xena: Warrior Princess*, *Hercules: The Legendary Journeys* (as "Zeus"), *A Twist in the Tale*, *Dark Knight* and *Legend of the Seeker*.

Henri Vernes

Influential Belgian-born French writer and journalist Henri Vernes (Charles-Henri-Jean Dewisme) died on July 25, aged 102. In 1953 he created the

Marie Versini

character of adventurer "Bob Morane" for a series of pulp novels (beginning with *La Vallée Infernale*) and, from 1959 onwards, comics books ("*bandes dessinées*"). The series ran for more than 200 volumes, which spanned fifty years and sold well over 15 million copies. The Bob Morane books often combined science fiction and fantasy themes with those of the lost race or weird menace novels. Vernes' (who wrote many different series under various pseudonyms) was the subject of a documentary, *Henri Vernes, un aventurier de l'imaginaire*, in 1997, and his autobiography, *Mémoires*, appeared in 2012. From 1964–65 there was a live-action French TV series starring Claude Titre as "Bob Morane" and Billy Kearns as his companion "Billy Ballantine", and the characters were adapted for a French/Canadian animated TV series in 1998. There was also a short film, *L'espion aux cent visages* (1961), which appears to be lost today.

French leading lady Marie [Claude] Versini, who co-starred with Christopher Lee in *The Brides of Fu Manchu* (1966), died on November 22, aged 81. Two years earlier, Versini had a serious fall in her Paris apartment and suffered several broken bones and a head injury.

Emi Wada

Oscar-winning Japanese costume designer Emi Wada (Emiko Noguchi) died on November 13, aged 84. She worked on *Princess from the Moon*, *Dreams*, *The Bride with White Hair* and *The Bride with White Hair II*, *The Storm Riders*, *The Restless* and *The Warrior and the Wolf*. Wada also created John Gielgud's cloak for Peter Greenaway's *Prospero's Books*.

Jessica Walter

American leading lady Jessica Walter died in her sleep on March 24, aged 80. She was in *Lilith*, *The Immortal*, *Play Misty for Me*, *Home for the Holidays*, *Dr. Strange* (1978, as "Morgan LeFay"), *Vampire* (1979), *She's Dressed to Kill*, *Ghost in the Machine*, *Temptress* and *Doomsday Rock* (aka *Cosmic Shock*). On TV, Walter appeared in episodes of *Diagnosis: Unknown* ('The Curse of the Gypsy'), *The Alfred Hitchcock Hour*, *The Sixth Sense*, *Wonder Woman*, *Babylon 5*, *Poltergeist: The Legacy* and *Touched by an Angel*. Her second husband was actor Ron Leibman from 1983 until his death in 2019.

Gloria Warren

Hollywood actress and singer Gloria Warren (Gloria Weiman) died September 11, aged 95. Discovered by a local radio producer in the early 1940s, she was signed to a contract with Warner Bros., who saw her as a potential rival to Universal's Deanna Durbin. However, after co-starring in a handful of movies for mostly other studios—including the Monogram "Charlie Chan" mystery *Dangerous Money* in 1946—Warren retired from the screen the following year.

Norman J. Warren

British film director Norman J. (John) Warren died on March 11, aged 78. His credits include the cult classics

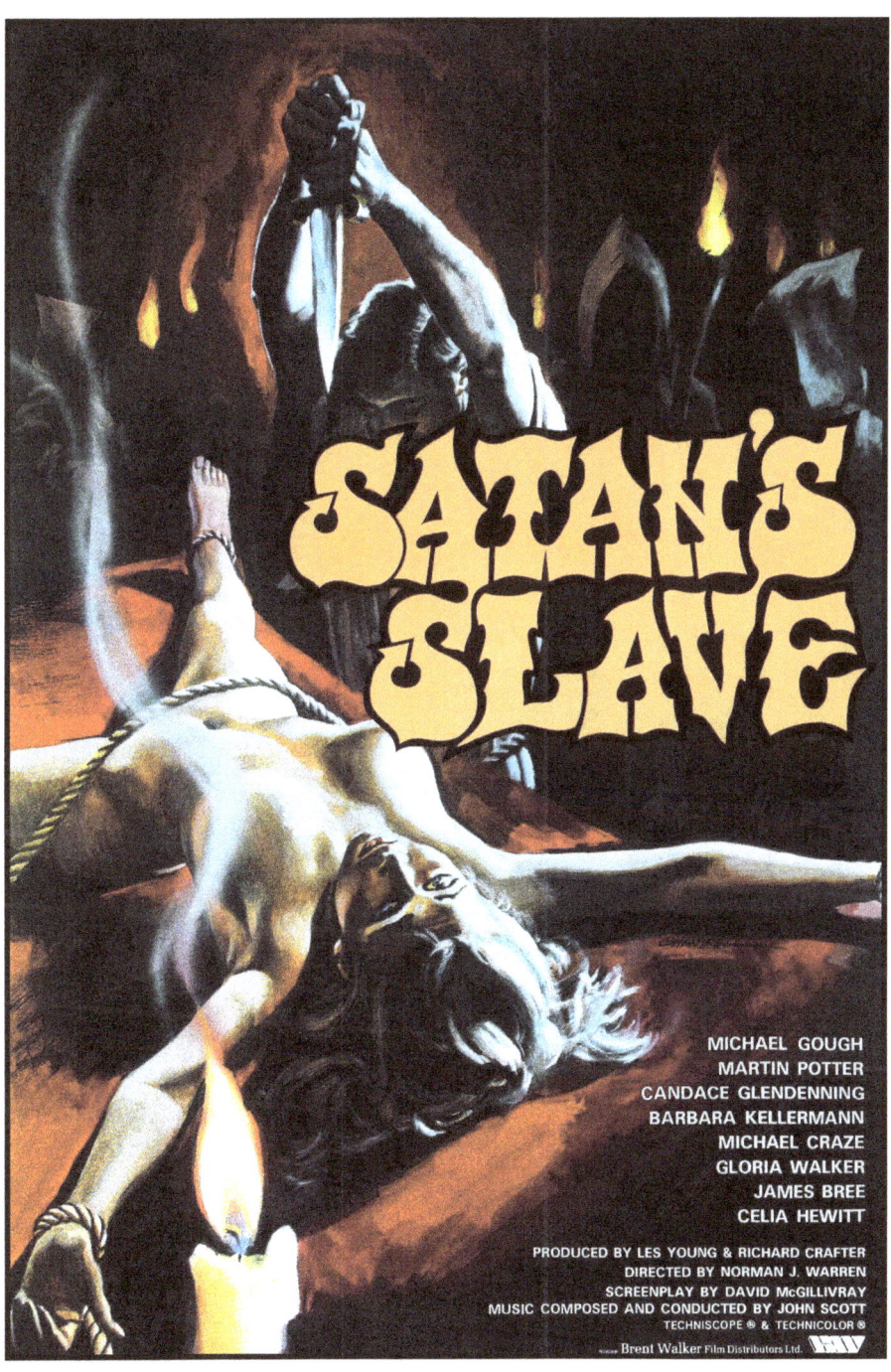

Norman J. Warren (1942–2021) directed the low-budget British film
Satan's Slave (1976), which starred Michael Gough as a creepy cult leader.

Satan's Slave (with Michael Gough), *Prey*, *Terror*, *Spaced Out*, *Inseminoid* (aka *Horror Planet*) and *Bloody New Year*.

Joan Washington

Scottish voice and dialect coach Joan Washington died in America on September 1, aged 71. Her many credits include *Greystoke: The Legend of Tarzan Lord of the Apes*, *Highlander*, *101 Dalmatians* (1996), *The Borrowers* (1997), *Star Wars Episode I–The Phantom Menace*, *102 Dalmatians*, *Star Wars Episode II–Attack of the Clones*, *The Nutcracker in 3D* (aka *The Nutcracker: The Untold Story*), *Cinderella* (2015), *Crimson Peak*, *The Little Stranger* and *The Witches* (2020). Washington married British actor Richard E. Grant in 1986.

Dilys Watling

British actress Dilys Watling (Dilys Rhys-Jones), the adopted daughter of actor Jack Watling and the half-sister of Deborah Watling, died on August 10, aged 78. Amongst her credits is the 1967 film *Theatre of Death* (aka *Blood Fiend*) starring Christopher Lee. She retired from the screen in 1994.

Peter Watson-Wood

British documentary filmmaker and producer Peter Watson-Wood died on November 1, aged 92. As a producer, his credits include *Dream*

Demon (1988), *Forbidden Sun* (aka *The Bulldance*), *Tales of the Riverbank* (2008) and *The Wicker Tree*. In 1956, Watson-Wood and Cornish tourist photographer Mike Courtney erected the now-iconic "Land's End" signpost and charged people to have their pictures taken.

Woody Welch

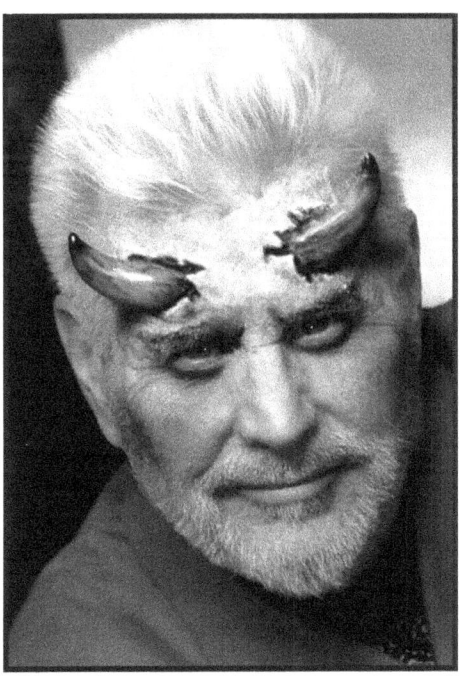

68-year-old American artist Woody Welch died of complications from a heart attack and diabetes in early January. His mother, Jewel Flowers Evans, was a model for pin-up artist Rolf Armstrong and, after seeing *The Animal World* (1956), he began creating his own artworks of horror, SF, and fantasy (using photos from *Famous Monsters of Filmland* and *Castle of Frankenstein* magazines for reference). Welch created most of the covers for *Space Monsters* magazine (2013–15) and he worked as a storyboard artist on *Halloween: Resurrection* (2002).

Joan Weldon

Singer and Hollywood leading lady of the 1950s, Joan Weldon (Joan Louise Welton), who co-starred in the classic 1954 giant ant movie *Them!*, died on February 11, aged 90. In a screen career that only lasted between 1953 and 1958, she appeared in ten movies and several TV shows.

Italian 4-foglio poster by Luigi Martinati for Them! *(1954), which co-starred Joan Weldon (1930–2021) as a scientist battling gigantic mutated ants.*

Lina Wertmüller

Italian screenwriter and director Lina Wertmüller (Arcangela Felice Assunta Wertmüller von Elgg Spañol von Braueich), the first woman to be nominated for an Academy Award as Best Director, died on December 9, aged 93. As "Lina Wertmuller Job" she co-scripted the stone-age comedy *When Women Had Tails* (1970) and came up with the original story for the sequel, *When Women Lost Their Tails* (1972).

Betty White

Emmy Award-winning American TV actress Betty [Marion] White died on December 31, a little more than two weeks before she would have turned 100. Best known for co-starring in such classic sitcoms as *The Mary Tyler Moore Show* (1973-77) and *The Golden Girls* (1985-92), she also appeared in the movies *Lake Placid*, *Return to the Batcave: The Misadventures of Adam and Burt* and *The Third Wish*, along with

the 1987 TV special *ALF Loves a Mystery*. White's screen career lasted for eight decades.

Jack Whyte

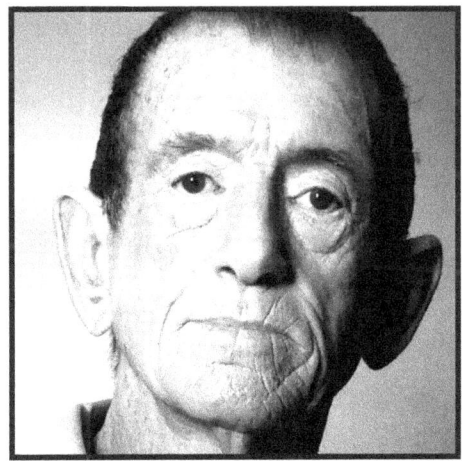

Scottish-born Canadian author Jack Whyte died of cancer on February 22, aged 80. His Arthurian and other historical fantasy series include "The Camulod Chronicles"/"Legends of Camelot", the "Knights Templar Trilogy" and the "Guardians Trilogy".

Yvonne Wilder

American supporting actress Yvonne Wilder (Yvonne Othon), who was a regular on the 1970s sitcom *Operation Petticoat*, died on November 24, aged 84. She made her movie debut in *West Side Story* (1961), and went on to co-star in *The Return of Count Yorga* (which she also scripted with her then -husband, director Bob Kelljan) and appear in an episode of TV's *The Girl with Something Extra*. After retiring from the screen in the early 1990s, Wilder became a painter and sculptor.

Bergen Williams

American character actress Bergen Williams (Laura Lynn Williams), who appeared as housekeeper "Alice Gunderson" in more than 150 episodes of ABC-TV's daytime soap opera *General Hospital* (2002-15), died of Wilson's disease (a rare inherited disorder that causes copper to accumulate in the body) on July 20, aged 62. Often cast as nurses or security guards, she also had small roles in *Mom and Dad Save the World*, *Wishman*, *Younger and Younger*, Clive Barker's *Lord of Illusions* and *Killer Pad*, along with episodes of TV's *Lois & Clark: The New Adventures of Superman*, *Babylon 5* and *FreakyLinks*.

Cara Williams

American supporting actress and singer Cara Williams (Bernice Kamiat, aka "Bernice Kay"), who had her own CBS-TV show from 1964-65, died of a heart attack on December 9, aged 96. In a screen career that stretched back to the early 1940s, she appeared in *Laura* (1944), *The Spider* (1945) and *The White Buffalo*, along with four episodes of *Alfred Hitchcock Presents*. The second (1952-59) of Williams' three husbands was actor John Drew Barrymore. After retiring from the screen in the late 1970s, she had a career as an interior designer.

Clarence Williams III

African-American actor Clarence Williams III, best known for co-starring as undercover cop "Linc Hayes" in ABC's *The Mod Squad* (1968-73), died of cancer on June 4, aged 81. He was in *The House That Dies Drear*, *Perfect Victims*, *Maniac Cop 2*, *Tales from the Hood*, *The Silencers* (1996), *Encino Woman*, Disney's *The Love Bug* (1997), *Mindstorm* and *American Nightmares* (aka *Mr. Malevolent*). On TV, Williams also appeared in episodes of *Tarzan* (1968), *Orson Welles Great Mysteries*, *The Highwayman*, *Shades of LA*, *Twin Peaks* (1990), *Tales from the Crypt*, *Star Trek: Deep Space Nine*, *Millennium* and *Miracles*.

Karl Williams

Longtime Paramount Pictures publicist Karl Williams died of liver complications on February 7, aged 52. For fifteen years with Paramount, he worked on the campaigns for the first two *Transformers* movies, *Indiana Jones and the Kingdom of the Crystal Skull*, *Star Trek*, *Iron Man* and *Iron Man 2*, *Thor* and many other titles. Williams went on to serve as Head of Publicity for Digital Domain, as well as working at 20th Century Fox, CBS Films and Amazon.

Michael K. Williams

54-year-old American actor Michael K. Williams, best known for playing gay criminal "Omar Little" in HBO's *The Wire* (2002–08), was found dead in his Brooklyn apartment on September 6 from an apparent heroin overdose. He appeared in *The Incredible Hulk* (2008), *Tell Tale*, *The Road*, *RoboCop* (2014), *The Purge: Anarchy*, *Ghostbusters* (2016) and *Assassin's Creed*, and portrayed the Devil in the 2013 short film *The Devil Goes Down*. On TV, Williams also co-starred as "Leonard Pine" in the 2016–18 TV series *Hap and Leonard*, based on the books by Joe R. Lansdale, and "Montrose Freeman" in *Lovecraft Country* (2020), based on the novel by Matt Ruff. The distinctive scar on his forehead was from a bar fight on this twenty-fifth birthday.

Betty Willingale

British TV script editor and producer Betty [Kathleen] Willingale died on February 15, aged 93. She began her career in the early 1960s and worked on *A Christmas Carol* (1977), *Wuthering Heights* (1978), *The Woman in White* (1982) and the long-running ITV series *Midsomer Murders*.

Marc Wilmore

American TV writer and executive producer Marc [Edward] Wilmore, who worked on scripts for a dozen episodes of *The Simpsons* (including a couple of 'Treehouse of Horror' episodes) died of complications from COVID-19 on January 30, aged 57.

His other credits include an episode of *Harry and the Hendersons*.

Mark Wilson

Pioneering American magician [James] Mark Wilson, a founding member of the Magic Castle in Hollywood, died on January 19, aged 91. He had the first magic show (with his wife, Nani Darnell) on network TV in the early 1960s and guest-starred on episodes of *The Six Million Dollar Man* and *Wonder Woman*. Wilson was also a magic consultant on a 1979 episode of *The Incredible Hulk*.

S. Clay Wilson

American underground comix artist S. (Steve) Clay Wilson died on February 7, aged 79. He had been suffering from dementia, brought on by a build-up of fluid on the brain in 2012. Inspired by EC horror comics such as *Tales from the Crypt*, Wilson began drawing as a child. An early

contributor to *Zap Comix* (along with other counterculture figures such as Robert Crumb, with whom he collaborated), he created his most famous character, "The Checkered Demon", for the publication in 1967. He went on to contribute to such titles as *Yellow Dog*, Art Spiegelman's *Arcade*, *Weirdo* and *Graphic Classics 4: H.P. Lovecraft*. Wilson's cartoons were invariably violent and sexually explicit, and in later years his work became even more horrific, featuring zombie pirates and rotting vampires. He not only illustrated German editions of William S. Burroughs' *Cities of the Red Night* and *The Wild Boys*, but also works by Hans Christian Anderson and the Brothers Grimm. *The Art of S. Clay Wilson* was published by Ten Speed Press in 2006.

Romy Windsor

American actress Romy Windsor (Romy Walthall) died of cardiac arrest on May 19, aged 57. She co-starred in *Howling IV: The Original Nightmare* and *The House of Usher* (1989), and had supporting roles in *Howling: New*

Spanish VHS video cover for Howling IV: The Original Nightmare *(1988), which starred Romy Windsor (1963–2021) and had a troubled production.*

Moon Rising and *Face/Off*. On TV, Windsor appeared in episodes of *Quantum Leap*, *Early Edition*, *The X Files* and *The Nightmare Room*. She retired in 2011 and became an acting teacher in the San Fernando Valley.

Jane Withers

1930s Hollywood child star Jane Withers (Jame Ruth Withers), who was Shirley Temple's closest rival at the box office, died on August 7, aged 95. She made her first screen appearance in 1932, and her later credits include episodes of TV's *The Alfred Hitchcock Hour* and *The Munsters*. Following the death of Mary Wickes, Withers took over the voice of gargoyle "Laverne" in Disney's *The Hunchback of Notre Dame* (1996), along with two spin-off video games and the sequel, *The Hunchback of Notre Dame 2: The Secret of the Bell*. During the early 1940s, Whitman Publishing Company featured the actress in three mystery novels: *Jane Withers and the Hidden Room*, *Jane Withers and the Phantom Violin* and *Jane Withers and the Swamp Wizard*.

Robin Wood

American writer and gaming artist Robin Wood died of cancer on April 19, aged 68. She illustrated the Anne McCaffrey tribute *People of Pern* (1989) for The Donning Company/SFBC, the Robin Wood Tarot Deck and several covers of *Dragon* magazine.

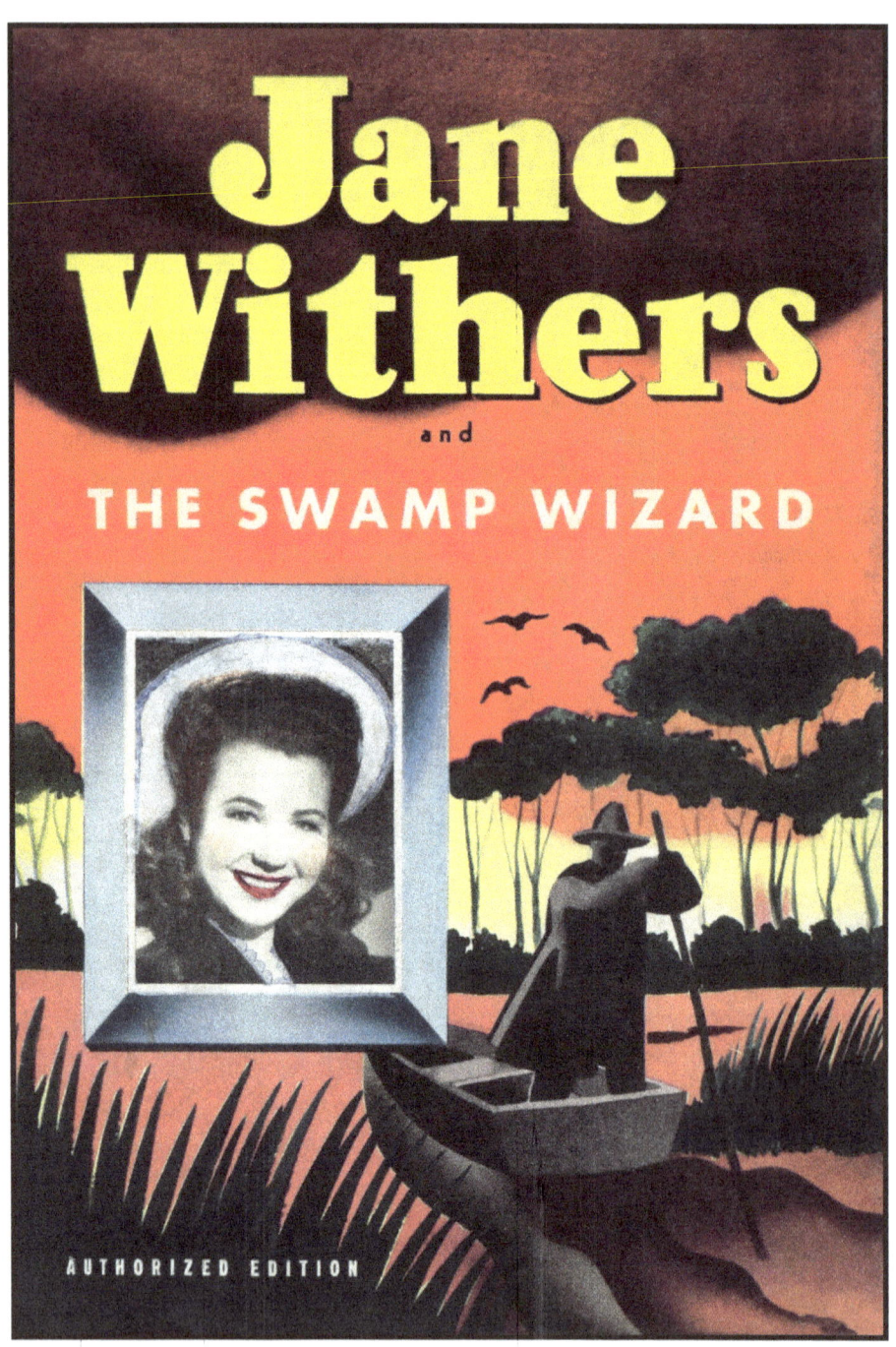

Cover of the juvenile mystery Jane Withers and the Swamp Wizard by Kathryn Heisenfelt (Whitman Publishing Co., 1944), which featured the teenage film star (1926–2021) as the heroine.

Wood also created the art for a 1989 Tor edition of Fritz Leiber's *Ship of Shadows* and *The Writer's Complete Fantasy Reference*, and contributed articles to *Stigmata: An Anthology of Writing and Art* ('Burying the Undead: The Use and Obsolescence of Count Dracula') and *The Shape of Rage: The Films of David Cronenberg*.

Victor Wood

Filipino actor and singer Victor Wood died of complications from COVID-19 on April 23, aged 75. He played the titular caped crusader in *Fight! Batman, Fight!* (1973), and his other screen credits include another knock-off, *Jesus Christ Superstar* (1972). In the 1960s he was known as the Philippine "Jukebox King" because he had so many hit songs playing on jukeboxes across the country.

Henry Woolf

Diminutive British character actor Henry Woolf died in Canada following a series of heart operations

on November 12, aged 91. A lifelong friend of the playwright Harold Pinter, his film credits include *Marat/Sade*, *The Bed Sitting Room*, *The Ruling Class*, *The Rocky Horror Picture Show* (as "A Transylvanian"), *The Hound of the Baskervilles* (1978) and *Superman III*. On TV, Woolf was in the *Doctor Who* serial 'The Sun Makers' (1977), and he portrayed "Dr. Cornelius" in the C.S. Lewis "Chronicles of Narnia" adaptations *Prince Caspian and the Voyage of the Dawn Treader* (1989) and *The Silver Chair* (1990) for the BBC. In the early 1990s Woolf moved to Canada, where he taught acting at the University of Saskatchewan.

Samuel E. Wright

American actor and singer Samuel E. (Ernest) Wright, who voiced "Sebastian", the Jamaican-accented crab in Disney's *The Little Mermaid* (1989) and various sequels and spin-

offs, died of prostate cancer on May 24, aged 72. Wright also portrayed "Mufasa" in Disney's Broadway version of *The Lion King*.

May Wynn

American actress May Wynn (Donna Lee Hickey) died on March 22, aged 93. The former dancer and beauty queen co-starred as "Concha Ramsey" in *The Unknown Terror* (1957). Wynn retired from the screen in 1960 to work as a real estate broker. Her first husband (1956-64) was actor Jack Kelly.

Andy Yanchus

Longtime Marvel comics staff colourist Andy P. Yanchus died on September 11, aged 77. In 1965, he began working for the Aurora Plastics Company, where he became project manager for their hobby-kit line. During the nine years he was with Aurora, he launched the "Monster Scenes" line of snap-together toy kits, which was eventually canceled after complaints from parents. Yanchus joined Marvel as a colourist in 1976, where he worked on such titles as *Uncanny X-Men*, *Incredible Hulk*, *Amazing Spider-Man*, *Nick Fury Agent of S.H.I.E.L.D.*, *Doctor Who* and *G.I. Joe*. In 2014, he co-wrote the official history and reference guide *Aurora Monster Scenes: The Most Controversial Toys of a Generation* with Dennis L. Prince.

Masayoshi Yasugi

Japanese science fiction and fantasy author Masayoshi Yasugi apparently killed himself on December 12, aged 49. He had reportedly told his younger brother that he hardly had any work due to COVID-19. In 2003, Yasugi won the fifth Nihon SF Shinjin-Shō (New Japanese Science Fiction Writer Prize) from the Science Fiction and Fantasy Writers of Japan for his novel *Yume-Miru Neko wa, Uchū ni Nemuru* (The Dreaming Cat Sleeps in Space). He also wrote the novelisation of the *anime* film *Expelled from Paradise*.

Viktor Yevgrafov

Russian actor and stuntman Viktor [Ivanovitch] Yevgrafov, who portrayed "Professor James Moriarty" in two TV series twenty years apart— *The Adventures of Sherlock Holmes and Dr. Watson* (1980) and *Vospominanie o Sherloke Kholmse* (2000)—died of a blood clot on October 20, aged 73. He also starred in the 1990 horror film *Dominus*, based on Ray Bradbury's stories 'The Black Ferris' and 'The Scythe'.

John Sacret Young

American TV producer, writer and director John Sacret Young died of brain cancer on June 3, aged 75. He wrote and directed several episodes of the 1995-97 Fox series *VR.5* and UPN's *Level 9* (2000-01), and scripted the 1977 TV movie *The Possessed*, which co-starred Harrison Ford.

Jeanne Youngson

Dr. Jeanne [Keyes] Youngson, who founded the first Count Dracula Fan Club in 1965, died on August 15, aged 96. Over the years, it grew into

an international organisation with fifteen active divisions around the world, which she mainly initiated. For a decade, Youngson also acted as curator for the society's Dracula Museum in New York City before it moved to Vienna, Austria, in 1999. After thirty-five years, the name of the organisation was changed to The Vampire Empire. Youngson's many vampire-related publications include *Count Dracula and the Unicorn*, *The Count Dracula Chicken Cookbook*, *The Further Perils of Dracula*, *A Child's Garden of Vampires*, *The Count Dracula Book of Classic Vampire Tales*, *The Count Dracula Book of Classic Vampire Stories*, *Freak Show Vampire*, *The Bizarre World of Vampires*, *Private Files of a Vampirologist: Case Histories & Letters* and *Do Vampires Exist? A Special Report from Dracula World Enterprises* (with Shelley Leigh-Hunt). She was married to Oscar-winning documentary film producer, writer and director Robert Youngson from 1960 until his death in 1974.

May Wynn (1928–2021) played the wife of a mad scientist who had created a flesh-eating fungus that looked like soap bubbles in The Unknown Terror *(1957).*

Index by Date

Month Not Known

Linda Boyce
John Logan

January

    Jeffrey Dempsey
    Woody Welch
1   Ron Dominguez
    Mark Eden
    George Gerdes
2   Vladimir Korenev
4   Tanya Roberts
    Barbara Shelley
    Gregory Sierra
5   John Richardson
6   Antonio Sabáto, Sr.
7   Michael Apted
    Christopher Little
    Marion Ramsay
8   Steve Carver
    Mike Henry
    Steve Lightle
    Diana Millay
    Ivo Niederle
9   Carmine Capobianco
    John Reilly
10 James Follett
    Julie Strain
11 Stacy Title
13 Lail Finlay
14 Storm Constantine
    Peter Mark Richman
15 Dale Baer
    Timothy Lane
16 Charlotte Cornwell
18 Perry Botkin, Jr.
19 Kellam de Forest
    Mark Wilson
20 Nathalie Delon
    Mira Furlan
21 Bob Avian
    Rémy Julienne
22 Walter Bernstein
23 Tony Ferrer
    Alberto Grimaldi
    Hal Holbrook
    Larry King
    Bruce Kirby
24 Gunnel Lindblom
25 Marie Harmon
26 Richard Arnold
    Cloris Leachman
    Leslie Newman
    Peter Vere-Jones
27 Don Harley
28 Kathleen Ann Goonan
    Darroll Pardoe
    Cicely Tyson
30 Allan Burns
    Marc Wilmore

February

David G. Barnett
Meloney Crawford Chadwick
Bill Titcombe
1 Dustin Diamond
Robert C. Jones
3 Haya Harareet
5 Christopher Plummer
6 Harry Fielder
7 Michael G. Adkisson
Giuseppe Rotunno
Karl Williams
S. Clay Wilson
8 Jean-Claude Carrière
9 Gerald Feil
John Hora
10 Victor Ambrus
Larry Flynt
Christine Morrison
Ina Shorrock
11 Reg Lewis
Frank Mills
Rowena Morrill
Joan Weldon
12 Christopher Pennock
Lynn Stalmaster
13 George Mandel
Yvonne Rousseau
14 Wanda June Alexander
Catherine Belsey
15 Andreas Teuber
Betty Willingale
16 Harry V. Bring
Si Spencer
18 Alan Curtis
Frank Lupo
21 Peter S. Davis
22 Jack Whyte
23 Peter Harris
Geoffrey Scott
24 Alan Robert Murray
Ronald Pickup
28 Johnny Briggs

March

3 Nicola Pagett
4 Dean Morrissey
5 Edward L. Plumb
6 David Bailie
Nikki Van der Zyl
7 Frank Thorne
8 Norton Juster
Trevor Peacock
9 Jeffrey M. Hayes
Cliff Simon
Isela Vega
11 Isidore Mankofsky
Norman J. Warren
14 Henry Darrow
Yaphet Kotto
18 Richard Gilliland
22 May Wynn
23 Steve Lines
George Segal
24 Jessica Walter
25 Robert Rodan
Bertrand Tavernier
26 Alan Marques
28 Blade Braxton
30 Gérard Filipelli
Myra Francis
31 Cleve Hall

April

1 Lee Aaker
   John A. McGlashan
3 Lois de Banzie
   Penny Frierson
   Gloria Henry
   Biff McGuire
   John Paragon
4 Derrick Ferguson
5 Phil Eason
   Robert Fletcher
   Joye Hummel
   Frank Jacobs
   Paul Ritter
6 John Clabburn
   Mark Elliott
   Walter Olkewicz
7 Anne Beatts
   James Hampton
8 Margaret Wander Bonanno
   Richard Rush
   Walter Schneiderman
9 DMX
11 Giannetto De Rossi
   Enzo Sciotti
12 John C. Pelan
13 Dr. Aaron Stern
14 Trader Faulkner
   Timothy Patrick Quill
15 Ira Keeler
16 Helen McCrory
   Anthony Powell
   Liam Scarlett
   Felix Silla
19 Fred Jordan
   Douglas Livingstone
   Jim Steinman
   Robin Wood
20 Monte Hellman
21 Charles W. Fries
   Bernie Kahn
23 Victor Wood
24 Nathan Jung
   Shunsuke Kikuchi
26 Charles Beeson
28 Anish Deb
29 John Bush
   Frank Cox
   Johnny Crawford
   Billie Hayes
   Libertad Leblanc
   Frank McRae
30 Claudia Barrett

May

   Peggy Spirito
1 Olympia Dukakis
   Tom Hickey
   Willy Kurant
   John Paul Leon
2 Wynn Hammer
3 Richard Halliwell
4 Chuck Hicks
6 Kentaro Miura
   Guillermo Murray
7 Tawny Kitaen
8 Jean-Claude Romer
   Bill Starr
   Jan Stirling
10 Neil Connery
   Tony Harding
   Kevin Jackson
   Norman Lloyd

11	"Buddy" Van Horn	5	Richard Robinson
12	Kathy Burns	7	Douglas S. Cramer
	Blackie Dammett		Larry Gelman
	Jesse Hamm	9	Linda S. Touby
13	Marvin Kaye	10	Ray MacDonnell
15	Gary Littlejohn		Joyce Mackenzie
	Roy Scammell	11	Peter Adams
16	René Cardona III		Kay Hawtrey
17	Don Sakers	12	Dennis Berry
18	Charles Grodin	13	Ned Beatty
19	David Anthony Kraft		John Gabriel
	Romy Windsor		David Lightfoot
23	Milton Moses Ginsberg	14	Paul Alexander
	Gerardo Moscoso		Lisa Banes
24	Desiree Gould	16	Norman S. Powell
	Robert Hall	17	Frank Bonner
	Samuel E. Wright	18	Joe Praml
25	Gary Compton	19	Leon Greene
26	Lorina Kamburova	20	Joanne Linville
	Paul Soles	23	Jackie Lane
27	Shane Briant	24	Clare Peploe
	David Butler		Steve Sherman
	Robert J. Hogan	25	Olga Barnet
29	John Gregg		John Erman
	Joe Lara	26	Fernand Guiot
	Gavin MacLeod		Larry D. Johnson
31	Arlene Golonka	29	Stuart Damon

June

July

	Bob Brown	2	Kate Ferguson
	Mike Don		Kartal Tibet
	Bob Haberfield	3	Desmond Davis
3	Robert W. Coye		Anne Stallybrass
	Damaris Hayman	4	Sanford Clark
	John Sacret Young	5	C. Dean Andersson
4	Clarence Williams III		Raffaella Carrà

			August
	Richard Donner		
	Paul Huntley		
	William Smith	1	Alvin Ing
6	Roger Cudney	2	Elizabeth Anne Hull
7	Robert Downey, Sr.	3	Jean Hale
	Chick Vennera		Fred Ladd
8	Kumar Ramsay	5	Alistair Durie
11	Colette O'Neil		Reg Gorman
	Robson Rocha	6	Peter A. Lees
12	Charles Robinson	7	Brad Allan
13	Sid Altus		Colin Fletcher
	Joe McKinney		Markie Post
14	Sally Miller Gearhart		Jane Withers
	Bill Tortolini	8	John Hitchin
15	Judi B. Castro	9	Alex Cord
	William F. Nolan		Pat Hitchcock
16	Steve Hickman		Ken Hutchison
	Biz Markie	10	Don Jones
17	Pilar Bardem		Victoria Paris
	Jane Morpeth		Dilys Watling
18	Milan Lasica	11	Lorna Toolis
19	Raymond Cavaleri	12	Scott Allen Nollen
20	David Dukas		Una Stubbs
	Bergen Williams	13	Don Poynter
21	Patricia Kennealy	15	Jeanne Youngson
22	Rick Boatright	16	Richard Lee-Sung
23	Bryn Fortey	17	Eddie Paskey
	Mike Mitchell	18	Mary K. Frey
24	Al Pugliese		Jill Murphy
25	Ed Meskys	19	Sonny Chiba
	Henri Vernes		Lisa Mannetti
26	Rick Aiello		Salman A. Nensi
	David Von Ancken	21	Masanari Nihei
	Wiktor Bukato	22	Marilyn Eastman
28	Clive Scott	23	Brick Bronsky
	Saginaw Grant		Michael Nader
	J.W. Rinzler		Rosita Quintana
30	Jay Pickett	25	Erle M. Korshak

Zdenka Procházková
26 Sompote Sands
27 L. Neil Smith
28 Catherine MacPhail
   Bill Taylor
29 Ed Asner
31 Michael Constantine

September

Langdon Jones
Denise Lee
1 Carol Carr
  George Martin
  Joan Washington
2 Mikis Theodorakis
3 Irma Kalish
4 Greta Tomlinson
5 Gil Lane-Young
  Tony Selby
6 Jean-Paul Belmondo
  Nino Castelnuovo
  Judith Hanna
  Michael K. Williams
7 Edward Barnes
8 Art Metrano
  Matthew Strachan
9 Jon Gregory
  Elizabeth I. McCann
11 Carlo Alighiero
   Gloria Warren
   Andy Yanchus
12 Fran Bennett
   Sondra James
13 Don Collier
14 J. Randolph Cox
   Reuben B. Klamer
   Norm MacDonald
15 Robert Fyfe
   Doris Piserchia
   Joel Rapp
   Ronald Roose
16 Graham Garfield Barnard
   Mike Humphreys
   Jane Powell
   Juli Reding
17 Maria Chianetta
   Avril Elgar
   Jimmy Garrett
   Basil Hoffman
19 William R. Beck
   John Challis
   Stephen Critchlow
   Tim Donnelly
   Morris Perry
21 Bob Couttie
   Willie Garson
   Luis Gaspar
   Anna Gaylor
   Al Harrington
   Peter Palmer
22 Jay Sandrich
   Melvin Van Peebles
23 David H. DePatie
24 Ota
   Takao Saitô
25 Douglas Barbour
26 Susan Bartholomew
   Ugo Malaguti
28 Vergena Fields
   Tommy Kirk
29 Ravil Isyanov
   Michael Tylo

October

     Carole Nelson Douglas
2   Richard Evans
3   Cynthia Harris
     Marc Pilcher
4   Michael Ferguson
     Alan R. Kalter
6   Lou Antonelli
     Patrick Horgan
7   Jan Shutan
8   Sally Gwylan
     Rick Jones
10   Bob Herron
     Ruthie Tompson
12   Brian Goldner
13   Gary Paulsen
14   Dorothy Steel
16   Denise Bryer
     Geoffrey Chater
     Alan Hawkshaw
     Betty Lynn
17   Toshihiro Iijima
18   Christopher Ayres
     Val Bisoglio
     Ralph Carmichael
     Jo-Carroll Dennison
     William Lucking
19   Jack Angel
     Leslie Bricusse
20   Jerry Pinkney
     Robert Thurston
     Viktor Yevgrafov
21   Halyna Hutchins
     Wes Magee
22   JoAnna Cameron
     Peter Scolari
24   Mamat Khalid

26   Linda Carlson
     Allen Payne
27   Jonathan Reynolds
28   Phil Lonergan
     Camille Saviola
29   Kit Berry
30   Joe Cornelius

November

     Gene D'Angelo
1   Peter Watson-Wood
3   Bob Baker
4   Lionel Blair
5   Silvio Laurenzi
6   Clifford Rose
7   Enrique Rocha
     Dean Stockwell
8   Vegar Hoel
9   Jerry Douglas
     Roy Holder
     Simon Marshall-Jones
     Alec Monteath
     Gavan O'Herlihy
12   Henry Woolf
13   David Fox
     Wilbur Smith
     Emi Wada
14   Bart the Bear II
     Heath Freeman
17   Keith Allison
     Art LaFleur
19   Will Ryan
     Alex Rebar
20   Billy Hinsche
21   Lou Cutell
     Joey Morgan

22	Miquel Barceló	9	Lina Wertmüller
	Bernard Holley		Cara Williams
	Doug MacLeod	10	Michael Nesmith
	Paolo Pietrangeli	11	Jack Hedley
	Marie Versini		Anne Rice
23	Mary Collinson	12	Masayoshi Yasugi
	Larry Levine	13	William G. Contento
24	Ian Curteis	14	Henry Orenstein
	Yvonne Wilder	15	Bridget Hanley
25	Jeremy G. Byrne	16	Richard Citron
26	Stephen Sondheim		Doug Robinson
28	Kichiemon Nakamura II	17	Sung-Young Chen
29	Arlene Dahl	18	Gérald Forton
	David Gulpilil		Sayaka Kanda
	Howard Honig		Curt Meyer
	Tommy Lane	19	Nicholas Georgiade
			Sally Ann Howes
		20	Pierre Philippe

December

1	James R. Terry	22	Richard Conway
3	Diana G. Gallagher	23	Sharyn Moffett
	Andrei Izmailov		T. Mark Taylor
	Denis O'Brien	27	Andrew Vachss
	Antony Sher	28	Romaine Hart
4	Martha De Laurentiis		Lee Server
5	Inés Morales	29	Hugh Lund
	Peggy Neal	30	Denis O'Dell
	Scott Page-Pagter		Renato Scarpa
7	Benício	31	Gian Filippo Pizzo
8	Chris Achilleos		Jeanine Ann Roose
			Betty White

About the Author

Stephen Jones

British writer and editor Stephen Jones lives in London, England. A Hugo Award nominee, he is the winner of four World Fantasy Awards, three International Horror Guild Awards, five Bram Stoker Awards, twenty-one British Fantasy Awards and a Lifetime Achievement Award from the Horror Writers Association. One of Britain's most acclaimed horror and dark fantasy writers and editors, he has more than 160 books to his credit, including the illustrated histories, *The Art of Horror*, *The Art of Horror Movies* and *The Art of Pulp Horror*; the film books of Neil Gaiman's *Coraline* and *Stardust*, *The Illustrated Monster Movie Guide* and *The Hellraiser Chronicles*; the non-fiction studies *Horror: 100 Best Books* and *Horror: Another 100 Best Books* (both with Kim Newman); the single-author collections *Necronomicon* and *Eldritch Tales* by H.P. Lovecraft, *The Complete Chronicles of Conan* and *Conan's Brethren* by Robert E. Howard, and *Curious Warnings: The Great Ghost Stories of M.R. James*; plus such anthologies as *Terrifying Tales to Tell at Night: 10 Scary Stories to Give You Nightmares!*, *The Mammoth Book of Folk Horror*, *The Mammoth Book of Halloween Stories*, *The Lovecraft Squad* and *Zombie Apocalypse!* series, and thirty-one volumes of *Best New Horror*. You can visit his web site at www.stephenjoneseditor.com or follow him on Facebook at "Stephen Jones-Editor."

THE ALCHEMY PRESS
BOOK OF THE DEAD 2020

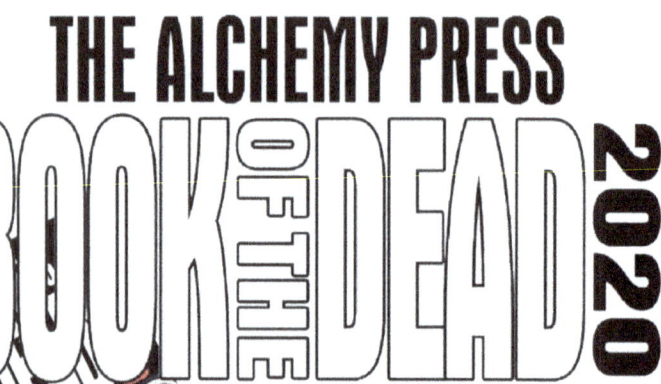

Celebrating the careers of more than 450 individuals who made significant contributions to the horror, science fiction and fantasy genres during their lifetimes. Compiled by award-winning writer and editor **Stephen Jones**, this first volume in a new annual series includes tributes to a trio of Hollywood legends ... possibly the last star of silent pictures ... the screen's best James Bond ... a pair of British actresses who were both "Bond girls" and *Avengers* ... two British actors who played – but did not voice – iconic *Star Wars* characters ... an author who did for crustaceans what James Herbert did for rodents ... and a forgotten pioneer of "sword and soul" fantasy ... all illustrated with numerous photographs and associated images.

This is not only a welcome reference volume, but also an informative and entertaining tribute to those we lost in 2020 and who left their mark on books, movies and popular culture in unusual and often fascinating ways.

The Alchemy Press Book of the Dead 2020
Compiled by Stephen Jones
ISBN 978-1-911034-12-4 £14.99

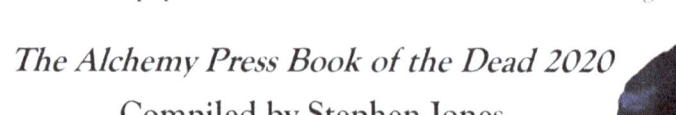

Available from Amazon and other good booksellers

alchemypress.wordpress.com/books-of-the-dead/botd2020/

Coming in 2023 . . .

www.ingramcontent.com/pod-product-compliance
Lightning Source LLC
Chambersburg PA
CBHW080546230426
43663CB00015B/2727